When Religion Matters

When Religion Matters

Practicing Healing in the Aftermath
of the Liberian Civil War

Annie Hardison-Moody

☙PICKWICK *Publications* • Eugene, Oregon

WHEN RELIGION MATTERS
Practicing Healing in the Aftermath of the Liberian Civil War

Copyright © 2016 Annie Hardison-Moody. All rights reserved. Except for brief quotations in critical publications or reviews, no part of this book may be reproduced in any manner without prior written permission from the publisher. Write: Permissions, Wipf and Stock Publishers, 199 W. 8th Ave., Suite 3, Eugene, OR 97401.

Pickwick Publications
An Imprint of Wipf and Stock Publishers
199 W. 8th Ave., Suite 3
Eugene, OR 97401

www.wipfandstock.com

PAPERBACK ISBN: 978-1-62564-589-0
HARDCOVER ISBN: 978-4982-8644-2
EBOOK ISBN: 978-1-5326-0535-2

Cataloguing-in-Publication data:

Names: Hardison-Moody, Annie.

Title: When religion matters : practicing healing in the aftermath of the Liberian Civil War / Annie Hardison-Moody.

Description: Eugene, OR: Pickwick Publications. | Revision of author's dissertation (doctoral)—Emory University, 2012.

Identifiers: ISBN: 978-1-62564-589-0 (paperback) | 978-1-4982-8644-2 (hardback) | 978-1-5326-0535-2 (ebook)

Subjects: LCSH: Pastoral theology. | Theology, Practical. | Intercultural communication. | Liberia—History—Civil War, 1989-1996—Women. | Liberia—History—Civil War, 1999-2003—Women.

Classification: HM1211 H38 2016. (print) | HM1211 (ebook)

Manufactured in the U.S.A.   OCTOBER 10, 2016

For Sophie, my sunshine

Contents

Acknowledgments | ix
Abbreviations | xii

Introduction | 1
1 Women, War, and Peace | 13
2 Memory and Migration | 34
3 Forgetting the Past | 64
4 Women's Leadership from Local to Global | 87
5 Mothering Practices | 112
6 Practices of Transformation: Making a Way | 131
7 Transformation Is | 150

Appendix A: Interview Participants and Research Methods | 163
Appendix B: Interview Protocol | 168
Bibliography | 169
Index of Names | 175
Index of Subjects | 177

Acknowledgments

I am so grateful to everyone who has supported and encouraged me along this journey, including the women who are the focus of this book. Their willingness to engage this process and talk with me about their lives and experiences has been a gift for which I am forever grateful.

This work began in graduate school at Emory University. My friends and colleagues there were a generous support to me during this process, notably the women of the Person, Community, and Religious Life (PCRL) course of study and the staff of *Practical Matters*. I feel lucky to have experienced such a true endeavor at interdisciplinarity through my time at Emory, and I'm grateful to my PCRL and *Practical Matters* colleagues for modeling this for me. I also want to thank my dissertation writing partners, both near and far: Abbie Holland Conley and Brandi Denison, who both made meeting to write a joyous event; and Jenna Supp-Montgomerie, whose friendship sustained me during the rough times. Thanks to the continued generous mentorship of Bonnie Miller-McLemore, I was connected to Kate Lassiter and Mindy McGarrah Sharp, who have been integral to the birthing of this text. Their edits, positive encouragement, and beautiful scholarship (read their books!) have made this book so much better than it was. Additionally, my dear friends Brittany, Justine, Megan, Brooke and Miriam have always encouraged me and my work. I love you all so much.

I was able to travel to Liberia, Ghana, and Kenya over the course of my work at Emory thanks to the generous financial support of Emory University's States at Regional Risk Program, Emory's Initiative in Religious Practices and Practical Theology, and the Social Science Research Council (SSRC). Through a Dissertation Proposal Development Fellowship with the SSRC, I was able to interact with both faculty mentors (Vincent Pecora and Jonathan Sheehan) and an interdisciplinary group of graduate student colleagues who helped to shape this work into a concise and coherent project. I am thankful to each of these programs and funders for their support.

In addition to such wonderful colleagues and friends, I was blessed with a dissertation committee that pushed me to do the work I was meant to do. Elizabeth Bounds is one of my favorite conversation partners, particularly around issues of women's religious lives. Wendy Farley has been a wonderful mentor; her writing and way of being in the world are a reminder to do work that matters. Pamela Scully is the kind of feminist scholar I aspire to be: one who is generous in her engagement with others and passionately committed to feminist work on the ground. And finally, working with Emmanuel Lartey, my advisor, helped me to see what practical theology can be: a liberative discourse that engages global issues and healing practices. I am forever grateful for his continued support, and for his pep talk that helped me to (finally) finish this book.

As I left Emory, I found another interdisciplinary community that has become just as important to me, in the Department of Youth, Family, and Community Sciences at North Carolina State University. My colleagues at NC State (in YFCS and beyond) are just marvelous. They help me love coming to work every day (truly). I am particularly grateful to my department head, Carolyn Dunn, whose mentorship has profoundly shaped my career in religion and health. Thank you, Carolyn, for believing in me all these years.

The chapter on mothering in this book was shaped by the conversations I have had over the past five years with my (now) co-editors and friends, Claire Bischoff and Elizabeth Gandolfo. Our many Skype conversations about theology, religious practices, and the day to day realities of mothering have been life-giving.

This book would have been a bit of a mess without the very talented editorial skills of Ulrike Guthrie. Thank you, Uli. Thank you to K. C. Hanson and the editorial team at Wipf & Stock for extending grace and support along this process.

It is difficult to write about how important my family is to me. Will's family has been my family for the past eighteen years, and Susan, Wilton, Seth, and Meredith have been there for me every time I have needed them. To Larry and Libby—thank you for caring for and loving Sophie so that I could work and write. Jenny Drossner, although we are not related by blood, has been a part of my family since the day I met her in the fourth grade. I am so glad that I went to Emory so that I could see you, David, and

Acknowledgments

Emma more often. Our families have so many fun times ahead. My parents are incredible people who have supported me from the beginning—letting me know that whatever I chose to do with my life, they would be right behind me. My sister, other than Will, is the person who knows me best in the world, and her unwavering support and reminders that my work is not all that I am, helped me to see that there is more to life than this often strange academic world. To Will, my best friend and partner—I don't know how any of this would be possible without you. And along the way, we had Sophie—a little ray of sunshine after several years in the dark clouds. You and Sophie are my life and my loves. Thank you.

Abbreviations

CEDAW	Convention on the Elimination of Discrimination Against Women
DDR	Disarmament, Demobilization, and Reintegration
ECOWAS	Economic Community of West African States
FCC	Friendship Community Church
ICAN	International Civil Society Network
IDP	internally displaced person
INPFL	Independent National Patriotic Front of Liberia
IRHAP	International Religious Health Assets Programme
LFS	Lutheran Family Services
LURD	Liberians United for Reconciliation and Democracy
LWI	Liberia Women's Initiative
MSF	Médicins Sans Frontières
NGO	non-governmental organization
NPFL	National Patriotic Front of Liberia
SSRC	Social Science Research Council
TRC	Truth and Reconciliation Commission
ULIMO	United Liberation Movement for Democracy in Liberia
UN	United Nations
UNCSW	United Nations Commission on the Status of Women
UNHCR	United Nations High Commission on Refugees
UNIFEM	United Nations Development Fund for Women
UNFPA	United Nations Population Fund
UNSCR	United Nations Security Council Resolution
WIPNET	Women in Peacebuilding Network
WONGOSOL	Women's NGO Secretariat of Liberia

Introduction

In January 2009, I went to Liberia for two weeks, primarily to attend a conference on post-conflict transformation and regional stability offered by Emory University's States at Regional Risk initiative.[1] After the conference I talked with leaders from women's organizations, non-governmental organizations (NGOs), and the government about gender-based violence and the ways women were working together to promote healing and transformation. It was eye-opening.

One such conversation occurred during a brief three-day stay in a small village in Lofa County when I sat with Sonnie, who was sorting rice to prepare for the afternoon meal.[2] After some small talk she volunteered: "The women here suffered during the war,"[3] and told me how women were dragged into the bush by rebel soldiers to be raped. She herself had been their prisoner, "out there," she said, pointing to the immense stretch of rain-

---

1. Emory's States at Regional Risk project brings together scholars, policy makers, practitioners, and students in five key world regions with the aim of increasing practical understanding concerning the reduction of state risk and the increase of effective public governance and services. For more, visit http://sarr.emory.edu/. I am grateful to Emory professor Bruce Knauft for the opportunity to attend this conference.

2. All names have been changed throughout this text to protect the anonymity of the women with whom I worked. The names of the organizations and faith communities where I worked in the Liberian community in an urban city in North Carolina have been changed as well.

3. As the Liberian Truth and Reconciliation Commission Report "Women and the Conflict" notes, Lofa county was one of the top seven counties that experienced the majority of violations as reported to the TRC. As the report goes on to note, "Sexual violence against women was of a particular nature involving brutal acts of rape, gang rape and multiple rapes, vaginal and anal rape and also with objects, guns, cassava plants, sticks, boots and knives." Republic of Liberia Truth and Reconciliation Commission, "Volume Three: Appendices Title 1: Women and the Conflict," 40.

forest that encircled the village. Women were left to find their own way back to the village through the treacherous terrain. The rebels burned the entire village save for two homes in 2000, forcing the villagers to retreat to the bush, where many lived for several years.[4] Others trekked across the border to Guinea or south into Monrovia, the capital. When I asked Sonnie how she was able to endure such trauma, she said "Only God. God was there."

This conversation sparked a series of questions that ground this text: How might starting with the fact that "God was there" frame how we think about violence, suffering, survival, and healing, and the role of religion and religious practices in bringing these things to bear? Why is it that God must be present in the moment of rape or wartime violence? Does God provide a witness to the event? Does God provide a promise of future healing? If so, what does that healing look like? Does God provide a sense that someone cares about what has happened?

These questions that coalesced around Sonnie's response started with several ethnographic experiences I had while studying at Emory University.

Beyond Institutional Religion: Studying Religion and Health

I came to Emory University after spending two years working in North Carolina for the Division of Public Health. My research direction changed profoundly as a result of ethnographic research that I conducted for the Reproductive Health and Religion Project at Emory. Although the project addressed the effects of women's religious beliefs on their reproductive health decisions, my own analysis and writing began to focus on the prevalence of violence in the narratives of the women at the homeless shelter where I worked.[5] I followed this up with ethnographic research in a domestic violence shelter in North Carolina. There, I focused on the various systems and organizations that women affected by violence must navigate, each with its own expectations of who the survivor is and each with its own vision for how justice and human rights are performed, created, and maintained. I

---

4. The TRC "Women and the Conflict" report notes that "approximately 300,000 Liberians were internally displaced by 2003 and another 320,000 were refugees in neighboring countries; an estimated 80% were women and children." Republic of Liberia Truth and Reconciliation Commission, "Volume Three: Appendices Title 1: Women and the Conflict," 34.

5. Hardison-Moody, "Getting This Off My Chest."

Introduction

found myself wondering how people survived, endured, and even thrived in spite of this kind of intense violence. What does it mean to envision healing in the midst of pain, woundedness, and suffering? How do understandings of flourishing shift when they are placed in critical conversation with women's experiences of violence? How do women experience and survive trauma—not only in the moment of violence, but as it "unfolds" in everyday life?[6] And how should we think about what care looks like for women who have experienced this kind of trauma?

In those same years, I attended the United Nations Commission on the Status of Women (UNCSW) meetings where I focused on the ways that religion emerges (or fails to emerge) when women, peace, and violence are discussed.[7] I found that a human rights perspective often failed to recognize religion as a legitimate frame of reference, despite the fact that for many grassroots activists and, perhaps most significantly, survivors of violence, religion is often a guiding frame for all of life (particularly in an African context).[8] As anthropologist Sally Engle Merry found in her work on the UNCSW, international human rights actors often assume that secular approaches based in the legal or political system will (and should) ultimately triumph over "traditional" or "religious" practices for ending gender-based violence.[9] By contrast, I have found that activists and survivors increasingly draw upon religious traditions and practices to address the complicated nature of violence and conflict.

Subsequent fieldwork with survivors of conflict-related violence in a Liberian church in domestic violence shelter in North Carolina confirmed that for many survivors of violence, religion mattered in their healing processes. In these two settings, as well as in the homeless shelter, where I conducted fieldwork for the Religion and Reproductive Health Project, like Sonnie, I heard women talk about the fact that "God was there" in the moment of violence (or the threat of it), helping them to get through it. All these various experiences suggested that there is a need for a more nuanced understanding of religion in frameworks, practices, and programs that address healing as it relates to conflict and violence.

---

6. Das, *Life and Words*, 1.

7. My thanks to Emory University's Initiative in Religious Practices and Practical Theology for the funding to attend these meetings.

8. See Magesa, African *Religion*; Olupona and Nyang, eds., *Religious Plurality in Africa*; Horton, *Patterns of Thought in Africa and the West*.

9. Merry, *Human Rights and Gender Violence*, 15.

In this book, I argue that religion matters in situations of conflict and their aftermath. When religion is addressed in a public health or human rights frame, it is often only parsed in its institutional forms (i.e., in terms of religious leadership, doctrine, or institutions). Here, I bring to the fore the everyday practices that women engage as they seek healing. This intervention can benefit from language about healing and transformation also used by theologians with feminist and practical commitments to care and gender justice.

Why Liberia?

One key question that I feel I need to answer this early on in the book is, "Why focus on Liberia?" First, because Liberia has become somewhat of a case study for international conversations about women, war, and peace. The adoption of UN Security Council Resolution (SCR) 1325 has led to international attention on the role women play in peacebuilding work.[10] A report released in the fall of 2010 by the International Civil Society Action Network (ICAN) and the MIT Center for International Studies, titled "What the Women Say: Participation and UNSCR 1325," noted the invisibility of women's peacebuilding practices—to funders, international agencies, and national governments—as a major barrier to the implementation of UNSCR 1325 on women, peace, and conflict.[11] The invisibility of women's peacebuilding work and, significantly, a lack of attention to the ways women think about peace and healing, has had concrete implications for women's lives and for the future of peace processes worldwide. Liberia was a case study for this report.[12] Second, the success of the 2008 film *Pray the Devil Back to Hell* and the selection of two Liberian women, activist

---

10. According to the United Nations Office of the Special Advisor on Gender Issues and the Advancement of Women, Security Council Resolution 1325 "reaffirms the important role of women in the prevention and resolution of conflicts, peace negotiations, peace-building, peacekeeping, humanitarian response and in post-conflict reconstruction and stresses the importance of their equal participation and full involvement in all efforts for the maintenance and promotion of peace and security." United Nations, "Landmark Resolution."

11. International Civil Society Network and MIT Center for International Studies, "What the Women Say."

12. The Global Network of Women Peacebuilders is a civil society organization dedicated to increasing women's participation in peace work. They have produced a detailed report on cost and financing of SCR 1325. See Cabrera-Balleza and Popovic, "Costing and Financing Implementation."

Introduction

Leymah Gbowee and Liberian President Ellen Johnson Sirleaf for the 2011 Nobel Peace Prize, has brought renewed attention to women's experiences of violence and their role as peacebuilders in this country.

When I returned to the US from Liberia in early 2009 and was volunteering for the United Nations Development Fund for Women (UNIFEM), I met and befriended Laura Paynes, the Executive Director of an organization working on Liberian issues in North Carolina. Laura and I hit it off immediately, and soon I was working with her organization, studying their process, and interviewing women in her networks. Working with Laura led me to Friendship Community Church, where I conducted fieldwork for this project. I spent nine months with this church, attending weekly services, interviewing members, and attending women's prayer meetings and events. I subsequently partnered with Friendship Community Church and Laura's foundation to develop a "women's empowerment group" to address some of the issues of trauma and healing that were present in the Liberian community.

During my 2009 trip to Liberia, I attended a conference, which focused on post-conflict regional stability and heard international and national academics and dignitaries discuss a way forward for the Mano-River region of West Africa, which had been terrorized by years of national civil wars that profoundly affected regional stability. In her opening address, Liberia's President Sirleaf asked us to think about regional and national stability as "a question of transformation," noting that if Liberia and its neighbors "do not go through transformation, we simply repeat the mistakes of the past, and we find ourselves sinking back into these old practices."[13] This book draws on this fieldwork, and focuses on one key concept that has been central to post-conflict theory: transformation. I explore how, with the help of religion, transformation happens in and through the course of everyday life as women narrate and enact healing for self and community.

Besides trauma and hardship, conflict and war provide a particularly intense opportunity for transformation and growth at individual, communal, and national levels. The devastating effect of conflict is not all that remains in its "aftermath"[14]; new possibilities for transforming individual, communal, and national life also emerge, and specifically the question of

13. Transcript of remarks made by Her Excellency, Ellen Johnson Sirleaf, President of Liberia at "Mano River Region at Risk?: Post-Conflict Conversations Within and Across Borders," a "States at Regional Risk" Conference sponsored by the Institute of Critical International Studies (ICIS) of Emory University. Monrovia, Liberia. January 13–14, 2009.

14. Meintjes, Pillay and Turshen, *There is No Aftermath for Women*, 7–8.

what it means to reconcile, heal, and thrive. Through fieldwork—and specifically interviews and participant observation—conducted with Liberian communities in the United States and in Liberia, I explore the role that religious traditions, beliefs, and practices play in the ways that this transformation and healing occurs.

In Liberia, Christian, Muslim, and African traditional beliefs and practices shaped the ways the war was lived and described[15] and the ways that the women's peacebuilding movement functioned.[16] In response, this book asks how religious practices and beliefs have affected the ways that reconciliation and healing are imagined in this post-conflict period. This interdisciplinary project demonstrates the intersections of religious, political, and cultural meanings on practices of reconciliation and healing. As such, this project will be of interest to scholars thinking about African religions and religions in Africa, the intersections of religion, conflict, and peacebuilding, and gender and religion. Though this project represents fieldwork in one particular context and community, it has ramifications for the emerging discipline of religion and health, specifically that it points toward new languages for healing that are attentive to the intersections of religion and practice in everyday life.

Grounding Assumptions

Several assumptions shape this book: 1) that we should look beyond the "traditional" avenues of redress or power for the ways in which healing and transformation emerge; 2) that women's religious lives are multiple and layered; and 3) that research with communities should begin with a participatory stance from the researcher.

Regarding the first assumption, that transformation and healing often happen beyond the purview of traditional or institutional sources of power, I note that issues of post-conflict transformation and transitional justice have recently emerged as a vital concern for feminist scholarship.[17] Much of this work has focused on the role of the state in mediating justice for women. However, feminist theorists are beginning to recognize the

15. Ellis, *The Mask of Anarchy*.
16. Moran and Pitcher, "The 'Basket Case' and the 'Poster Child.'"
17. Scanlon, "Foreword," *African Journal of Conflict Resolution*. See also Scully, "Should We Give up on the State?"; and Bell and O'Rourke, "Does Feminism Need a Theory of Transitional Justice?"

Introduction

"fundamental misfit" in working for justice and healing through these avenues only.[18] In line with this, I argue that we should examine the ways that healing and transformation happen outside of these traditional avenues of redress of the state and the law. So while the Liberia Truth and Reconciliation report recommends memorialization practices and rituals on a larger scale in Liberia, I focus on the ways that healing and peace are negotiated among Liberian women now living in North Carolina.[19] These practices include women meeting to talk about their experiences during the war through trauma healing workshops and practices of leadership, prayer, and mothering. My experience with women in the Liberian community in North Carolina as well as memoirs about women's experiences of the Liberian Civil War, suggest to me that often healing happens not in any grand public way but as women go about their everyday lives.[20]

The second assumption that grounds this work is that women's religious lives are multiple and layered. In this, I follow in the footsteps of scholars like Tracy Hucks, who describes African-American women's "multiple religious allegiance[s]," whereby women blend together traditions and practices "for accessing spiritual power and for obtaining alternative modes of healing and recovery."[21] Similarly, womanist theologian Monica Coleman deftly analyzes materially and theologically the ways in which women's religious experiences often defy traditional systematic theological categories. She begins her text, *Making a Way Out of No Way: A Womanist Process Theology*, by telling two stories. The first story is of a women's sexual assault survivors group. The women in the group are braiding the hair of one of their members who has just been assaulted by her partner. For the woman who is bleeding and crying, the hair braiding is a practice of care; through the women's tender ministrations, she feels embraced by God.[22] The second story is of a Yoruba-based dance class that Coleman attends, where women experience healing through the movement of their bodies and the pulsing rhythm of the drum.[23] Noting that womanist theology has traditionally been written from an explicitly Christian perspective, Coleman develops a theological position that is able to speak to both of these

---

18. Scully, "Should We Give Up on the State?," 30.
19. See, Republic of Liberia, "Women and the Conflict," 57–58.
20. See Das, *Life and Words*, 216.
21. Hucks, "Burning with a Flame in America."
22. Coleman, *Making a Way*, 1–3.
23. Ibid., 3–6.

groups: the sexual assault survivor and the women in the African dance class.[24] Coleman argues that the postmodern womanist theology she develops is "a verb"; it is active and moving.[25] It is a metaphysical theology that starts with experience and endeavors to form a system of ideas that explains our experience. It represents "our best ideas given what we know."[26]

Coleman, like Hucks, finds that women's religious identities are often capable of adapting to and incorporating from multiple religious traditions. Because this is the case, she argues, "that activity is primary, with meaning ascribed *after* practice."[27] Like Coleman and Hucks, it is helpful to think of women's religious lives as being born out of their own practices and narratives. This is in keeping with observations of anthropologists of religion like Joyce Burkhalter Flueckiger, who argue for an indigenous understanding of religious practice. As Flueckiger found in her work with Amma, a Muslim healer in Hyderabad, India, rather than understanding Amma's work in terms of some conception of "true Islam," we arrive at a more nuanced comprehension of the particularities of a religious tradition (and the blendings women make among traditions) when we bracket this claim to authenticity.[28]

Like these anthropologists, religious studies scholars, and theologians, I argue that before viewing a practice of belief through an analytic or systematic theological lens, we do well to listen to and observe how women narrate and practice their sense of what it is to be religious, to experience peace, and to find healing.

The third assumption that grounds this book is closely related to the second of beginning with women's experience and expression of their religious lives: in my research I adopt a participatory stance that puts the community at the center of the research project. Linda Tuhiwai Smith, in her book *Decolonizing Methodologies: Research and Indigenous People,* notes that research supposedly *with* indigenous peoples often actually has been research *on* indigenous peoples. Rather than beginning with the indigenous communities' concerns, desires, and issues, researchers often approach a community or society with their own questions that they have developed independent of any conversation or dialogue with those among whom they

---

24. Ibid., 8.
25. Ibid., 169.
26. Ibid., 43.
27. Ibid.
28. Flueckiger, *In Amma's Healing Room,* 11.

work. Smith encourages researchers to "decolonize" their methodologies by adopting a more participatory model of research, which includes: asking members of the community to serve on the research team, designing research protocols in concert with the community, and sharing theoretical constructs and findings with the community.[29] Smith advocates for sharing research, for having an active dialogue between researcher and community, and for assuming a reciprocal relationship in which each contributes something to the eventual "product" (the research, community development plan, health intervention, etc.) that is created.[30]

In what I describe in this book I attempted to take such a participatory stance. Rather than assuming the causes and remedies for violence, I began by talking with communities and individuals about their experiences of violence and the ways in which they understood violence, healing, and transformation. Based on what the women told me, I also mapped out the places in the community where individuals sought out redress, reconciliation, healing, and justice, including through religious institutions, traditions, and practices.

I suggest that by paying attention to the ways that women define and practice peace and healing (in their words and on their terms), we might learn a great deal about the ways that peace is lived and learned despite the traumatic horrors that violence imposes upon a life. Tracing women's narratives and faith practices helps us to see the ways that religion matters for women who have survived violence. And it matters in remarkably ordinary ways—in the prayers women say as they express hope for the future, in the ways they turn to God in an effort to survive and "make a way out of no way," and even in the ways they imagine and create new families. I pay attention by placing women's narratives and practices in conversation with theories of transformation, peace, and healing—many of which emerge out of feminist post-conflict literature or human rights frameworks. I look for where ideas of transformation overlap with actual practice. I also look for the gaps and fissures between the international frameworks or theories and women's actual practices and lives, so that women's lives and practices can correct how healing and transformation are defined. This complicated understanding of the ways religion matters as women negotiate healing is a necessary and vital part of the larger conversation about women, violence, and peace.

29. Smith, *Decolonizing Methodologies*, 142–61.
30. Ibid.

Chapter Structure

To be attentive to women's healing practices following a conflict we must be attentive to the everyday ways in which these healing practices emerge within local contexts and communities. The women chronicled in this text have found themselves in a situation that is far from ideal but they have made the moral, theological choice to live in ways that restore both self and community. These healing processes are not just physical, but affective as well, and are infused with the belief that there is good in the world despite the horrific evidence to the contrary. Their spirituality derives from both their Christian faith (all of the women discussed here are Christian) and their African religious sense of self and community. In that it reflects these ordinary, spiritual ways that women are reclaiming life after violence, theological language is a particular asset to the post-conflict work of transformation.

With women's narratives grounding this discussion, the next chapter contextualizes the Liberian Civil War and then makes the two key points on which this work depends: 1) Religion matters to many survivors of violence—a fact that international women's rights work must take into account; and 2) The ways in which women talk about and practice peace and healing should direct our theoretical and theological explorations of what healing is and how it emerges in women's lives.

The second chapter focuses on experiences of migration that so profoundly shape women's experiences of transformation and healing post-conflict. It begins with the stories of survivors of the Liberian Civil War and shows how for these women healing becomes possible because "God was there" in and after the moment of trial. This understanding of God's presence is a significant way that religion matters for the women from Liberia. By seeing God in and through their stories of hardship, they envisage healing as a real possibility in their lives, communities, and the world. This is not a naïve vision of healing; rather, it is complicated by the realities of violence and trauma they continue to experience as immigrants in North Carolina.

Chapter three explores the ways that healing happens in the body for many of the women with whom I worked. For healing is not only affective, but also bodily. I examine two particular practices: a trauma healing group that used art-therapy as a way for women to work through (rather than speak of) trauma, and prayer practices that allow women to "make a way" for healing after violence—both important because some people find

Introduction

it difficult to speak of trauma and so we must find other ways to do post-conflict transformation work.

By following the stories of three women who are leaders in the North Carolina Liberian community where I worked, chapter four examines the ways that women's leadership emerges in everyday contexts. These women's lives and practices allow us to see the moral and theological choices that women are making to pursue healing despite the reality of violence in their lives. They do this out of a care for self and community. I juxtapose these stories with international women's rights frameworks to show that we need to widen these frameworks to explore the ways that healing happens in and through everyday life.

Chapter five draws on the narratives and practices of mothering observed during fieldwork at the Liberian church to argue that mothering is one way that women experience healing of self and community after conflict. This chapter also draws on literature on the women's peace movement in Liberia that shows that the "strong mother" figure is a helpful archetype to understand how and why mothers are able to make claims on the community to promote peace and healing.

In chapter six, I look at more specifically Christian practices—the worship practices at Friendship Community Church—to see how they help the women to create new narratives of hope and life out of hardship and harm. Practices, gestures, and bodies—like narratives and stories—reveal the ways that religion matters in women's post-conflict transformation. The chapter begins with an exploration of religious practices and how they have been studied in both anthropology and theology. It then gives a thick description of worship practices at Friendship Community church to show how worship was one way women transformed life, or attempted to "make a way" after war and conflict. Finally, I unpack that phrase, "making a way," noting both its indigenous uses in the church and its theological origins in womanist theology. The languages and practices of "making a way" were some of the everyday ways that women from Friendship Community Church sought healing and transformation in this post-conflict community.

The text that follows is the result of my academic and personal journey to discover the ways women who have been affected by violence think about and practice healing. I learned that

1. Religion matters to many survivors of violence.

2. Women's everyday practices of peace and healing should be at the center of our theoretical and theological explorations of post-conflict transformation.

No representation of another person can ever be completely "truthful" or "authentic" (and any study of trauma forces us to realize that the "truth" of memory is incredibly complex).[31] However, I hope that what follows reflects the ways the Liberian women with whom I worked have transformed their selves and their communities following the violence they endured, and the role that religion plays in this transformation.

---

31. There are always difficulties in representing other people, particularly when it comes to survivors of violence. As Susan Brison writes, "traumatic memory, like narrative memory, is articulated, selective, even malleable, in spite of the fact that the framing of such memory may not be under the survivor's conscious control," 31. She goes on to write that representing survivors of trauma can perpetuate harmful victim stereotypes, and "may inadvertently perpetuate stereotypes of one's group as weak and helpless," Brison, *Aftermath*, 35.

Additionally, as Mercy Amba Oduyoye writes, much of what has been written about African women in a theological context has been about their victimization. In this text I have attempted to work against victimization narratives by writing about the ways women both experience and react to violence, including the ways that they survive, thrive and work for change in their worlds (see Chapter Three, particularly). See Oduyoye, *Beads and Strands*. See also Sharp, *Misunderstanding Stories*.

1

Women, War, and Peace

In March 2010 I attended my first United Nations (UN) Commission on the Status of Women (CSW) meeting. From around the world it brought together thousands of women representing hundreds of Non-Governmental Organizations (NGOs) to strategize about how to improve women's human rights globally. I was a representative from what was then the United Nations Development Fund for Women (UNIFEM), United States Chapter, and as such was able to attend several of the official delegate events on site. I spent much of my time observing how language about religion is framed, shaped, and crafted at the UN and the ways that this is then translated and disseminated by local programs and organizations. I attended numerous NGO-sponsored events (called "parallel sessions") at the Church Center Building and the Salvation Army where I realized that religion had become a "buzz word" for international women's human rights work, heard that international women's human rights activists must be "vigilant" in working against "religious fundamentalisms," and was told that we should recognize and build upon the "valuable" work of faith-based organizations.

At the 2010 CSW, particularly at official UN meetings that I attended, gender equality was touted as the best strategy to end gender-based violence internationally. In other words, legal and political reforms were given priority over strategies that were (problematically) described as "cultural," "traditional," or "religious." Despite this fact, talk about religion circulated at the various meetings I attended and seemed to function in two ways: 1) "Religious fundamentalisms" were presented as a problem that women's human rights actors needed to overcome; and 2) "Faith-based organizations" were offered as a promising institutional space for gender equality programmatic work. In this way, faith communities that affirmed the ideals of gender equality could be mobilized to support and carry out international gender justice work. On the one hand I heard that dogmatic and anti-feminist religion was something to be feared and combated and on the other that religion offered valuable institutional space and programmatic support.

A particular human rights story also emerged in conversations about gender-based violence. It began like this: Studies show that between one quarter and three quarters of all women worldwide will be affected by domestic violence or sexual assault. Gender-based violence is an epidemic across the world.[1] The story continued usually with a particular contextual situation—women in Africa, women in post-conflict countries, women in refugee or internally displaced person camps, women and global migration. The story then suggested policy and programmatic solutions for ending violence, with most of these solutions based on legal or political frameworks. In other words, the assumption was that to control and prevent gender-based violence, the state needed to assume its proper role in the "protection" of women as "vulnerable" subjects.[2] The aim of these stories, offered by those who work on international women's human rights, was toward gender equality throughout the world. This idea of gender equality, as anthropologist Sally Engle Merry emphasizes, is often directly contrasted to strategies or solutions that are "traditional," "cultural," or "religious."[3] In fact, at UN CSW in 2011, I heard one presenter from the United Nations Population Fund (UNFPA) state that "religion and culture are interlinked"; together they form the "basis for violence against women" and "harmful cultural practices."

My fieldwork at CSW left me wondering: 1) What discursive and practical work does a turn to "religion" do for women's human rights activists? 2) Is that role different from the role religion plays in the lives of those with/for whom these activists work?

---

1. World Health Organization, "Fact Sheet: Violence Against Women."

2. For more on the "vulnerable subject" see Fineman, "The Vulnerable Subject." Fineman posits a turn to the vulnerable subject rather than the autonomous individual of liberalism. Vulnerability points out that we are all capable of being harmed by one another, or being subjected to diseases or disorders that attack from outside. Pamela Scully has written a salient critique of the use of the frame of vulnerability and protection in international women's human rights work. See also Scully, "Vulnerable Women."

3. Merry, *Human Rights and Gender Violence*, 15, 44.

The United Nations Commission on the Status of Women: Between Feminist Theory and Theology

Yet how religion functioned at CSW becomes more complicated when examined from the standpoint of practice rather than discourse alone. Following Courtney Bender's study of lived religion at an AIDS organization, my focus is on the ways "religion and spiritual things are made manifest daily" through practice, words, and actions.[4] Each morning at CSW, I attended worship services planned and organized by the members of Ecumenical Women, a coalition of Christian denominations committed to gender equality and social justice.[5] These services highlighted in visual form the intersections of religion and human rights, performatively blending the "stories" of human rights work such as the Beijing Platform for Action and the Convention on the Elimination of All Forms of Discrimination Against Women with the stories of women exemplars, saints, and prophets from the Christian tradition.

I found myself in a world that wanted to talk about the impact of religion on women's lives, but by framing it only in terms of the ways in which religious institutions discriminate against or oppress women, or the ways that religious organizations could be harnessed to do vital human rights work. Religion was talked about as if it existed only in its doctrinal or institutional forms; conversations didn't capture the complicated and everyday ways that religion actually matters in women's lives.

I realized that scholars of religion can contribute to this conversation a language and a way of understanding the role of religion in and through daily life that speaks to and with women's experiences. My own work in this area is profoundly shaped by the field of feminist practical theology, which I believe offers a particularly apt theoretical lens through which to consider these practices of health and healing.

As Mary McClintock Fulkerson notes, "the practical theological task has to do with the way Christian faith occurs as a contemporary situation."[6] Feminist theologians like Serene Jones have examined life and practice in their theological scholarship. In her article "Transnational Feminism and the Rhetoric of Religion," Jones elaborates on the "nitty gritty play of our

---

4. Bender, *Heaven's Kitchen*, 3.

5. For more on Ecumenical Women at the United Nations, visit http://ecumenical-women.org/.

6. Fulkerson, *Places of Redemption*, 7.

everyday practices" that engender a "transnational feminism that seeks the flourishing of women."[7] When rhetoric breaks down, as it often does when people are working across great discursive and community divides, this everyday practice can sustain us, can call us back to practices of hospitality and solidarity, which are fundamental to healing.

Jones and Fulkerson point out that life and practice are not measurable, and they point us toward a way of understanding human experience that is illustrative for both theory and theology. Finding myself in the midst of international conversations about women, violence, and peace, I started to see that my particular training had something to offer these conversations. I wondered: How might conversations about women, war, and peace shift if we start by looking at the ways that women talk about peace and healing in their own words? What might we learn about the ways women are able to survive after violence by being attentive to their practices? Theologians provide an alternative language of healing and peace that offers a pointed intervention into international conversations about women, war, and peace. In other words, theologians can help these international and local human rights actors to see the ways in which *religion matters* for women who have survived violence.

When Religion Matters: Thesis and Background

As my time at the UN highlighted, there is a need for increased conversation about how, when, and why religion matters for women who have faced experiences of violence. We need to hear what women say about how they negotiate peace and healing in the course of their everyday lives. Theology that is both practical and feminist can contribute to this growing conversation about women's experiences of war and its aftermath. This book therefore centers on the lives and practices of religious people, providing a paradigm for understanding the ways religion matters in women's lives. This text is an intercession into the conversations about women and violence that I heard at the United Nations and the ways that institutional religion was talked about as either a danger or a potential instrument of change. As a scholar of religion and health and as someone trained in practical theology, I believe that theologians have much to contribute to these broad-sweeping international conversations. Not only are practical theologians equipped to pay attention to the intricate ways that religious practices

---

7. Jones, "Transnationalism and the Rhetoric of Religion," 104.

emerge from, challenge, and shape communities and individuals, but our disciplinary lens can help to develop a theological language of healing that can provide a valuable counterpoint to the measurable, quantifiable way in which health and transformation are often talked about. This language can also more closely mimic the indigenous ways that the women with whom I worked describe the moral choices they make and the practices in which they engage to find healing for self and community.

In what follows, I explore the ways that religion matters to women who have survived the Liberian Civil War. I look at both their narratives and practices to discern how healing and peace emerge in their lives, families, and communities. By hearing what women say and by understanding how they practice their faith, a complex picture of peace and healing emerges that describes a process in the midst of ordinary life, a process in which women take in the resources of their religious traditions and practices and harness them for survival, resilience, and hope for the future. From these Liberian women's practices and narratives, I develop a vision of healing in conversation with practical, feminist, and womanist theologians. Because it is not based on quantifiable objectives or measurements of health or peace, it offers an alternative view of the ways in which peace and healing emerge in and through women's everyday narratives and practices. This chapter lays some of the groundwork for the text through its introduction both to the historical context of the Liberian Civil War and to the women's human rights and feminist post-conflict transformation literature that will serve as a conversation partner for the ethnographic experiences and interviews highlighted throughout this text.

The Liberian Civil War: Women's Experiences

The context for this text is the Liberian Civil War and its effects on Liberian women now living a world away in an urban city in North Carolina. Liberia is a small country in West Africa, founded in 1822 by slaves emancipated from the United States and from slave boats bound for the United States. The connection with the United States has, through the years, remained strong, particularly in the minds of many Liberians. Leymah Gbowee describes it as a "blood tie," and notes other connections between the countries:

> Our constitution was modeled on America's; our capital was named after President James Monroe. Until the 1980's, our official currency was the US dollar, and even after we had a Liberian

dollar, US money was both accepted everywhere and desirable. My friends and I grew up on shows like Sanford and Son, Good Times, Dynasty and Dallas.[8]

Although not always recognized by U.S. Americans, Liberia's sister country played a significant role in both its political and cultural history.

From its founding in 1822 until 1980, Liberia was governed by descendants of the American settlers known as Americo-Liberians or "Congo" Liberians. These settlers lived mainly in and around Monrovia and developed a system of indirect rule over the indigenous Africans already living in Liberia.[9] This system became a source of profit for the growing nation of Liberia, but the resultant wealth did not reach most of its indigenous people.[10] It was only in 1963 that this system of indirect rule was abolished, although the effects of the "colonial-style system of government" lingered. Consequently, as historian Stephen Ellis has recounted, non-Americo-Liberian families born before the 1960s would have been raised under a system of government in which "national power and prestige lay with an oligarchy of people, most of them with some American ancestry, who professed Christianity, were literate in English, and made a public display of what they themselves called 'civilisation.'"[11] Until the military coup of 1980, which established Samuel Doe as the first "native born" Liberian President, indigenous families and traditions were often disparaged and oppressed.

Doe came to power in 1980 as a result of a military takeover. As anthropologist Mary Moran writes, Doe and "the young military men who took power violently in 1980 represented themselves as acting in the interests of the disenfranchised: the rural and urban poor, the 'tribal' people who had been excluded from real power for the previous 30 years."[12] Doe's government set out by killing several dozen Americo-Liberians, including prominent ministers and government officials. In her memoir, *The House at Sugar Beach: In Search of a Lost African Childhood*, journalist Helene Cooper talks about her family's experience of the brutality of the Doe government. On the first anniversary of a series of riots that had occurred over the price of rice (a staple product in Liberia), Cooper's family home was overrun by a group of soldiers who raped Cooper's mother. Soon after, her

---

8. Gbowee, *Mighty Be Our Powers*, 7.
9. Ellis, *The Mask of Anarchy*, 37.
10. Ibid., 42.
11. Ibid.
12. Moran, *Liberia*, 8.

uncle Cecil was shot at Barclay Beach, along with eight other men.[13] Her family left for the United States exactly one month after the coup. Their experience was common among the several Americo-Liberian women in North Carolina with whom I worked.

Not surprisingly, many other Liberians of Americo-Liberian descent left for the United States in the early 1980s, fearing retribution, harassment, imprisonment, and even death at the hands of the new government forces. Marie, one of the women I interviewed for this project, who later founded a shelter for Liberian survivors of gender-based violence, recounted to me how her family left Liberia in 1980, but how she was unable to make the last flight out of the airport with her family, and how she was left with an uncle in Monrovia until she was able to escape in the mid-1990s. Ella, another woman I interviewed, told me of her time as a young woman living in Doe's Liberia. Her mother, like Ella, a "Congo woman" or descendant of the settler class, was arrested. Her family moved to the United States (like Cooper's family) in the mid-1980s to escape the persecution.

When Doe came to power, individuals from rural areas, who previously had not been a part of the Monrovia establishment, took up residence in the capital city, particularly individuals from Doe's homeland of Grand Gedeh county, and became ministers and government officials.[14] As those who had held power fled to the United States or other countries, Doe's government welcomed indigenous Liberians who had previously been shunned from political life.[15] One such person was Aletha Meah, now the pastor of Friendship Community Church. Pastor Meah, from Grand Gedeh county, served in the Doe government as a high level Assistant Deputy Minister. In this position, she was able to travel the world, experiencing new places and people she had never met before, like Europe, and many countries in Africa and the United States. She also served as an assistant minister in a Baptist Church in Monrovia, and took care of her own children as well as nieces and nephews who lived with her and her husband in Monrovia. After the coup things "settled down," she said, but not for long.

By 1983, the support for the military government was beginning to slip. A coup attempt on Doe's government in 1982 led him to become increasingly paranoid; although the original 1980 cabinet was "multiethnic," Doe became "fearful of ambitious young soldiers like himself" and began

13. Cooper, *The House at Sugar Beach*, 175–78.
14. Ellis, *The Mask of Anarchy*; Moran, *Liberia*, 80.
15. Ellis, *The Mask of Anarchy*, 56.

"the systematic purge of all but members of his own Krahn region from the ranks of the elite military forces and strategic government posts."[16] This Krahn-dominated government, and the increasing retribution Doe perpetrated against anyone who opposed him, "prompted the formation of ethnically defined resistance groups, with no political ideology beyond opposition to Doe and led by men like Charles Taylor, whose sole ambition was to gain control of the apparatus of the state."[17] These conditions of repression and favoritism led to what would become the Liberian Civil War.

The first stage of the war began in 1989 when Charles Taylor and Prince Johnson, then both leaders of the National Patriotic Front of Liberia (NPFL), launched a coup. Supported financially by individuals in the United States (including current President Ellen Johnson Sirleaf[18]) and militarily by the Gaddafi government in Libya (where rebels received training and arms),[19] Taylor and Johnson launched an attack on their country. Despite the presence of troops from the Economic Community of West African States (ECOWAS) in 1990, Samuel Doe was tortured and killed by rebels, reportedly on the orders of Johnson. While Johnson and Taylor ended up parting ways, their campaigns that moved from the northeast and northwest respectively toward Monrovia marked the beginning of a brutal Civil War during which more than 200,000 Liberians were killed.

It was at this point that members of Doe's government, and notably, members of the Krahn ethnic group, began trying to leave Liberia en masse. Among them was the aforementioned Assistant Deputy Minister Meah, now Pastor Meah. Though she was preparing to leave her home, her husband, and the nieces and nephews she had living with them, Pastor Meah sent her children back home to Grand Gedeh county, with the hope that it would be easier for them to escape to Ivory Coast when things "got bad." Pastor Meah then left with her driver for Sierra Leone, unwittingly without her government passport (which she believes was stolen)—something that would make getting away from this increasingly regional conflict all the more difficult. When she got to the Sierra Leonean border, she heard from the officials there that she would not be able to cross, that all government ministers must return to Monrovia. There, at the border, she prayed, trusting that God would "make a way out of no way." Pastor Meah felt that

16. Ibid., 138.
17. Ibid.
18. Sirleaf, *This Child Will be Great*.
19. Ellis, *Mask of Anarchy*, 69–71.

she was delivered from Liberia by God,[20] was able to continue through to Sierra Leone and north to Guinea, and then took a plane to Ivory Coast. This circuitous route to Ivory Coast was due in most part to the way that the war progressed in Liberia. Rebels were entering the country through Ivory Coast and beginning to set up deadly check points where they would often murder, on the spot, those they suspected of being from certain ethnic groups.[21] As the rebels began to bear down on central Liberia toward the capital, the routes out of the country became increasingly perilous.

The war was perilous—and not only for those women and men who were a part of the Doe government. As the war raged on, other ethnic groups, organizations, and national and regional bodies became involved. Doe's death did not mean the end of fighting, as government forces along with ECOWAS, INPFL, and NPFL forces continued to struggle for control of the country. As a response to the violence of the NPFL and INPFL, other factions like the United Liberation Movement for Democracy in Liberia (ULIMO) emerged in 1991. The country was spiraling into a brutal Civil War.

This brutality was felt particularly by women and by children, many of whom were conscripted into armed service with rebel fighters.[22] For Laura Paynes, a Liberian woman from Caldwell just outside of Monrovia, her

20. It is important to note that Pastor Meah and others in the church describe God in male gendered language. I am citing her words here.

21. As Ellis writes, "While Taylor was waiting to make a final assault on Monrovia, he was building an impressive personal fief [outside the city]. All roads in NPFL territory, the greater part of Liberia, were sealed with numerous check-points where travelers were liable to be stopped and interrogated and have their goods looted by those on duty. Many Monrovians derive some of their worst memories of the war from the period in mid-to-late 1990, when the NPFL was establishing itself outside the city. All over its territory, the NPFL set up check-points known as 'gates' along the road, usually consisting of a piece of rope stretched between two poles, manned by gun-toting NPFL fighters, sometimes no more than children. Often these check-points were decorated with ghastly trophies such as human skulls . . . The US embassy estimated that at one NPFL check-point known as 'No Return,' no fewer than 2,000 people were killed in the course of 1990, their bodies often remaining unburied in the surrounding bush. No one would touch them for fear of being considered a government collaborator." Ellis, *Mask of Anarchy*, 89.

22. As the TRC "Women and the Conflict" report notes, the TRC collected more than 20,000 statements, of which 51% were from women. The TRC designated 23 kinds of violations, of which "forced displacement stands out and represented one third of the reported violations, followed by killing, assault, abduction, looting, forced labor, destruction of property." Women were significantly more likely to be raped. See the Republic of Liberia's "Women in the Conflict" report for more detailed statistical analysis of women's varied experiences during the conflict, particularly 28–51.

current work as an advocate for Liberian youth living in the United States was fueled by her own harrowing experiences, and the experiences of children she helped in these early stages of the war. Laura and her family were held captive in their hometown of Caldwell by some of Charles Taylor's soldiers as they made their way to Monrovia. Eventually the young soldiers took the townspeople of Caldwell with them on the road, shutting them inside a church between Caldwell and Monrovia. Laura and her family were imprisoned there for several days, until the soldiers heard that Prince Johnson's soldiers were headed their way. The group inside the church felt some relief when the soldiers fled, but they did not step outside of the church until several days later. Laura, her mother, and her little brother then traveled to Monrovia, where they were eventually separated, only to find each other again a year later. She was able to return to her job in Monrovia, working for the US Embassy, but she felt compelled to do something about what she had seen and escaped. She told me that living near the Embassy were dozens of homeless children displaced by the war. Discreetly (because of her job) she began to take care of these children, finding them a place to stay and giving them food from what little money she had. This was the beginning of Laura's humanitarian work. These "children" (now grown) still call Laura on holidays and for her birthday, and to Laura, they will always be "her kids."

During the first stage of the war (which Liberians called "World War I"), a series of peace accords was reached, ending in 1997 with democratic elections in which Charles Taylor was elected President of Liberia in 1997 with 75% of the vote; his outrageous campaign slogan, "He killed my ma, he killed my pa, I'll vote for him," reminded Liberians that if Taylor were to lose the election, he would continue to wage war for control of the country.[23]

During and after "World War I," women like Laura, Marie and Pastor Meah were playing multiple roles in an attempt to save their families, their children (whether biological or not), and themselves.[24] Though all three women were able to make it to the United States before the second phase of the war ("World War II" as it was known) began, nonetheless that war had a profound effect on their lives as well. For example, Marie's work for women affected by gender-based violence was a result of her own experiences and

---

23. Ellis, *The Mask of Anarchy*, 109.

24. As Agnes M. Fallah Kamara-Umunna writes, "We called the first war, the one fought from 1989–1996, 'World War I.' We called the second war, the one fought from 1999—2003, 'World War II.' Which goes to show you just how horrific they were." Kamara-Umunna and Holland, *And Still Peace Did Not Come*, 4.

hearing the stories of women she came in contact with at refugee camps or at home in Liberia. Women were traumatized as a result of the violence they suffered at the hands of fighters during the war. As she told me:

> It was important to open [the shelter] because there was no shelter, and you had survivors who had been raped during the Civil War and also after the war . . . and also after the war, post-conflict Liberia. There was an alarming rate of children who were seven to thirteen [in age] who needed a place where they could go to because the community would you know, shun them, you know, so they needed a place.

This account echoes what has been reported in the Liberia TRC's "Women and the Conflict" report, which noted that the continued effects of violence against women and girls during the Civil War caused many women to feel ashamed, corroding their "self-worth and dignity."[25]

In 2000, what became known as "World War II" broke out between new warring factions, including Liberians United for Reconciliation and Democracy (LURD) and Taylor's government. In the early 2000s, some of the most dangerous years of the war, fighting outside of Monrovia caused massive displacements, with thousands of internally displaced persons (IDPs) fleeing to Monrovia to overcrowded IDP camps and, in desperation, eventually the national football field. In 2003, due to pressure from West African leaders, the international community, and, significantly, women's peace movements within Liberia, the warring factions were finally brought together in Accra, Ghana to bring an end to the fighting and develop a roadmap for the way forward.[26]

The film *Pray the Devil Back to Hell* (2008), directed by Gini Reticker, tells the story of women in the Women in Peacebuilding Network (WIPNET) in Liberia who worked together across religious divides to confront and convince President Charles Taylor and rival warlords to bring peace to their country in the midst of this Civil War.[27] In the film, we hear the stories of

---

25. Republic of Liberia, "Women and the Conflict," 52.

26. See Fuest, "This is the time to get out front" and Fuest, "Liberia's women acting for peace."

27. It is important to point out that women are only portrayed in this film as victims of violence and peacemakers; however, women played multiple roles during the conflict, something that I describe in the next section of this chapter. Women were also combatants during the Liberian Civil War, and one of the most notorious female fighters, Black Diamond, was profiled in the BBC audio documentary. See Samura, "West African Journeys: Part Three." As Pamela Scully writes, Security Council Resolution 1325 and

Leymah Gbowee, Etweda "Sugars" Cooper, Vaiba Flomo, and Asatu Bah Kenneth, leaders of WIPNET who brought Liberian women together to encourage a ceasefire and to push forward the peace process. Working for peace through more traditional avenues of politics and the law was dangerous, and because the women could have been severely persecuted and punished for criticizing Taylor or the warlord leaders of Liberians United for Reconciliation and Democracy (LURD), they decided instead to work for peace through their religious institutions. As Gbowee recalls:

> Taylor went to church, and the leadership of LURD went to the Mosque. Taylor could pray the devil out of hell. And we said, if this man is so religious, we need to get to that thing that he holds firmly to. So if the women started pressurizing the pastors and the bishops, the pastors and the bishops would pressurize the leaders. And if the women from the mosque started talking to the Imams, they would pressurize the warlords also.[28]

This allowed them to bring together a significant contingent of leaders and supporters from throughout Liberia. It also gave their project legitimacy in the eyes of the people and leaders of Liberia, for it drew upon accepted avenues of redress and representation, including mediation, prayer, and the women's status as mothers.[29] The women were not naïve about the process. As Gbowee recounts of the Disarmament, Demobilization, and Reintegration (DDR) process, women brought special skills to the work of peace: "We know the history. We know the people. We knew how to talk to an ex-combatant and get his cooperation, because we know where he comes from. To outsiders like the UN, these soldiers were a problem to be managed. But they were our children."[30]

The women of WIPNET drew on the memory of Christian-based coalitions, bringing in Muslim and women who practiced African religions as well, in order to work for peace and an end to violence. As the film portrays, through songs, prayer and mediation, the women of WIPNET were able to draw upon the resources of their congregations as well as indigenous

---

its accompanying resolutions focuses primarily on women's roles as victims of violence as opposed to considering them as "individuals legitimately aspiring to a variety of freedoms." See Scully, "Vulnerable Women," 120.

28. Reticker, *Pray the Devil Back to Hell.*
29. Moran and Pitcher, "The Basket Case," 506–7.
30. Gbowee, *Mighty Be our Powers,* 172.

traditions of women's ritual and political authority to work for peace.[31] Gbowee's memoir, published in 2011, details the religious motivations of this movement and the women's work for peace, which was accomplished both through the work of WIPNET and the Liberia Women's Initiative (LWI). The LWI attended the Accra Peace Conference in 2003 and conducted letter writing campaigns to African First Ladies to "impress upon their governments to intervene in ending the war in Liberia."[32] Eventually, the women's work paid off, and a peace deal was brokered at the Accra Peace Conference.

Taylor resigned the presidency on August 11, 2003, and a transitional government was appointed, headed by Chairman Gyude Bryant. Ellen Johnson Sirleaf won the 2005 elections, and was inaugurated in 2006, making her the first African woman to serve as head of state. The war was over, but the women's work for healing had just begun, as Gbowee writes:

> The psychic damage was almost unimaginable. A whole generation of young men had no idea who they were without a gun in their hands. Several generations of women were widowed, had been raped, seen their daughters and mothers raped, and their children kill and be killed. Neighbors had turned against neighbors; young people had lost hope and old people, everything they'd painstakingly earned. To a person, we were traumatized. We had survived the war, but now we had to remember how to live.[33]

The work ahead for Liberians was immense. This text addresses the ways in which one community remembers "how to live" and the ways that healing emerges in the midst of this. As Gbowee continues, "Peace isn't a moment—it's a very long process."[34]

As a part of that long peace process, a Truth and Reconciliation Commission (TRC) was established in 2005.[35] In addition to working with the

---

31. For an analysis of women's ritual authority and political life in Nigeria, see Amadiume, *Male Daughters, Female Husbands*.

32. Republic of Liberia, "Women and the Conflict," 45.

33. Gbowee, *Mighty Be Our Powers*, 268.

34. Ibid.

35. The mandate of the TRC in Liberia was to "document and investigate the massive wave of human rights violations," to "establish the root causes of the conflict and create a forum to address issues of impunity," to "identify victims and perpetrators," to create a "forum to facilitate constructive interchange between victims and perpetrators," to address economic and other social human rights violations, to review Liberia's history to determine the causes of the war, to deal with the issues faced by women and children

Liberian community in Liberia, the TRC engaged the Liberian Diaspora in the process, the first TRC in history to do so in such a sustained manner. This process provided a forum for 1,631 Liberians living outside of the country to participate in the statement-taking process of the TRC. This was important because key actors in the conflict (including witnesses, perpetrators, and victims) were known to be residing in the United States, Europe, and West Africa.[36]

Complicating the Ways We Talk about Women and Conflict

Women in Liberia experienced numerous acts of violence during the conflict, including rape, sexual assault, forced displacement, sexual exploitation, murder, and assault.[37] One woman told this story to the TRC:

> Sixteen armed men jumped over the fence, burst the gate and came into our apartment. They took cell phones, money—everything. I had my children—my son, my daughter, my two nephews and my nurse—with me. A boy with a hammer came toward me and said, "This woman is for me." He hit my head with the hammer. He pulled down my jeans in order to rape me. My little daughter started screaming. And the man grabbed my screaming child from my side and knocked her down and started raping her. He just grabbed her from me, raped her to death and laid her to the side.[38]

The gravity and magnitude of women's experiences of sexual violence during the war was a key focus of the TRC, which established a gender committee in 2006. Yet as the former TRC Gender Advisor Anu Pillay writes, this led to a "tendency to focus on victimhood, especially sexual and physical violations" in the work of the Commission, and the "full spectrum

---

during the conflict, to create a report, and to "make recommendations to the Government of Liberia for prosecution, reparation, amnesty, reconciliation and institutional reform." Republic of Liberia Truth and Reconciliation Commission. "Consolidated Final Report."

36. Young and Park, "Engaging Diasporas in Truth Commissions." As Young and Park write, "Diasporas have long played a role in movements to precipitate transitions in nation states. Those who have been forced—or who have made the difficult choice—to flee a regime are those who often have the greatest interest in pushing forward a transition," 348.

37. Republic of Liberia, "Women and the Conflict," 30.

38. Ibid., 41.

of women's involvement with their multiple identities did not fully emerge from the hearings."[39]

Pillay and others have noted that this focus on women solely as victims of conflict completely "ignores their role as accomplices in a negative sense or as activists and comrades in a positive sense."[40] The TRC report, "Women and the Conflict," provides a more comprehensive reading of the multiple roles women played during the conflict, including as combatants (either forced or voluntary). For many women combatants it was either "kill or be killed": "I wanted to help the rebellion. I thought that if my brothers could do it, well so could I. I wanted to do like my brothers. When you are little, you want to do as if you were tall. When you are a girl, do as if you were a boy."[41]

In her memoir, *And Still Peace Did Not Come: A Memoir of Reconciliation*, peace activist Agnes Fallah Kamara-Umunna describes her work with these young Liberian women who either joined or were conscripted into service. Her book describes how women who served as combatants were also abused sexually and forced to cook and clean for the male fighters. Hearing their stories caused Kamara-Umunna to wonder "if they had it worse in the war. Their jobs weren't done when they left the battle field."[42] She found these young women after the war, squatting in an old government building in Monrovia, "raising babies of rape and struggling to get by. Many were alcoholics. Some were sex workers. Others were on the verge of entering the sex trade. 'What choice do we got?' they asked me."[43] Struggling to get by both during the war and after, these former fighters did what they had to to survive, and often became quite self sufficient. As one woman, Comfort, told Kamara-Umunna, "I don't want no man to help me. I can support myself. Myself can help myself."[44]

Conflict can provide a nation and its communities with an opportunity to redefine and transform its political and religious structures and practices to build upon gains made by oppressed groups, like women,

---

39. Pillay, "Truth Seeking and Gender," 97.

40. Pillay, "Violence Against Women in the Aftermath," 39. See also Codou Bop's essay, "Women in Conflicts, Their Gains and Their Losses" and Sheila Meintjes's essay "War and Post-War Shifts in Gender Relations" in the same volume.

41. Republic of Liberia, "Women and the Conflict," 49.

42. Kamara-Umunna and Holland, *And Still Peace Did not Come*, 231.

43. Ibid.

44. Ibid.

during the conflict.[45] The women's movement in Liberia's role in moving forward the peace process and helping to elect the first African female president have been lauded internationally as a positive example of this type of transformation that can occur in and after conflict. Certainly women experienced significant hardship and trauma during the war. But that is not all that remains in the "aftermath" of war. New possibilities for transforming individual, communal, and national life also emerge. In what follows, I demonstrate how:

1. Women experience violence and work for peace in a variety of ways. They are not only victims of violence, but also carry it out. They not only suffer violations, but also actively work for peace on international/national/local scales and as a part of everyday life.

2. The "aftermath" of violence is a pivotal stage for women who are working to transform society. To harness this transformative power, women's full experiences of violence—the harms and the gains experienced—must be accounted for.[46]

The above brief points provide a framework for understanding the post-conflict practices of peace and healing that follow in this text. They demonstrate that while conflict is incredibly damaging, it also offers significant opportunities to transform self and community.

While the two points above have been addressed in feminist literature on post-conflict transformation and peacebuilding, they pose a quandary for specifically Christian theological scholarship on women and peace. In part this can be attributed to what Shelly Rambo has named as the tendency toward a "redemptive gloss" in Christian stories of suffering and redemption.[47] Mary McClintock Fulkerson echoes this when she states that, "The very conviction of God's redemptive presence tempts the theologian to map sense and order onto the worldly." Instead, she argues for a theology that provides "ever-fuller attention to the complexity of the world."[48] Often the first impulse when faced with suffering is to make it understandable, preferably by placing it within a frame of spiritual reference in which good triumphs over evil in a linear fashion. But what does this sort of story, this

---

45. See Meintjes, Pillay and Turshen, "There Is no Aftermath for Women"; also Fuest, "This Is the Time to Get out Front"; and Fuest, "Liberia's Women Acting for Peace."

46. Meintjes, Pillay, and Turshen, "There Is no Aftermath for Women," 7–8.

47. Rambo, *Spirit and Trauma*, 8.

48. Fulkerson, *Places of Redemption*, 6–7.

type of remembering violence, do to and for survivors? Does this speak to their experiences of violence, pain and (possibly) peace? To address these questions, I begin by arguing that feminist, practical theologians have an important contribution to offer this literature and discourse, notably through their understanding of and language about the complicated ways religion matters for women who have experienced violence.

Where Is Religion?

The first question that could be asked of this book is: Why religion? Why not situate such a conversation about women, peace, and violence within its more traditional disciplinary bounds: feminist theory and women's studies? Because *religion matters*.

A better picture of the ways religion functions for women who have experienced violence is important for two reasons, the first of which is that religion often plays a significant role in women's mobilization for peace, as it did in Liberia. Leymah Gbowee gives an example when she tells of a vision that she had in 2001, while sleeping in the WIPNET offices:

> I didn't know where I was. Everything was dark. I couldn't see a face, but I heard a voice, and it was talking to me—commanding me: "Gather the women to pray for peace!"
>
> Gather the women to pray for peace! I could still hear echoes as I woke up, shaking. It was 5 a.m. What had just happened? What did it mean? . . .
>
> In some ways, that dream, that moment were the start of everything. We knelt down on the worn brown carpet and closed our eyes. "Dear God, thank you for sending us this vision," said Sister Esther. "Give us your blessing, Lord, and offer us Your protection and guidance in helping us to understand what it means." My dream became the Christian Women's Peace Initiative.[49]

Gbowee tells about how women worked together across religious lines to broker peace during and after the Civil War, and how prayer, hymns, religious practices, and scriptures were significant in that work. Researchers have noted the presence of widespread religious networks that encouraged cross-class cooperation among women before and after the Civil War.[50]

---

49. Gbowee, *Mighty Be Our Powers*, 122.
50. Moran and Pitcher, "The 'Basket Case' and the 'Poster Child,'" 501–19.

Additional research on the resurgence of these movements is necessary in this post-conflict period.

In addition to understanding the role religion plays in women's peacebuilding movements, focusing on the ways religion matters for women who have survived violence also prioritizes the voices of survivors themselves. Many women in Liberia and in the Liberian community in North Carolina have told me that "God was there" in the moment of violence or that "only God" can help Liberia to heal. For many survivors of violence, religious practices and beliefs and a sense of healing and reconciliation are intimately intertwined. As Marie stated, it was "faith," that enabled her to survive the rape she experienced at the hands of family members before the war and by strangers during it. To get through what she went through entailed, "just letting God. You know, you have to trust [God]."[51] Such harrowing experiences of violence make us wonder how women are able to, as anthropologist Veena Das writes, "make the everyday inhabitable."[52] For some women that was only possible through their religious practices, beliefs, or a sense of divine care or healing. Though this is by no means the case for all women, we must pay attention to what the appeal to religion or spirituality does for women who are responding to or who have experienced violence.

Although hotly debated among scholars of secularization and religion, the question of what "counts" as religious becomes all the more complicated when in conversation with scholars of African religion. Theologians like Laurenti Magesa and theorists like Kwame Gyekye and Jacob Olupona have argued that in an African context religion is infused into all aspects of life, including the legal and political systems.[53] Likewise, as researchers involved in the International Religious Health Assets Programme (IRHAP) have noted, in some African contexts, it is impossible to separate what is meant by "religion" and "healing" because these two terms are used synonymously.[54] Magesa writes that African religion is far more than a system of beliefs that informs life. It is, rather, a " 'way of life' or life itself, where a distinction or separation is not made between religion and other areas of human existence."[55] If religion is a part of life itself—constitutive

---

51. Marie's story is told in more detail in chapter three.

52. Das, *Life and Words*, 16.

53. See Magesa, *African Religion*; Gyekye, *African Cultural Value*; Olupona and Nyang, *Religious Plurality in Africa*.

54. Germond and Molapo, "In Search of Bophelo in a Time of AIDS."

55. Magesa, *African Religions*, 25.

of rather than incidental to who we are as human persons—then a more complicated picture of the intersections of religion, violence, rights, and healing is necessary.

Given that the focus in much of feminist theory, theology, and women's human rights practice has been on the institutional functions of religion[56] and acknowledging the presence of African religions in all aspects of life, this project probes the ways that activists and survivors navigate and define healing at a more local level. While it is important to understand the ways that religious organizations function and intersect with human rights work, this project focuses on the ways that people navigate religious systems, institutions, and communities and the ways that religion emerges in the stories that they tell about their own experiences of violence. We must, in short, investigate the ways that women *live* their religion in the local and individual context, and the ways they negotiate transformation and healing as a process of integration that emerges over time.

Theology birthed of women's experience has long been a central tenet of feminist, womanist, and mujerista theologies. I draw on women's experiences of violence as they are remembered through interviews and in small groups and through practices of peace and healing that women engage in their local church in an urban city in North Carolina To do this, I conducted seven interviews with women in this community; participated in worship, education, and prayer practices for nine months at a Liberian church; and helped to create and observed a six-week women's empowerment group that dealt with issues of trauma and healing.

But what of theology? I have begun with the practical theological task which, as Emmanuel Lartey writes, "entails critical, interpretive, constructive and expressive reflection on the caring activities of God and human communities."[57] I follow Lartey's praxis methodology that moves from concrete experience to social analysis to hermeneutical analysis and finally to pastoral praxis of liberation.[58] Additionally, an intercultural pastoral theological paradigm extends to the global community, not merely resting in individual, church, or community concerns. As Lartey affirms, such a pastoral theology reveals that "Something can be known about both the divine and the human through an examination of the caring activities

---

56. See Merry, *Human Rights and Gender Violence*, 44; Nussbaum, *Women and Human Development*. 182–83.

57. Lartey, *Pastoral Theology in an Intercultural World*, 28.

58. Ibid., 123.

of human communities."⁵⁹ This includes the ways that women experience violence and the healing practices they engage as they go about re-creating their lives.

Indeed, pastoral theologians like James Poling, Christie Neuger, and Pamela Cooper-White have argued, based on their experiences as pastoral counselors, that to bring about justice for women affected by violence, women's voices and experiences of violence must be heard and validated, and perpetrators must be held accountable.⁶⁰ Their predominant focus on the United States benefits from considering what might be learned in a global, "intercultural" theological conversation about "issues of global justice specifically including matters of race, gender, class, sexuality and economics... This approach is polylingual, polyphonic and polyperspectival."⁶¹ Further, African feminist theologian Mercy Amba Oduyoye not only helps us to think about the concrete (social, political, religious) practices of justice that must be brought to bear in the world, but also reminds us that the resources for this work (both "religious" and so-called "secular") are vast and wide. We must look for practices of peace that exist outside of the more traditionally recognized arenas. For practical theologians, this might be the church; for feminist theorists, this might be the state and the law. A feminist theological activist praxis is thus attentive to practices of healing *wherever they exist*. It is alert to the political as well as the religious realms of healing, noting that women's participation as full members of the divine community in the world is not limited to their participation in the work of the church. It is aware of the ways the women I worked with for this text are increasingly widening the space for women to participate in the work of peace: by telling their stories, by providing spaces and practices that offer healing, by being a shoulder to cry on, and by setting the example for what women can and will do to work for peace and justice in the world.

Conclusions

I began this book with an argument to hear "what the women say," despite the fact that women's voices and practices are often ignored in international

---

59. Ibid., 18.

60. See Cooper-White, *The Cry of Tamar*; Poling, *The Abuse of Power*; Neuger, "Narratives of Harm"; Neuger, *Counseling Women*.

61. Lartey, *Pastoral Theology in an Intercultural World*, 124.

women's rights and peace work.[62] As Hellena Moon has argued, practical and pastoral theologians are apt contributors to international women's rights conversations, because of their inherent care for "dignity for human beings." She goes on to write that they are particularly gifted for contributing to human rights work, in that their attention to "story-listening, mutuality, reciprocity and advocacy" can contribute to the continued democratization of global women's rights work.[63] The work of practical theology is not only work done on behalf of those within the walls of the institutional church; instead, it is work done for the world. The women's voices and practices included here encourage us to widen the space for conversations about the ways in which religion matters in international women's rights conversations about peace and healing.

By paying attention to the ways that women define and practice peace and healing in their words and on their terms, we might learn a great deal about the ways that healing is lived and learned despite the traumatic horrors that violence imposes upon a life. Tracing women's narratives and faith practices helps us to see the ways that religion matters for women who have survived violence. Religion matters in remarkably ordinary ways—in the prayers women say as they express hope for the future, in the ways they turn to God in an effort to survive and "make a way out of no way," and even in the ways they imagine and create new families. As I explore the ways that religion matters for women, I build a language of healing and transformation out of women's words and practices. Understanding healing in this seemingly chaotic way offers a vital alternative to the ways that health and peace are often described and measured internationally. As such, this complicated understanding of the ways religion matters as women negotiate healing is a necessary and vital part of the larger conversation about women, violence, and peace.

---

62. International Civil Society Network and MIT Center for International Studies, "What the Women Say."

63. Moon, "Transforming the Paradigm of Wo/men's Human Rights through Intercultural Pastoral Care," 61.

2

Memory and Migration

I met with Evelyn on a fall afternoon to talk with her about her experiences in a trauma-healing group, held at a Liberian church where I carried out nine months of ethnographic fieldwork. We began our conversation by talking about the workshops, which Evelyn found to be "nicely organized." She recalled that the group "[made] you think about the past," which, was "not just a bad moment because someone died, [but] you remember that person." Evelyn struggled with the fact that her children, who were born in the United States, did not go through the civil war in Liberia. She noted that she told them, "I wish you would have gone through the war." She did not (of course) want her children to remember dodging bullets or running for their lives, but instead, she wanted them to know that experience in order "to know where [they] came from." For Evelyn, this sense of memory was crucial to building a sense of community: We all want to "connect with [our] people."

Looking back on the trauma and hardship she endured, Evelyn reflected, "Why complain? It's gonna be. Everyone will die." While to some this might sound like fatalism, this understanding of life as survival through hardship demonstrated the profound sense of resilience among many women at the church. For these women, memories of their homeland in Liberia—including memories of the war and its aftermath—were a crucial part of the way that they were able to "make a way" where there often seemed to be none. The past—although traumatic at times—they recounted and remembered as a way to mark their survival in spite of it. As Evelyn stated, "you came from somewhere to get to where you are now."

Memory and Migration

In this chapter, I explore how memories of war shaped and were shaped by a congregation of Liberians who resettled to the United States at various points during a prolonged civil war in their country that ended in 2003. Migration, like conflict, is a period of transition and transformation. The process of leaving one's home, loved ones, and most of one's worldly possessions is an incredibly difficult and fraught one, particularly for refugees or other displaced persons escaping war. The women with whom I worked were very frank about these difficulties, but they also drew upon these hardships to craft a narrative that expressed their ability to endure and survive despite these intense challenges, drawing on words like "empowerment" and "making a way" to name the transformative process. This sense of "making a way" was imbued with divine presence, and many women noted that God "was there" as they were escaping danger or dealing with traumatic events.

In what follows, I begin with the stories of several women I met during the course of my fieldwork. Several key themes emerged: 1) the women emphasized "empowerment," drawing attention to the ways that God helped them to overcome serious trials and provided strength so that they could in turn help others; 2) their desires for healing reflected what might be seen as mundane or "everyday" practices and needs; 3) their healing was always relational, dependent on another (divine or human) to be fully realized; and 4) they embraced rituals as a way to memorialize what had been lost and celebrate the "blessings" they had been given.

This chapter explores these themes, and offers a foundation for theorizing about transformation that will be elucidated in future chapters. Here as there, I begin with fieldwork and interviews, then turn to international human rights frameworks and practices to explore the overlaps and gaps between "what the women say" in one local context and how transformation is encouraged on a more international scale. In this chapter, I focus on truth and reconciliation commissions, as they are often the primary vehicle employed to build collective memory about what happened during a war in order to repair old wounds and heal a divided country. While a vital strategy in post-conflict transformation, truth commissions often fail to see the key elements of healing that I have identified above. Given this gap, I argue for a more robust theory of post-conflict transformation—one that sees the everyday, relational practices that encourage what women here name as "empowerment."

Migration Stories

The research that grounds this text begins with a small Liberian church in an urban city in North Carolina, where I conducted fieldwork. At the time of my fieldwork, Friendship Community Church[1] was made up of seventy to ninety Liberians (approximately 95% of the church was Liberian; other Africans and spouses also attended). It was housed in a small run-down strip-mall building close to downtown, a location that few people noticed. A small sign that read "Friendship Community Church" peeked out from behind the only (barred) window in the storefront. From the late 1980s, this small community of Liberian Christians has been coming together every night of the week to worship, to pray, to read scripture, to share stories, to eat, and to repair and restore hope and life. The pastor, Aletha Meah, and assistant pastor, Felicia Jones, provided leadership, comfort, and support to their parishioners, working with a large leadership team made up of about a dozen Sunday School administrators and teachers, deacons, missionaries, and other appointed leaders.

When I first started interacting with the members of Friendship Community Church, I asked people how they had come to live in this city. As I heard from a program coordinator at Lutheran Family Services (LFS), it was difficult to estimate the numbers of Liberians living in the this area of North Carolina at the time of my fieldwork. Most of the Liberians I talked with at the church estimated the size of the community between 2,000 and 4,000. Almost all of them came here from Liberia, from refugee camps, or from other locations in the United States. From Liberia, most came through the LFS refugee services program, where they were greeted at the airport by a volunteer family who offered them a hot meal and some sense of social support. They were placed in an apartment, given some spending money, and offered job training or language classes. Liberians resettled by LFS in the late 1990s and early 2000s came to North Carolina for a number of reasons: because family members already lived in the area, because of the LFS resettlement agency, and in response to directives from national offices (like those of Lutheran Immigration and Refugee Services) that sought to place refugees in communities with economic growth and opportunity.[2] As I learned, the issues faced by Liberians coming to the United States were in

---

1. The name of the church has been changed to protect the anonymity of its parishioners.

2. Jason Payne, interview by author, Raleigh, North Carolina, March 2, 2012.

many ways typical immigrant and refugee issues: adjusting to a new culture, finding a job and income, dealing with transportation and language barriers, and missing family members back home. However other issues they faced were more intimately related to their experiences of war and conflict in Liberia. With the assistance of their case manager, they figured out how to find a job, put their children in school, enroll in school themselves, and connect to the larger Liberian community and vital services like healthcare and food assistance. As the refugee program coordinator at LFS told me, their refugee resettlement program focused on "empowerment," helping refugees to "translate their dreams and desires into what will work in the US."[3]

In addition to the already staggering issues they faced as refugees, Liberians coming to this urban city also entered a community that was rife with conflict. As Pastor Meah related to me, people coming here thought that life would be great in America, but then realized, "there is still a war here! You come from war, you go into a war." Gang violence, intimate partner violence, poverty, and other forms of systemic and personal violence continued for Liberians in the Diaspora, even after peace was declared at home in Liberia.[4]

This continued state of conflict was what brought together Laura Paynes and Pastor Meah, two strong community leaders. When I attended a meeting held by both organizations (Laura's non-profit and FCC) in January of 2011, the assembled group decided that the biggest hurdle facing the Liberian community was the trauma that lingered after the war was over. The two organizations decided to organize a trauma healing program—informal, small group discussions where men and women could talk about and process what they had been through.[5] As Laura told me:

> Look at the faces of the women and you tell me that these people have not been through a whole lot and . . . something is not going on in their lives . . . when you look at the faces of the women you should know that deep within they are—some of them you know

---

3. Ibid.

4. For more on the experiences of Liberians in New York, including experiences of gang violence, poverty and disenfranchisement, see Jonny Steinberg, *Little Liberia*.

5. These trauma healing groups serve as a significant research site for this project. As I will elaborate in the next chapter, small informal discussion groups were chosen because of the community's mistrust of Western psychotherapeutic approaches. As I have heard many times, if you tell someone from the church that a therapist is coming in or that they should go to counseling, no one will show up.

> [fighters] killed their entire family? They were the only person who survived. Some of them have one child, they killed that child. You know all those things. Mentally look at the women's faces and tell me, that there is not something going on with them. And those are the things I think, OK, how can I help these women? To be able to move forward with their lives, mentally, to not think about the things. I know it is difficult, but we could help, there's a way that if they could talk about it, there's a way that would help them to move forward.

Laura saw the impact of violence on her communities and, along with the church, set about the task of repair.

The women I got to know had varied experiences of migration, had come to the United States at different time points during the Liberian Civil War, but had all been shaped by their experiences of the war and its aftermath. Their understanding of what healing looked like was affected by these experiences. For Laura, her social work started with children left homeless after their parents were killed or displaced during the conflict; Ruth struggled with alcoholism as a result of her journey and hearing about all that her children had endured as they tried to escape the war; Ella's memories of life before the war helped to ground her post-war sense of the possibility of peace; Evelyn came to be named "Mother Theresa" at FCC because of her care and concern for others; and finally, Pastor Meah's journey out of Liberia, and the sense of displacement she experienced helped her to create and sustain a new "family" at Friendship Christian Church. For each of the women I worked with, memories of the war profoundly shaped their present realities, helping them transform self, life, and community.

In addition to its deleterious effects, conflict can also provide opportunities for change and growth. As stated by the Liberian Truth and Reconciliation Report:

> The strong links between transitional justice, development, and gender equality have been overlooked and underdeveloped in both theory and practice. Transitions are rare periods of rupture that offer opportunities to re-conceive the social meaning of past conflicts in an attempt to reconstruct their present and future effects.[6]

The women's stories highlighted below offer examples of how that transformation happened in one post-conflict migrant community.

---

6. Republic of Liberia, "Women and the Conflict," 1.

Memory and Migration
Laura's Story

Laura's commitment to social work grew out of her experiences during the first Civil War in Liberia in the early 1990s:

> During the Civil War, 1990 . . . I was stuck; I was with my family and my mom. My dad was somewhere around the market. My mom and all the children . . . were in Caldwell. The first 1990 war was May 4th . . . when the first rebels came to our town. The rebels captured us and they took us . . . [The rebels] would look at you and think that you worked for the government and they would slaughter you . . . They brought me out, I was sitting in front of my grandmother, in front of my mom . . . we didn't know where the rest of the younger people [were]. I could hear my grandmother asking my mom, because she was deaf, what happened? And my mom was so scared [because], she had already lost one of her kids . . . [The rebels] asked me a couple of questions, If I worked for the government . . . I never worked for the Liberian government, I was just a student . . . one of the guys, he said she doesn't look like anyone who could work for the government, "she [is] struggling" . . . I was really dirty, I hadn't taken a bath . . . [So] for nine days I was held hostage with my family [by these rebels]

[Annie] How did you get out? They left?

> No, after nine days of being captured . . . they heard that Prince Johnson and his group were coming . . . they were afraid of Prince Johnson . . . According to them Prince Johnson's group would kill anybody they would come across. So we could not go back because the Doe soldier[s] [were] looking for people who were rebels, and the rebels [we were with] were afraid of Prince Johnson . . . so they started pushing us back [away from Doe's and Prince Johnson's soldiers] . . . and [one night,] in the middle of the night . . . we heard gunshots . . . [so] the rebels left [and left] us in a church by ourselves. For three days, no food no water. We couldn't go outside; they just left us in that building . . . [Finally,] someone came up with the courage [to leave the church]. . . then me my mom and my little brother we decided to go to the city [Monrovia], and that's how we got separated.

Laura was, at different times, forcibly abducted and held by rebel forces, displaced from her home, and separated from her family.

Despite—or because of—these events, after she escaped the church Laura found shelter and food for a dozen young children left homeless and orphaned on the streets of Monrovia, where she got a job working with several Americans: "And that was, you know, the beginning of some of the things that I do. And since I came here [to the U.S.] . . . some of the kids most of the kids we had they all grew up. You know, they grew up." She pulled out an enormous suitcase overflowing with photographs—pictures of her family back home and of the children she helped during the war, recounting:

> I have a whole suitcase, this is my suitcase full of pictures. Most of the kids were in the street, they lost their parents, their family. And I wanted to, you know, I wanted to do something because they would be hungry, hungry, and nothing to eat. So I started going all around, asking the marines to give me MREs [Meals Ready to Eat] and I would give them to the children at night when I got off work. I would just give them for them to eat. And they would have to sleep on the street again.

Eventually, through the help of an American she knew, Laura was able to find an apartment to rent where some of the children could stay. Although she left for the U.S., they continued to call her on holidays and birthdays. Watching these children grow up, and hearing their healthy, strong voices when they called, kept her going.

Evelyn's Story

As noted in the introduction to this chapter, Evelyn wanted her children to know about the war in Liberia in order to "connect with [our] people." For Evelyn, the memories of the war and what she went through back home in Liberia are a part of who she is today. It connects her to home, to the place she "came from." As our conversation progressed, Evelyn told me about how difficult life has been for her since moving to the United States as a young girl. Now a mother of three, 29 years old and married, Evelyn was in school at a local university, studying to be a teacher or a social worker. She also worked full-time as an in-home aid in order to pay the rent and bills for the small apartment she shared with her husband and children. Evelyn's drive to work two jobs and finish school came, in large part, from watching her own mother leave school early to escape to the United States during the war. Her mother was escaping not only the violence of the war but also an abusive relationship.[7] When Evelyn was able to join her mother

---

7. As Codou Bop writes, "assault on the bodily integrity of women, of adolescents and of little girls is a central and universal fact of all wars," "Women in Conflicts," 26.

in the United States, she watched her mother work until midnight each night to provide for her family. This made Evelyn determined to get an education and to provide for her children and godchildren. Evelyn worked night shifts as a medical assistant for elderly patients, got home at 7:00 in the morning, got her children ready for school, went to school herself, and then met the children again when they get home from school only to start the cycle over again with work that evening. Evelyn said that the other girls in the church called her Mother Teresa because she did not get involved in their talk about sex, and she acted "so old" for her age, despite being only twenty-nine. Looking back on what she went through and where she was when we talked, Evelyn was proud, but acknowledged that life was hard.

Ruth's Story

Children played a strong role in Ruth's migration journey as well, although by her account her memories of leaving the war were shaped more profoundly by her children's experiences than her own. Ruth and I met through Friendship Community Church where she was a missionary and elder. She attended most of the women's empowerment groups as well. We met for our interview at her home. While we chatted at her kitchen table, Ruth's grandchildren and children came in and out of the house, making snacks after school, picking up food, and chatting with their mother and grandmother. Ruth came to the United States by way of "Little Liberia" in Staten Island[8]; unfortunately, as she related, she was unable to bring her children with her. Ruth had to leave one child behind in Liberia; one was in a refugee camp. While she was in Staten Island, Ruth knew that her children were going through tremendous traumas. When they were able to call, they told her about seeing dead bodies in their local river, watching pregnant women being mutilated, and other horrors of war.[9] She found herself unable to sleep, instead waking up to nightmares filled with the visions of her children's

8. See Steinberg, *Little Liberia*.

9. Mary Moran describes the elaborate phone tree networks that developed during the Liberian Civil War, as relatives tried to call each other from different countries around the world (and inside Liberia). She writes of conversations with her foster brothers during the 1996 battles in Monrovia, when they were trapped inside an apartment, "The Internet was providing me with information not just for my personal or scholarly use, but with a life-or-death importance to the people I was in contact with. Ironically, I sometimes knew more about what was going on in any given section of Monrovia than people who were physically there." Moran, *Liberia*, 11.

daily life in a war zone. At the time of our interview, Ruth's children were in the United States with her—a daughter and a son, both fully grown. They participated in church life as well; her son was a pastor (not at FCC, but at another church) and her daughter sang in the FCC choir.

For Ruth and the other women from FCC with whom I talked, the church was another family, one to which she was devoted. As she said, "I like all my family to go to church, because why? We've got six days in the week to rest, to do what we have to do. What about the one day where we're going to serve God for two to three hours? [It's a day] just for you to say Lord, "Thank you." For Ruth, the healing process was a partnership with God. "When you want God to help you to do something," she said, "you got to do it with all your mind, your body, your soul . . . You don't doubt Him, knowing that He will heal you. If you put trust in God to say He will do it, He will do it. Yes, He will. Don't doubt it." Ruth has felt this healing presence in her own life, notably in her ability to overcome an addiction to alcohol:

> When I came to this country, me, I used to like pleasure. I used to drink, I used to do everything . . . I don't care, when you tell me about church, I say I don't care, I'm not going . . . but I was laying down one day in my house with my husband that passed away, my husband I been with 34 years, not this one I just married. I was lying down, in my house, I had went to a party. I was laying down, I had had a bottle of, cans of Heinekens. When I drank that drink, I was laying down in the house, and I see something in the room and I say "Aii!" It was white as snow, like a snow ball. I was between sleep and awake, and I said, "What is this?" I said, "Lord, what kind of devil coming to disturb me in my room?" So I turned my back because I didn't want to see the thing. Then I turned, [and] I said, "What is this?" I said, "Please," I said, "This is the devil, the devil is busy!" Then I went to sleep, but the thing came to me again, and I heard a voice saying, "Ruth, I'm telling you this." I ignored it . . . but [then I] went to a party, drank a can of Heinekens and I was sick, sick sick. Since then, any time I sit by someone drinking I want to throw up. Since then I never drank again. Like that, like that. I never touched liquor again, and I just devote myself to the church. And it was sudden, but I wanted to go to church and understand the Bible, like that.

Although she did not state this, Ruth's alcoholism was most likely a symptom of the secondary trauma she experienced, worrying about what her children were enduring without her.[10] As Ruth noted above, since that moment of healing she has been devoted to the church: "I have to go to the church before I feel good . . . I know there is a faith in the church that is good for me. You know, there is nothing on the outside [of the church] that is good for me." Ruth felt God's presence in her life and talked about how she was always in communication with God. She recounted, "You know when God wants to call you, he call you like me and you talking . . . that's how God comes to people."

Being thankful for what you have was something that came up repeatedly in Ruth's interview, whether she was talking about her children's survival of the war, her miraculous cure from alcoholism, or her more recent healing of a pain in her hands. Her sense of healing was grounded in her sense of faith in God's continued presence. As she told me, "You just have to have the faith that God's going to do something for you, and He will do that for you." This faith allowed Ruth to be thankful for what she had—namely, the ability to wake up each day. As we closed our time together, Ruth reflected on this fact, saying:

> When you go to sleep, it's like you're dead, and He touch you to wake you up. Wake you up and see the day and say, "Oh thank you Lord!" Some people they go to sleep and they don't wake up. We are no better than them. But, you know, if you get up, you be the lucky one. [So you should] say, "Thank you." That's me.

Ella's Story

One fall afternoon, I met Ella at her home to interview her for this project. Like Ruth, Ella talked a good deal about being grateful, yet in contrast her gratitude was shaped by her experiences of pre-war Liberia, where community was the center of life and everyone helped one another as best they could. Ella and I had met several times at events Laura organized for her foundation. As we sat down together on the luxuriously overstuffed couch in the living room of her apartment, Ella told me what it was like for her growing up in Liberia. It was nothing like her life in the United States, but they "didn't even know there was a different life here." In Liberia as a child, Ella's mother would leave for work in the morning, dropping Ella off with

---

10. For those who are unable to "spontaneously dissociate" from traumatic events, they may use drugs or alcohol to numb the pain. See Herman, *Trauma and Recovery*, 44.

a neighbor. Everyone would "take care of one another." These feelings of mutual support were ruptured during the war, and Ella's tears flowed as she recounted, "When the war broke out, people acted like they never knew what it was to love or care for one another."

Ella told me about how her family, "Congo people," felt increasingly persecuted after Samuel Doe took power in 1980. Her mother was arrested. As a young girl during this time she "felt like [she] saw too much." She began to experience problems in school, trouble concentrating, and lack of desire to participate in her regular activities, because she was worried about her family and what they might go through. As a young woman, Ella decided to leave Liberia and she was able to do so in the mid-1980s to attend college in Texas. She left her family behind, not knowing that she would not return to Liberia for over a decade.

When she got to the United States, Ella was frustrated by the lack of knowledge of Liberia that she encountered among her fellow students at the university in Texas. She recounted to me that her classmates asked her if she lived in a "tree house" in the jungle. Her quick witted response was that yes, she did, and that in fact when U.S. officials visited Liberia they were placed in the nicest tree house of them all. One of her professors noticed her frustration at her classmates' ignorance about both Liberia and Africa more generally, so he showed her a high school history textbook. When Ella realized that there was almost no mention of America's sister country, Liberia, her frustration with her classmates diminished because, in her words, "they didn't know." Now to her America "is like a big brother. It's like me in my family. You can't do everything for everyone."

Ella told me how proud she was of the work Laura was doing in the community to help people heal. "Some people," she said, "are not over the trauma they have been through [but] if you only get to one person, you did something." Ella called back home to Liberia constantly, trying to help her family when she could. As she told me, although she had "not joined a group" that was formally addressing what went on during the Civil War, she was "not causing any war either." For Ella, talking about what she had been through was healing. As she told me, "I believe the more you talk, the less it becomes a weight on you . . . Talking is very good, but not everybody is able to talk, but they can move on." However, moving on was difficult because "people don't forget" what happened during the conflict. Of the memories of war, she reminded me that people might "suppress them, but it triggers and comes out. [What I went through] was 30 years ago, but I still remember." Although these memories never left, Ella believed that people could "grow and accept the situation."

Ella's healing was accomplished through her faith. As she told me, "I wouldn't be who I am if I wasn't a Christian. It molded me a lot, my conscience, knowing right from wrong, being able to forgive." After her mother was arrested and members of her family were harassed and harmed by Doe's government, she "went back to the same school" and worked hard to forgive the people who had derided and hurt her family. Difficult times reveal our faith, she recounted, saying that "when war was going on, I prayed more, I looked to a higher power for peace . . . Religion offers a peace of mind." For Ella, her faith offers a sense that "it's okay, everything that I go through."

I asked Ella how she felt about current prospects for peace in Liberia. She explained that, "when I left, it was the early destruction. There were not a lot of people in the cities. Then I went back after ten years and it was really shocking." Though there were "too many people, kids, in the streets, . . . development had started." When you are in a situation, you "don't see it as bad. I didn't even know [at the time] that it could get worse." It is often only after you experience a different reality that you notice the difference.

She was cautiously optimistic about the future when she told me, "What do I wish? I would like to go back home, but I'm worried that someone will go crazy and disrupt [the peace.] I pray it doesn't happen." She hoped that Liberians would be able to disagree without having to "kill one another" over their disagreements. "We are not all going to agree," she said, "we are human beings; we think we know everything!" Ella relayed her frustration with those who wanted a quick solution to Liberia's problems. "You expect development in five to six years when it took so much time to destroy [Liberia?]" Instead, she argued, Liberians should focus more on the way of life they nurtured before the war—the times when neighbors watched out for neighbors, when family members lived close by, and when a sense of community was central. As she told me, "I don't think we are taking care of each other like we are supposed to." Peace, for Ella, comes through this change of heart, this ability to see the other as a friend. In our final moments together, Ella summed it up, "Peace comes with love. If you can have love for your neighbors, you can find peace."

Telling Truths, Remembering War

For the women above, experiences of the war shaped their ability to heal—and, importantly, their understandings of what healing and transformation were and how they emerged. For some women, to engage this transformation process en route to recovery meant speaking about the violence that occurred. In her seminal work *Trauma and Recovery*, Judith Herman writes that such "public truth telling" events help survivors to feel that the violence they endured will not be forgotten and that they are not alone:

> Survivors understand full well that the natural human response to horrible events is to put them out of mind. They may have done this to themselves in the past. Survivors also understand that those who forget the past are condemned to repeat it . . . Survivors undertake to speak about the unspeakable in public in the belief that this will help others.[11]

This type of testimonial work has a long history in the Christian tradition. Drawing on Elizabeth Castelli's work on martyrdom, Shelly Rambo writes, "witnessing, truth-telling, testimony . . . Perhaps the figure of the 'martyr' that we need to mobilize here is not the one who sacrifices him- or herself but the one whose compulsion is to witness and to provide testimony."[12]

This idea of a shared narrative is also central to international transitional justice mechanisms like Truth and Reconciliation Commissions (TRC). Truth commissions "are efforts to create a public and systemwide accountability for crimes and atrocities committed within the period of recent violence."[13] Although the international community is still in the midst of "exploratory and experimental efforts to create adequate public truth and accountability," truth commissions represent the most current "social, political, and legal initiatives that attempt to bring into the public sphere a collective acknowledgement of what happened, who suffered, who was responsible, and how they are accountable."[14] Catherine Cole notes that although others have argued that truth commissions are "too legalistic," her performance-based exploration of South Africa's Truth Commission found

---

11. Herman, *Trauma and Recovery*, 208. See also Pillay, Speare, and Scully, "Women's Dialogues in Post-Conflict Liberia."
12. Rambo, *Spirit and Trauma*, 16.
13. John Lederach, *The Moral Imagination*, 143.
14. Ibid.

that "in the 2,000 testimonies given at public hearings, the unruliness and specificity of the lifeworlds this testimony represents—as well as the idiosyncrasies of individual subjectivities—had a fuller expression in the TRC process."[15] In fact, she finds in her work that although the TRC held a notion of "factual/forensic truth" that demanded a positivist approach—one that sought to combat a past record of lies and half-truths with 'hard,' authenticated, accurate and comprehensive data, or 'cold facts'—it treated personal/narrative truth as innately expressive of complexity, multiple layers of experience, and emotional density and a way of conveying the dignity of the individual giving testimony."[16] Indeed, the Liberia TRC drew on such alternative narrative practices, notably through the participation of women in community dialogues, therapeutic sessions, and sensitization programs.[17]

Liberia's TRC was established as a provision of the 2003 Comprehensive Peace Agreement. Its mandate was to "investigate gross human rights violations and violations of international humanitarian law covering the period 1st January 1979 to 14th October 2003 in order to identify the root causes of the conflict and establish the truth about the past."[18] As Gender Advisor to the TRC, Anu Pillay noted, the Liberian TRC was significant in its attention to women's participation. Over half (51%) of statements taken during the TRC process were from women; however, Pillay points out that the TRC narrowly interpreted "gender" to mean women and children, which led to a "tendency to focus on victimhood, especially sexual and physical violence."[19] This led to a first version of the TRC report that was largely "gender-blind." Together with civil society groups, Pillay worked to remedy this by creating a series of community dialogues held around the country with over six hundred women. These dialogues revealed that, "women were less concerned with redress and reparations for sexual violence, but were rather concerned with the loss of their livelihoods and the

---

15. Cole, *Performing South Africa's Truth Commission*, xv.

16. Ibid., 164. As she writes, "narrative was also a way that the commission connected individual stories to a larger collective narrative. While the TRC sutured together information from multiple statements to create a macronarrative of larger patterns of violence, personal/narrative truth spoke to the discrete, the particular, and the individual. The TRC's personal/narrative truth was subjective and valued subjectivity as a valid form of knowing and knowledge."

17. Republic of Liberia, "Women and the Conflict."

18. Ibid., 10.

19. Pillay, "Truth Seeking and Gender," 97.

day to day struggle they were currently facing including lack of safe water, housing, health care, and education."[20] These "everyday" concerns reflected some of the same issues that women in the North Carolina community relayed to me: they wanted to know that their children were safe and would have access to an education and jobs; they wanted to feel connected to a community that cared for them; they wanted to know that they would be able to provide for their families and create a new life in the United States. Beyond that, the women also explicitly named the role of religion and religious practices in this reparative work.

While human rights instruments and practices like truth commissions carry a great deal of power and are able to tell a broad story of injustice and harm, by doing so they can neglect to see the specific ways that women's religious lives affect how they understand and practice peace and healing.[21] As Veena Das points out, women's strategies of resisting, speaking, or embodying violence might emerge far from the expected contexts of truth commissions or the halls of the United Nations. Instead, she argues for a turn to the "everyday" to chronicle and understand the ways that violence and recovery happen in real life.[22] Das's reminder to look beyond the traditional arenas of justice asks us to expand what "counts" as human rights practice, opening the discourse to others who have been denied participation, often because of their inability or refusal to speak a human rights language, or to regard what has been denigrated as "culture" or "tradition" as valuable paths to reconciliation and justice. Like Pillay and the women who created the gender dialogues in Liberia, this text is an effort along these lines—an effort to hear what women say in order to place their thoughts, practices, and desires at the center of the post-conflict healing and transformation process.

---

20. Pillay, "Truth Seeking and Gender," 98.

21. As Talal Asad writes, "True, the 'proper domain of religion' is distinguished from and separated from the state in modern secular constitutions. But formal constitutions never give the whole story. On the one hand objects, sites, practices, words, representations—even the minds and bodies of worshipers—cannot be confined within the exclusive space of what secularists *name* 'religion.' They have their own way of being. The historical elements of what come to be conceptualized as religion have disparate trajectories... The unceasing pursuit of the new in productive effort, aesthetic experience, and claims to knowledge, as well as the unending struggle to extend individual self-creation, undermines the stability of established boundaries." Asad, *Formations of the Secular*, 201.

22. Das, "Violence, Gender and Subjectivity," 283–99.

While truth commissions have significant political benefits, they have "inherent limitations for psychosocial healing."[23] They do not address the long-term needs of survivors to incorporate traumatic memory into life and the ways they go about rebuilding and repairing life after conflict.[24] It is these other, more ordinary modes of remembrance and repair that the women highlighted in this chapter undertook and sought out. Communities of faith, like Friendship Community Church, were places where women could find a group of people willing to bear the burden of suffering along with them. As Pastor Meah told me:

> Most of us are from very big families. Now we are on this side where we do not have a lot of our families. So the church is our family. I thank God for the church. We are an extremely loving church. A few years ago I lost my mother, and I had to go home to bury her, and the church was by my side.

This religious community helped women to re-create their narratives, drawing on elements of faith, to envision—or witness to—hope for the future. Their work was not done out of a political need to rebuild or reconstitute the nation, but rather out of a need to rebuild and restore life. In what follows, I describe how that happened through the creation of a "women's empowerment group" by Laura's foundation and Friendship Community Church. While telling the story of what happened was an important part of bearing witness to all they endured, through the empowerment groups women were also able to imagine beyond the horrific things they had seen to consider a new, hope-filled future.

Trauma Healing Group: Privileging Empowerment

One winter afternoon, I entered Friendship Community Church where representatives from Laura's foundation and the church were meeting to plan some events. I shrugged off my winter coat and sat down and engaged in small talk with the rest of the people gathered around the front of the sanctuary. We pulled chairs together in a circle and started the meeting. The ten of us assembled—a couple of the leaders from both organizations,

---

23. Sideris, "Problems of Identity," 59; see also Ross, *Bearing Witness*.

24. As Veena Das writes, "Unlike the nostalgia for public space marked by the clear separation of the perpetrators and victims, most close studies of truth commissions have shown how much the notion of testimony have excluded certain other models of testimony and remembrance." Das, *Life and Words*, 220.

five young people ages eighteen to thirty, and me—were talking about how to encourage young people to feel engaged and empowered in their local communities. As we talked about offering educational programs, Reverend Grigsby, one of the leaders from the church, took the floor. This community suffered a great deal during the Civil War, he told us, and before they can be educated, people need to heal. Laura echoed Reverend Grigsby's thoughts. As these leaders spoke, the young men and women assembled began to move about anxiously in their chairs, some gearing up to speak, some seeming to wonder when this conversation would draw to an end. One of the young men agreed about their need to heal, noting that while trauma needed to be addressed, it was not only the trauma of the war that was affecting the community; there were also "things that are happening right now that [were] causing trauma." He continued by noting that people didn't want to talk about the war because some of the perpetrators now live here, too. How do you talk about experiences of victimization in a room where perpetrators of violence might be present, he asked? One of the young women nodded her head. How are we going to get people to talk, she wondered? How and why would someone come to a group to talk about trauma? Laura agreed that this would be a difficult task. No one would show up, she said, if you advertised a "trauma counseling" program. How then could healing happen if people didn't want to talk about it?

Conversations like these led us to create the women's empowerment groups, a way of addressing trauma and healing without forcing people to talk about what they had been through. For the women of FCC, an "empowerment group" seemed an apt route to accomplish some of what they expressed in interviews and during these meetings between Laura's group and FCC, namely that: 1) People wanted space to process what they had been through during the war, but they wanted to do it in a way that promoted "empowerment" and transformation; and 2) They didn't always want to *talk* about what they had been through in order to experience that sense of transformation or healing.

Together with Friendship Community Church, Laura's foundation, and a trauma counselor who works with refugee communities, I helped to create a six-week women's empowerment group, which drew on alternative practices of storytelling and narrative. The group met every Wednesday from August 10th to September 14th, 2011. Laura, Pastor Meah, Reverend Grigsby, and I thought that drawing on a strength-based name, rather than calling the group a "counseling" or "trauma" group, would bring more women to the table—and it did. Working with the trauma counselor, Angie, we designed a program that incorporated art as a healing practice, and explored the following six themes: 1) Inspiration/Who am I?; 2) Where do I come from?; 3) Remembering those I've lost; 4) Empowerment; 5) Gifts and visions for the future; 6) Peace.

Through storytelling, art-making, prayer, and reflection, this group of men[25] and women came together to provide comfort, care, and support to one another. We convened the group in the sanctuary of the church, gathering before Bible Study each week. The conversation was often very informal, and focused where participants led—which was often to talk of the Civil War. These practices of story-sharing created a shared group narrative of strength and empowerment, despite experiences of violence and loss, which reflects the ways that women talked with me about their healing process. Although we talked about the war, much of our time together was spent talking about the strengths and abilities that helped each of us to get through the hard times and to look forward to the future. We also joked about our lives, relationships, and families. As one woman told me, "just being together" was healing for her. Additionally, the artistic practices the group engaged reflected a non-verbal method of healing from trauma that allowed for growth through embodied practices (when speaking of violence was "too much").

Over the course of the six-week group, we had anywhere from eight to seventeen participants, men and women who attended Friendship Community Church but also others who heard about the group from Laura and her foundation. Several of the women highlighted in this text participated in the groups, namely Joyce, Ruth, Laura, Evelyn, and Pastor Meah. In addition, the core group of women who participated included Joanna (in her mid-fifties, a member of FCC), Tylah (Pastor Jones's daughter, in her early thirties), Reverend Grigsby (late forties; he is a member of the ministry staff at the church and a long time community leader), Pastor Jones (in her mid-sixties, Pastor Jones is the Assistant Pastor at FCC), and Adelaide (in

---

25. It is important to note that although this program was advertised as "Women's Empowerment," men showed up regularly. While this changed the group dynamic, I'm sure, it reflected I believe a real need for trauma healing in this community—the men also wanted to tell their stories, remember those they lost, and draw on their strengths to envision a positive future. While not the focus of this dissertation, I will explore this further in future work. This reflects what many womanist theologians argue, that liberation cannot happen without the participation of the entire community, men and women alike. See, for example, Williams, "A Womanist Perspective on Sin."

her sixties, one of the elders and missionaries of the church). Several of the young men attended the groups, including Laura's son, Jacob (early twenties), Evelyn's husband Joe (early thirties; the youth leader and praise leader at FCC), and Matthew, a friend of Jacob's (early twenties). The presence of two to four men no doubt affected the group dynamics and reflected these young men's expressed need for trauma healing work. Though their reflections in our groups were incredibly profound and moving, I'm sure that their mere presence prevented some women from talking about their experiences of gender-based violence during the war.

Several of the women in the empowerment group found that telling their stories about the war had a positive influence on their lives, despite the fact that it was often difficult and painful to do so. They noted that: 1) Hearing another person's story reminded them that they were not alone in what they had been through; 2) Telling their stories allowed them to see the areas where they felt empowered (in many cases, by faith in God) to persevere and survive; and 3) Talking with others allowed them to regain a sense of control over the memory and experiences. As I will elaborate through the descriptions of two of the sessions below, these positive effects of sharing a narrative relied on the presence of an empathic other, or group of others, to hear and affirm that story (and by extension, that person).[26] Participants also drew on ritual practices that resonated with the community in order to remember what they had lost and rebuild their life/story. Their descriptions pointed to the "everyday" ways that women envisioned healing of self and community.

Session One: Who Am I? What Is Empowerment?

It was the first meeting of the Women's Empowerment Group at Friendship Community Church. Angie and I arrived early to set up the room, placing the art supplies and snacks on the two large tables that Reverend Grigsby and James helped us to set up. Pastor Meah and Laura were both already

---

26. It should be noted that talking about experiences of violence is not always helpful or healing for women. When this kind of testimony is encouraged in order to obtain political, legal or judicial benefits and supports, the testimony that is obtained might appear to be frozen or forced rather than healing and empowering. See Brison, *Aftermath*; Das, *Life and Words*; Ross, *Bearing Witness*. However, talking about what one has been through—when the woman sets the term for what she will talk about—can be incredibly freeing and healing for some survivors of violence, as I experienced with the Liberian women with whom I worked.

there and Assistant Pastor Felicia Jones arrived just after us. Although we advertised that we would start at 4:00 pm, most of the participants made their way into the church around 4:30, something that we laughed about while waiting for everyone to arrive. "Liberian time," as everyone told me, was often later than U.S. time, so Laura and Reverend Grigsby had wisely advertised that the groups would start 30 minutes before we actually needed to begin. We were on a bit of a strict schedule, as Bible study was due to start just after our group at 6:30. There was a lot of laughter as the group settled down; all in all, seventeen men and women sat around the table. Laura welcomed everyone to the first meeting, followed by Reverend Grigsby, who gave a prayer. I then introduced Angie, who asked everyone to go around the room and introduce themselves.

Our first task as a group was to discuss what the groups were meant to be about—empowerment. We asked the group to tell us what they thought empowerment meant. Matthew, a young man about twenty-five years old, said that empowerment was about "not feeling inferior," even if you don't have an education. Empowerment is knowing that you are "just as good as someone else." This jumpstarted the rest of the group, and voices tumbled over one another, with ideas like: having what you need to succeed in life—education, healthcare, housing, and employment. Empowerment, Laura chimed in, is also "in your mind." Doing her part to connect the group to the issues of trauma that she and the leaders at Friendship wanted to discuss, Laura reflected that when you have things in your "past that you are not able to get over, like the Liberian Civil War, that is a barrier" to feeling empowered. She went on to say that empowerment cannot live when you "keep returning to" these past events, preventing you from moving forward in life. Angie used this as a jumping off point to explain that over the next six weeks our group would talk about the internal parts of empowerment, which include recognizing our strengths and moving forward despite what you have been through.

Angie then asked the group to talk a bit about the ground rules we would enforce during our time together. As she looked around and asked everyone to offer some basic rules for conversation, the once boisterous atmosphere became silent and stilted. People looked around, not answering her, fidgeting in their chairs. I started to worry, looking to Laura to check in about what we should do to move the conversation forward. After a somewhat forced conversation, some ground rules were established, including: keeping what we discuss confidential, promising to respect each other when talking, being quiet when others were talking, and showing positive support.

After this awkward moment, I helped Angie to get the art supplies out, and she explained that for the next few weeks, we would be making "empowerment books." These books, made out of felt, scraps of fabric, art supplies, paint and other art materials, would contain pages with different themes like inspiration, strength, the past, visions for the future, and peace. In this first meeting, we asked the group to create a collage or piece of art that reflected what inspires them. Angie began by asking about shapes that inspire people. The conversation livened up (I looked at Laura, saying "thank goodness for that," with my eyes) as people began chiming in: the colors grey and green, shapes like stars and diamonds. We moved on to animals that inspire, and heard lions, eagles, and bears. Then we put the materials out and let everyone create, asking them to think about what inspires them. During this art time, everyone was having fun, especially the younger people who were talking to each other, looking at everyone's books, and laughing about little mistakes we made with the supplies or in our representation ("that doesn't look like a palm tree!"). I noticed that despite this boisterous atmosphere, sitting by Pastor Jones were three older women, Ruth, Adelaide, and Rachel, who were quietly sewing pieces of fabric onto their felt. They had their needles and seemed content sitting together and making their projects. For a while I worried that they were not enjoying themselves like the younger folks, who continued to laugh with one another.

After about thirty minutes of crafting time, we went around the room to share what we had made. Not everyone ended up sharing, although most did, something that reflected both people's hesitancy to talk and also our lack of time (Bible study was almost upon us!). Justice went first. Although not a member of Friendship, Justice was good friends with Laura, and about her age (in her mid-forties). She held up her piece of felt, which had four dots on it—for north, south, east and west, she told us. In the middle of the dots was a heart. This represents, she said, that "no matter where you are, love is at the center." Pastor Meah held up her piece of red felt, which she had cut and sewn together into a child's dress. This is because children are the most important part of life, she said, reminding us that the Bible says to "go forth and multiply." She laughed as she said this, pointing her finger at the younger people in attendance. Pastor Jones had drawn a chicken on her page, because chickens are one of the major foods for Liberians. This chicken represents what we need in order to survive. She drew the chicken eating, "so that it would grow big and feed people." Baby chicks were scattered around the page, representing the food that would feed the next generation of people. Samuel had made an abstract piece replete with symbols. The square was God, because God is the basis of all things. At the center of the square was a circle, which represented Jesus. The star and the moon on the edge of the page are reminders of the light that we receive when we have God and Jesus as our foundation. "Jesus allows us to shine and be all we can be," he told the group. Jacob had made a palm tree out of felt. He made a palm tree because this is the most "important and vital plant to Liberians." So many things come from the palm tree—light, liquor, oil. It is a "source of life" for Liberians. Echoing the Liberia theme, Valerie had created the Liberian flag, cutting each of her stars out of felt. Matthew had made a church because he said the church was the "center of life;" if you "believe in God and are faithful then you will be granted abundance." The group laughed as he held his up, because the cross at the top of the church kept falling off. As we were about to close the meeting, Rachel, one of the three women who had been quietly sewing at the end of the table, raised her hand to talk. Her page was empty, except for a fish she had cut out of felt and onto it. The fish, she said, was an inspiration because though it had been a staple of the Liberian diet, "it was a luxury during the war." During those times, everyone was "eating whatever they could find." This fish, Rachel said, reminded her of those times, when she "didn't have anything," and yet was able to get by.

Laura and her son Jacob closed our time together as a group, thanking everyone for coming and encouraging them to come again next week. Reverend Grigsby reminded us that just being together, "sharing, talking is healing" and important for the community. As we hugged one another and cleaned up the art supplies, I breathed a sigh of relief. Laura and I looked over at each other, smiling tentatively about how things had gone. I walked out to the parking lot to talk with her briefly (since I was returning inside for Bible study), and we agreed that the first meeting had gone well. "We'll see," she said, "how things go next week." We hugged one another and I headed back inside to prepare for an hour of Bible study with members of Friendship Community Church.

Session Three: Remembering Those We've Lost

It was the third meeting of the "women's empowerment group" at Friendship Community Church. Angie, Laura, and I knew that it would be a difficult session, less boisterous and joyful than the last two meetings had been.

Angie came up with the idea to create memory boxes for someone that we had lost. We purchased small cardboard boxes that everyone could decorate with pictures, words, or other art supplies that represented the person. We would then write a prayer that could be placed in the box, along with any other tokens or mementos.

As Angie and I sat down with the group to begin our time together, talk turned on its own to "World War I" and "World War II" in Liberia. Ruth talked about her experience of being mistaken for a government minister on the side of the road in Monrovia. She described what it felt like to be held by a rebel soldier, to be waiting for him to confirm whether he would kill her or not. She explained that it was at moments like this, "when you think you might die," that you most feel the movement of God in your life. When the soldier came back to where Ruth was waiting, she assured him again that she did not work for the government. He agreed and sent her on her way and Ruth walked away, "faster than I ever walked before." "Praise God," she said, for being able to survive with her life intact. "The Liberian Civil War was like nothing you could imagine," another woman chimed in. Others went on to describe things that had happened to them during the war, including being taken hostage, being imprisoned, and watching friends and loved ones die and be killed. Shaking her head, Laura recounted that some women's "whole families died."

Angie looked around the group and asked them how it felt to share these stories about what they had been through. "I feel relieved to talk about it," Ruth said, because "the almighty God has carried me through." That made it "a little easier to talk about it," even though she hasn't completely "overcome it." Pastor Meah followed Ruth, saying that when she hears about what other countries, like Libya, are going through, it "brings back memories . . . it reminds you of yesterday."[27] As the conversation continued, the role of faith in helping a person to overcome trauma became a recurring theme. When talk turned to how one can live in a community where perpetrators and victims exist side by side (and where the lines between these two are complicated and blurry), Laura noted that this is "where faith comes in," faith that forgiveness and peace are possible, even in a new country and homeland where other kinds of violence are rampant. Pastor Meah agreed, echoing a theme that she had mentioned to me months before, "War is

---

27. The women's empowerment group, which ran from August—September 2011, occurred during the same time as the Libyan revolution, something that came up often in sermons at the church during these months.

right here in America. People are killing people." The group talked about how the church—and an individual life of faith in God's power to overcome violence—was what made it all bearable. The talk, which began on a horrific note, ended with a resounding chord of affirmation. Ruth closed her eyes and bowed her head slightly, her soft speech only enhancing the power of her words: "We will rise again."

A chorus of "Amens" echoed around the room.

When Angie asked the group how they felt about sharing their stories of the war, several of the women stated that conversations like this help them to feel "less alone." Indeed, as they shared stories about the various parts of the war ("Where were you during Octopus? That was the worst of the war!" "Were you in Liberia during World War II?" "I came to the United States in 1996") a common story of survival and resilience began to develop. They joked about the palm nuts that street sellers hawked when food became scarce. As they laughed about these nuts, which would crack your teeth if you weren't careful, Ruth shook her head, recalling how difficult it was to survive during those times. And when Ruth told the story about being held by the rebel soldier who thought she was a member of government, Laura jumped in with her own story of capture and eventual release. They nodded to each other as they remembered what it was like to "think you are going to die." These moments created collective memories of the hardships of war, and a shared narrative of survival among the group.

Our conversation that day started with a horrific story, shared by Ruth but echoed by Laura who chimed in with her own experiences of being stopped by soldiers during the war. These stories of fearing for one's life were followed by a group-wide realization that they had made it out alive and that God had helped them to survive. A sense of clarity emerged as the women reminded each other that this same God was present in their lives today. By noting, "We will rise again," the group was able to draw hope from this painful memory. I am not saying that through this process the trauma itself was erased. Rather, the group was able to weave a new narrative strand of empowerment and hope onto the "thickened" narrative/story about the war.[28] This was exemplified when Evelyn told our group about how empowered she felt by watching her mother raise four children on her own after

---

28. Pastoral theologian Christie Neuger develops a short-term feminist narrative approach to pastoral care and counseling that mirrors these methods. She writes that the old story of fear and abuse does not disappear, "it is, after all, part of the whole story – but one does want to lay alongside it a rich and detailed version of the new story so that it is available for generating new options and less pain." Neuger, *Counseling Women*, 190.

running for her life from her abusive husband. Despite being raised during the war[29] by a mother who survived domestic violence, Evelyn looked for the strength-filled parts of her story, building on the sense of empowerment that her mother's story offered.

We then created memory boxes for those we had lost, decorating them with pictures, words, and scraps of fabric and flowers that helped to commemorate those who were gone. Pastor Meah decorated her box with flowers, creating a "traditional tomb" for her father who was from Grand Gedeh County in Liberia. She prayed, "Daddy I love and miss you. May your soul rest in perfect peace." Ruth created a box for her husband who had died several years ago here in the United States. She wept softly as she talked about her "best friend" whom she misses dearly. They used to joke daily about who would cook the meals at dinner time. "When I sit down," she told us, "I shed a tear, but I know you are resting in Jesus." Laura created a box which she covered with the names of those she had lost; as others drew and pasted, she kept writing, names adorning the cover and sides of the cardboard box. In doing so, she noted that her brother who had died in the war is not buried in an identified grave; she doesn't know where his body is. "I have nowhere to see him," she said, as she echoed Ruth's statement that these are difficult things to talk about.

Evelyn was the last to present, and she showed us a box she had created for her sister and wished her "showers of blessings." "It makes me sad," she told us, when these difficult "memories come back." However, making this piece of art "felt good; it makes me feel like I can collect things to keep her close to me." Several of the group members, like Joyce, chose not to present, something that she discussed with us in the last meeting. We closed the group with a prayer offered by Reverend Grigsby.

Reframing Empowerment

When coupled with the gender dialogues and resultant practices of healing that emerged out of Liberia's TRC process, the women's empowerment groups and narratives presented here demonstrate the need for a robust

---

29 Pastoral theologian Christie Neuger develops a short-term feminist narrative approach to pastoral care and counseling that mirrors these methods. She writes that the old story of fear and abuse does not disappear, "it is, after all, part of the whole story—but one does want to lay alongside it a rich and detailed version of the new story so that it is available for generating new options and less pain." Neuger, *Counseling Women*, 190.

theory of transformation—and empowerment—that is attentive to relationality, the everyday, and the importance of memorialization and ritual. These elements might not fit every post-conflict reality; however, the correspondence between what was heard during and after the Liberian peace process and the words and practices of women in the North Carolina community affirm that these concepts need additional exploration in peace building and transformation work.

Philosopher Susan Brison writes that in addition to telling one's story to an "imagined other" (through writing to a person depicted on a photograph, for example), talking to other survivors of violence can be immensely healing, "in ways that go beyond the capacity of individual therapy." She goes on to say that talking with a group,

> can not only enable a survivor to feel empathy for her traumatized self (by first feeling it for another who experienced a similar trauma), but also make possible appropriate emotions, such as anger, that she was not able to feel on her own behalf. By first feeling empathy with other survivors and getting angry with their tormentors, she is better able to get angry with her own. Hearing others' narratives can also help trauma survivors to move beyond unjustified self-blame.[30]

Feminist theologian Serene Jones echoes Brison when she writes that for healing to take place, "it is crucial that the events of traumatic violence are testified to and then witnessed and believed by others . . . This healing involves, at least partially, the creation of a jointly authored story exposing the event of violence, which had been previously silenced, and then integrating this event into a broader life story . . . In an event of speaking, hearing and believing, a new future unfolds."[31] By sharing stories of the war together, in so doing overlapping each other's experience, and building a group narrative, the women in the group felt supported and empowered. They expressed that they felt a sense of camaraderie when hearing what others had gone through. Leymah Gbowee asks of her days doing trauma healing prior to her peacebuilding work in Liberia, "Does it sound like a small thing that the women I met were able to talk openly? It was not small; it was groundbreaking . . . Everyone [had been] alone with her pain . . . But holding in that kind of misery was as crippling as holding on to rage. I

---

30. Brison, *Aftermath*, 73.
31. Jones, *Trauma and Grace*, 79.

had found a way for us to squeeze it out."[32] Hearing what others had been through allowed the women to weave together a narrative that promoted what they named as empowerment, but what I (and the field of conflict studies) call transformation. This relational quality of healing, according to Brison, "reveals the extent to which the self is created and sustained by others and, thus, is able to be destroyed by them. The boundaries of the will are limited, or enlarged, not only by the stories that others tell, but also by the extent of their ability and willingness to listen to others."[33] The positive effects of sharing a narrative relied in large part on the presence of an empathic other, or group of others, who were able to hold that narrative and affirm that story (and thus, that person). As I describe in the next chapter, this makes cultivating communities of care that are able to bear such a burden particularly salient for post-conflict communities.

In addition to providing a shared story and a sense of common ground among the group, telling stories about experiences during the Liberian Civil War provided a narrative of resistance in the group. As Ruth's comment affirmed, it endowed the women with a sense that they would "rise again." Additionally, the women named God's presence at the moment of threatened annihilation as a moment of redemption—a positive and uplifting occurrence in a traumatic and terrible event. The group was able to recognize and claim an alternative narrative to the one that is often given about women's experiences of conflict—that of the victim. This is not to say that the women with whom I worked were not victimized (they were), but that their healing process involved reframing that narrative of victimization so that resistant and liberating strands were also present.

As Katharine Lassiter has pointed out, subject formation is a delicate and complicated process that is influenced by the ways we are recognized (or not) by others. While inherently harmful, processes in which we (or our pain) are not recognized or are mis-recognized by others also provide opportunities for agency and resistance; however, these are "not without

---

32. Gbowee, *Mighty Be Our Powers*, 106–7.

33. Brison, *Aftermath*, 62. Here Brison also argues that it is crucial to survival that a testimony be heard by others. She writes, "It is not sufficient for mastering the trauma to construct a narrative of it: one must (physically, publicly) say or write (or paint or film) the narrative and others must see or hear it in order for one's survival as an autonomous self to be complete." This is a crucial point in having empathy for oneself, Brison argues. "In hearing and supporting others' stories, we are more able to hear and be empathetic towards ourselves."

cost."[34] As the women in the group looked at one another and shared and listened to each other's stories, they drew on words like "empowerment" and phrases like "we will rise again" to remember and lament the horrors of war while acknowledging that their personal and collective becoming might create something new and more brilliant than what they had gone through. We will return to this point in a later chapter on mothering practices, but I point it out here to note that their understanding of "empowerment" (or agency or resistance) was intimately tied to practices of hearing, listening, and sharing that bound them together. The women's words and practices affirm that we are what Lassiter names as "selves-in-relation."[35] This relational understanding of self and subject formation is crucial for developing a robust theory and language for transformation and healing in the midst of and after violence and conflict.

The groups also drew on ritual and symbolization in order to help members to process in a healing way all that they had been through. As Shanee Stepakoff has written, "In the aftermath of war atrocities, symbolization—a process whereby an experience or emotion that has been unexpressed is given form—can provide survivors with a sense of relief and solace and can attenuate isolation by permitting traumatic experiences to be shared with and acknowledged by others."[36] Stepakoff worked in refugee camps in Guinea with Liberian and Sierra Leonean refugees, implementing a trauma healing program developed by the Center for Victims of Torture. Like our empowerment groups, they integrated artistic and ritual-based practices with story-telling and sharing, and used "memory books" (similar to our empowerment books) to help survivors to begin to integrate their narratives of war and trauma into their lives. Stepakoff notes that symbolization and ritual can be particularly powerful in post-conflict situations, for several reasons: 1) the symbolization of one's experiences of trauma can provide some relief, in that the survivor is finally able to express what they have been through; and 2) these practices open up "the possibility of being understood by another."[37]

While telling stories of violence in a way that envisions hope out of horror can be an important part of healing for many trauma survivors, some people find it impossible to speak of violence. As one woman recounted

34. Lassiter, *Recognizing Other Subjects*, 28.
35. Ibid., 15.
36. Stepakoff, "Healing Power of Symbolization," 400.
37. Ibid., 402.

during the same group conversation in which other women shared stories of the war, "it's just too much." How, then, do we "hear" violence that goes unsaid? In the next chapter, I focus on the ways healing and peace can emerge through rituals, gestures, and embodied practices that do not necessarily rely on speech. For some women, bearing witness to what remains after violence meant being attentive to the ways in which everyday life continues after trauma. Marcia Mount Shoop's eloquent description of re-membering after trauma has particular relevance here. She writes that:

> re-membering is not simple recollection or memory; re-membering is reconnecting body parts that have been severed, blocked, trivialized, compromised. When we re-member we do not only access the narratives that define us or simply finally find publicity for some hidden pain we have experienced. When we re-member we begin to integrate the threads of the untellable into the narrative of who we are and where we have been and how we live with truth and with authenticity. Re-membering does more than recollect; re-membering re-collects bodies and their broken, ingenious, tenacious parts into the sphere of how we pay attention.[38]

Re-membering as a renewed act of attention is the way that the women cited here see their work and stories; they bore witness to others' stories, sat with the complexity of their situations and our world, offered comfort through their words and practices, and took steps toward the repair of the lives and relationships in their communities. In the following chapters, I examine how that happened through several mechanisms: church practices, leadership, and mothering. I show how these simple moments and practices—the "stuff" of everyday life—assist in the reparative actions a survivor takes to transform a self that has fragmented as a result of violence. For the women with whom I worked, these transformations happened in and through their religious sensibilities and lives, because they felt God's presence in their struggles to "make a way" where life at times seemed impossible.

Conclusions

The women of Friendship Community Church detailed a process of transformation that was inherently relational and embedded in the everyday. They sought to better their lives in order to provide new opportunities for

---

38. Shoop, *Let the Bones Dance,* 48.

their children; they gave up alcohol because of their sense of a divine presence in their midst; they created healing communities to help others experience the type of personal and communal empowerment they continued to seek. Truth commissions, while necessary, are not always able to gather or hold these everyday practices of healing; instead, in an effort to rebuild a nation they focus on telling the story of what occurred (to build a shared memory of the atrocities and violations) and aim toward legal and political redress. That too is vital work. Yet my focus is deliberately on local women's narratives and practices as a way of exploring practices of transformation as they occur in and through everyday life. In what follows, I ask:

- What is necessary for these practices of self-transformation or empowerment to emerge?
- What kinds of robust community practices are able to hold survivors in such a way that they can express (or not) their memories in an effort to seek empowerment and healing?
- What is meant by the word "empowerment"? Despite describing its indigenous meanings for this group, how might that word be employed more broadly (or not) in healing and transformation work?
- How can theological language help us to craft a robust theory of empowerment or agency that can speak more clearly/closely to "what the women say" in the aftermath of violence?

As Laura told me, there are things her mom has gone through because of the war that still haunt her today. Laura's family still doesn't know whether her oldest sister is alive. "How can you live," she asked, "not knowing where your children are?" This, she noted, is why her family and friends turn to God. Her mother, she reminded me, prays "all the time." For, "when people have gone through so much violence and suffering, they need something to lean on." God was there for them, Laura told me, when no one else was. God was there, even when much of the rest of the world turned away during the Liberian Civil War. Frustrated that so few people in the United States knew where Liberia was, let alone that her home country was in the midst of a bloody Civil War, for women like Laura, the work of God was to remember and bear witness, even when no one else did. As we shall see in the next chapter, for some, telling stories of war was neither appropriate nor healing; in these instances, we must turn to the everyday ways people envision and enact healing, as a part of daily life.

3

Forgetting the Past

In a conversation I had with a women's rights and peacebuilding activist in Liberia at the United Nations Commission on the Status of Women meeting in 2010, I learned that Liberian women's organizations are increasingly turning toward everyday practice in their own healing and post-conflict recovery programs to mitigate the overwhelming violence women experienced during the war. One program offers gardening and small farm training to women who have been affected by gender-based violence and conflict. Its organizer, Mary, told me that the women in the program often do not want to talk about the violence they have endured. Instead, by working together on the farm, they build relationships and begin a healing process through embodied movements and gestures of love and friendship. After some time, she said, they may find the ability to speak of their experiences—or they may remain silent. Either way, they began to reconstitute their lives through the cultivation of the earth and of human relationship. Being attentive to healing and peace in practice seems particularly important for those who find it "too much" to talk about violence.

To bear witness to violence we must be attentive to what "remains"; more than the pain of trauma, it is also about healing.[1] To grasp these healing practices, I used ethnographic methods to glimpse the "everyday" ways that peace and healing were lived and experienced in the midst of relationships, practices and everyday life in a Liberian community in North Carolina. Veena Das argues that all violence embeds itself in relationship,

---

1. As Rambo writes, "'What remains in the aftermath of death' is the central question of witness," *Spirit and Trauma*, 44.

and it is the task of the anthropologist both to bear witness to violence that is hidden and to explore the ways that violence is not an event but is nonetheless entrenched in the recesses of life.[2]

The chapter explores how for some women telling stories about the war was a crucial part of the healing process in a post-war immigrant community, while for others telling stories of war was both dangerous and unsettling, not only because of reawakening memories, but because members of the same community had both endured and perpetrated violence. I draw on three ethnographic vignettes from my fieldwork: 1) the final session of our empowerment group; 2) a women's prayer meeting; and 3) conversations with youth and ministers about "forgetting" the past. Memories of Liberia—although conflicted and by no means universally shared among all members—were performed in various settings as an attempt to reconstruct and heal a community fractured by conflicts experienced both at home (Liberia) and in their adopted homeland (the U.S.). Despite a keen desire for transformation and healing that was professed weekly during sermons, or privately in interviews, this chapter explores the ways past and present violence often remained at the edges of (or invisible in) everyday conversations, hinting at fractures in the community that had not not healed.

Memory and Peace

The last meeting of the women's empowerment group was focused on peace. We talked together about what peace meant and how it emerges in our lives. Laura started the conversation by reflecting that to have peace you must "have something settled in yourself." "Even if you have been through negative things in the past," she noted, peace is being able to accept what you have been through. She recounted that in the past she always thought of herself as a "survivor," but that this meant that she was "always in survival mode." Now she calls herself a "contender." To her, a contender describes someone who is able to "move forward" and take positive steps in their lives, whereas a survivor is not able to "get over" what they have been through.

Reverend Grigsby went next, saying that peace was the "management of conflict" and the ability to "transcend surrounding circumstances." Pastor Meah followed by saying that there should be "peace in the community, peace in the family, peace in the home . . . No matter what you have been

2. Das, *Life and Words*, 218–19.

through, [you can have peace.] It is something that is in you." She reminisced about her family growing up, telling us that she was one of twenty-five siblings from three of her father's wives. It was hard to have peace in this family because there was "trouble when a man likes one woman" more than the other. Peace, she told us, must start within and live in the family in addition to the community and the world. "God has been good to me," she said. She looked around at the group and noted that many present had, during the Civil War, been "running away to save our lives. It is only by His grace that we are here today."

Joyce's understanding of peace was directly related to her own survival of violence during the Liberian Civil War. As she told our group, she particularly remembered one day during the war when she heard yelling and shouting on the Caldwell Bridge, close to her home, so went out to investigate what had happened. While there, she witnessed horrible things—bullets flying, women being killed—and yet, as she told us, "I can't remember how I got home." Looking back on that moment, Joyce knew that it was God who helped her to survive that horrific event: "I remember these things, how I have been delivered, and it brings peace." For that reason, she was thankful for everything that God had done in her life. "You go through so many hard times," she reminded us. We should always "take a minute and see what God has delivered you from. Some of us have been through all fourteen years [of the war]. God kept us alive. I was thinking about that a few days ago." She looked around the room and reminded us that by "thinking about what God has done for you, you will have peace."

"Who am I," Laura asked, to survive all that she had been through? She recalled yet again her own captivity, reflecting that "God has everybody here for a reason"; you are here on this earth because God "gives you a gift." Pastor Meah built on this, saying that everyone had a gift. "Who am I?" she asked the group rhetorically. "You are somebody! You are fearfully and wonderfully made." When they doubted this, she encouraged the group to "think on yesterday and what He has done for you." You can't "count all of your blessings—they are like the hairs on your head." Our group of eight paused to reflect on these powerful words before Angie brought us together again to create a piece of artwork to reflect what we had discussed. We created a peace flag, with each person contributing to the collage. It quickly became filled with images of the Liberian flag, drawings of Liberian women praying for peace, pictures of churches, there to "represent God, who represents peace." Joyce drew Jonah and the whale, reflecting that she was "not leaving here closing my mouth." The final person to present was Pastor Meah who had kept her drawing covered by a piece of paper once she finalized it, in order to reveal it with a dramatic flourish at the close of our meeting. She had written on it a single Bible verse: "Jesus wept." She said that Jesus wept because of "trouble in the world. He didn't make the world to be confused." Instead, "Jesus gives us peace, but we ourselves, because of envy, brought confusion. Jesus is grieving because this is not what he intended the world to be." As Reverend Grigsby closed our meeting with a prayer, we all placed our hands on the flag, and prayed for peace in our lives, in our families, in our communities, and in our world.

Healing as Collage: Weaving Counterstories of Hope

At the final meeting of the group, Joyce's painful recounting of her time on the Caldwell Bridge was layered with the conversation that followed between Pastor Meah and Laura about one's identity—in light of violence, and in light of being created in God's image. These moments of narrative reweaving—hearing a story of trauma, then layering it with stories of blessing and promise—cultivated a sense of healing among women in the group, bringing forward that which was difficult to bear, yet also finding what was worth salvaging in those memories. What was there to be thankful for? For these women it was life, God's presence, and hope in the future. The experiences of this group reflect the way in which group memories can help to create a narrative of hope and healing, woven together in ways that vary depending on who is listening and when and where the narrative is being relayed. Susan Brison writes:

> In contrast to the involuntary experiencing of traumatic memories, narrating memories to others (who are strong enough and empathic enough to be able to listen) enables survivors to gain more control over the traces left by trauma. Narrative memory is not passively endured; rather, it is an act on the part of the narrator, a speech act that defuses traumatic memory, giving shape and temporal order to the events recalled, establishing more control over their recalling, and helping the survivor to make a self.[3]

Retelling and re-weaving stories of trauma allows the survivor to reclaim her life in the face of traumatic memory. Like pasting together a

---

3. Brison, *Aftermath*, 71.

collage, with these practices of re-storying the self Laura and Pastor Meah poignantly described in their dialogue of identity, of being somebody. By affirming Joyce and others' survival, the women's comments helped to create a new narrative of strength and resilience. This creative work generates the "somebodies" that we all are, recalling Lassiter's notion of "selves-in-relation."[4] This narrative collage work happened in and through the recollection of traumatic memories, even in cases when they were not able to be verbally recalled.

Violence and the Everyday

While some survivors of violence are able to heal through narrative-based dialogic practices, for others this healing work happens through daily life and ritual practice. Veena Das reflects on this fact in her anthropological work, *Life and Words: Violence and the Descent into the Everyday*. Drawing on ethnographic experiences in India around post-partition violence and the 1984 Sikh massacres that followed Indira Gandhi's assassination, Das argues that violence is not merely a one-time event that ruptures life. Rather, the violent "event [attaches] itself with its tentacles into everyday life and folds itself into the recesses of the ordinary."[5] Violence reminds us that we can never truly have control over our lives or ourselves (we are always vulnerable to one another), and yet there is a hope we can find in relating to others that tells us that we are more than a victimized subject.[6] This work of reconstituting the self, which she likens to "the delicate task of repairing the torn spider's web," happens not through an "ascent into the transcendent," but rather in the midst of "everyday life."[7] This complicated, "everyday" work of "repairing" takes time and cannot always be articulated through speech and language. This resonates with theologian Marcia Mount Shoop's discussion of re-membering for trauma survivors. As she writes, "The body feels and is constantly processing experience in ways we cannot begin to characterize as extensions of rational thought. Our consciousness is often not the focal point of this processing of pain."[8]

---

4. Lassiter, *Recognizing Other Subjects*, 15.
5. Das, *Life and Words*, 1.
6. Ibid., 14.
7. Ibid., 15.
8. Shoop, *Let the Bones Dance*, 49.

What Das and Shoop point to are the ways that these remembering practices are embedded in the body. They are not always spoken. So looking toward the everyday practices of life that women embrace in order to survive and recover is crucial for those who work with survivors of violence. While many individuals are able to find healing through talking about their experiences of violence to an "empathic other,"[9] for some talking about violence is not possible, so practices of remembering and mourning became important ways of showing rather than telling of violence. In terms of healing, "there is no pretense here at some grand project of recovery but simply the question of how everyday tasks of surviving—having a roof over your head, being able to send your children to school, being able to do the work of the everyday without constant fear of being attacked—could be accomplished."[10] Although it is often assumed that to heal from violence requires speech, Das reminds us that it is problematic to assume that agency consists in forging the link between experiencing the pain of violence and talking of that pain. Rather, she points out that agency can also be seen in the "descent" into the everyday, where women are able to show, feel, recover, and resist violence through concrete, embodied relations and practices.

For Joyce, one way this happened was through the creation of the memorial box for her father, who died during the war. When I visited Joyce several weeks after the meeting at which we made those boxes, she showed me the one she had made for her father, which was set out in her living room. While she hadn't been able to talk much about her experiences during that session with the group, or even in her interview (she said she felt like Jonah, who was swallowed up by a whale for refusing to speak), she told me that she found a great deal of comfort in being able to memorialize her father. The box in her living room meant that she was able to remember him whenever she passed by. These small moments of recovery mark the non-narrative practices of healing that are invisible if we only think of healing from trauma as a recovery of voice. They also reveal the truly relational nature of memory, loss, and transformation.

The process of healing is just that—a process. Along the way, there are definite losses (something that we explored in the women's empowerment group)—loss of loved one, loss of home, loss of the self that once was, or of the idea of a coherent self at all. As Ella recounted, she felt the loss of the communal way of life most acutely; the sense that neighbors cared for

---

9. See Brison, *Aftermath*; and Hardison-Moody, "Getting This Off My Chest."
10. Das, *Life and Words*, 216.

neighbors. This was echoed by Liberia TRC's "Women and the Conflict" report, which notes that the long lasting effect of violence is its ability to weaken long-standing cultural and "value systems" of communities in Liberia.[11]

As the vignettes presented here suggest, however, these losses can also lead to an awareness of the profound connection between each of us as human beings. As Laura stated about the importance of healing work in the Liberian community, "We are all connected in so many different ways." The process of going through trauma can be, in this way, transformative. As Judith Butler writes:

> Many people think that grief is privatizing, that it returns us to a solitary situation and is, in that sense, depoliticizing. But I think it furnishes a sense of political community of a complex order, and it does this first of all by bringing to the fore the relational ties that have implications for theorizing fundamental dependency and ethical responsibility. If my fate is not originally or finally separable from yours, then the "we" is traversed by a relationality that we cannot easily argue against; or, rather, we can argue against it, but we would be denying something fundamental about the social conditions of our very formation.[12]

What Butler is saying is not a foreign concept among scholars of African religion, or indeed for the women with whom I have worked. The idea of a self that is intimately tied to others in its very being is central to African philosophy and theology. Because all of creation is imbued with the sacredness of God, "all creatures are connected with each other in the sense that each one influences the other for good or for bad."[13] The interdependence of all of life reflected in these women's stories derives from their experiences of violence, which remind us of our vulnerability, and thus, our susceptibility to others, and rests in a view of the self that is quintessentially relational. As Butler writes, "Let's face it. We're undone by each other. And if we're not, we're missing something."[14] Memories of violence and loss bring this connection to light—painfully, sharply. However (and the example of truth commissions from the previous chapter illumines this as well) practices of mourning and remembrance can be transformative in that bringing forth

---

11. Republic of Liberia, "Women and the Conflict," 15.
12. Butler, *Precarious Life*, 22–23.
13. Magesa, *African Religion*, 46.
14. Butler, *Precarious Life*, 23.

internal memories or experiences can prompt us to recognize our profound relationality and to act differently because of it.[15]

In her book *The Power and Vulnerability of Love: A Theological Anthropology*, Elizabeth Gandolfo draws on maternal narratives and practices to posit that human vulnerability is the existential condition that drives both the anxieties that lead to oppression and harm and the feelings of deep love that allow us to see the other as someone worthy of care and justice. She writes that "there is something about the memory of suffering in and of itself, that can empower individuals (or at least begin to empower them) for resilience and resistance to vulnerability and suffering."[16] Gandolfo draws on memorial practices to better understand the process through which this happens: memories "interrupt" our ideas about the world and our place in it; they help us to cultivate a new "identity" based in liberation and resistance; they encourage practices of "imagination" that help to envision a new future; and they present opportunities for action and resistance.[17] She builds out this theological conception of memory and resistance by drawing on spiritual and contemplative practices, arguing that a "contemplative framework . . . empowers and forms practitioners in an identity that opts for courage, peace, and compassion in the face of vulnerability, pain, and suffering".[18]

In what follows, I explore one such contemplative practice that was undertaken weekly at Friendship Community Church: the women's prayer meeting. Prayer, I contend, is one of the practices women drew upon both to remember harms done and to work to bring about a world and community that is more just, compassionate, and loving.

Prayer Warriors: Bodily Transformations through Prayer

Prayer is absolutely crucial in the life of the women with whom I have worked. Here, I provide a description of one meeting of the Women's Prayer

---

15. Katharine Lassiter, drawing on Butler, writes, "Without public grief, we become closed, static, and fixed. A refusal or inability to grieve forecloses moments of vulnerability when one may be truly challenged, rearranged, transformed . . . It is our ability to mourn and grieve that elicits the conditions for recognition" Lassiter, *Recognizing Other Subjects*, 98–99.

16. Gandolfo, *Power and Vulnerability of Love*, 275.

17. Ibid.

18. Ibid, 290.

service as indicative of the weekly meetings that happened over the course of my nine months with this community.

Women's Prayer Services: A Thick Description

Each Monday night at 7:30 pm, a group of five to fifteen women gathered in the sanctuary of Friendship Christian Church for the Women's Prayer Meeting. They offered their praises and concerns to a God they believed listened to and answered those prayers. The Prayer Warriors who organized and led the meetings were five women who pray together each Sunday to Thursday night at 11:00 pm on the phone, joined by Pastors Jones and Meah and Reverend Grigsby. They share the concerns of the church and pray for healing, sustenance, deliverance, and blessings. As Joyce told me later, she believes that this ministry made all the difference in the life of the church. They had "seen women get pregnant" who were thought to be infertile and their prayers brought jobs and money to people who desperately needed it. It was a "big commitment" (Joyce's words), but seeing the difference it made in the lives of members of the church made it worth her while.

When I attended my first prayer meeting, in very early spring of 2011, I walked in with some hesitancy. At this point in my work, I had been going to worship each Sunday as well as Bible study most Wednesday nights. I had also been working for a month and a half with the leaders of the church and with Laura's foundation, on the youth empowerment and trauma healing events. Pastor Meah invited me to the women's prayer services to "get to know the women," and to recruit women to participate in the interviews I planned to conduct. When I got there, Pastor Jones asked me to come and sit with her, Pastor Meah, and Missionary Dean in the cushioned seats to the side of the pulpit, those usually reserved for ministers.

The service began with some welcome and announcements from leaders of the Women's Ministry and Pastor Meah, letting everyone know when the next baby shower was, what they could bring for the next church event, and reminding everyone of upcoming events at the church. Then Joyce stepped forward to lead us in praise music. Her beautiful, full alto voice carried through the sanctuary space. When Joyce sang (as she did often during the praise and worship time on Sundays), she brought her whole self to the performance. The words of the songs often moved her to tears, her eyes closed and her arms stretched up to heaven. After several verses of a song, she led us all in the *a capella* singing of several hymns. At the women's prayer meetings, we sang hymns that everyone seemed to know by heart, songs like "What a Mighty God We Serve," "Count Your Blessings," and "Amazing Grace."[19] As the final notes of the hymn died down, Joyce, the designated prayer warrior, led us in about thirty minutes of communal prayer.

Joyce started with prayers for self and for family. She told us about Penny's uncle, who was struggling with an illness, and in so doing led us into the Pentecostal Prayer process. The "Pentecostal Prayer," as it is named at the church, is one in which everyone present joins in, concurrently speaking their own prayer, guided by a leader who offers topics to address and themes on which to focus. I grew up going regularly to my grandmother's Pentecostal Free Will Baptist Church in rural North Carolina, so I am very familiar with this type of prayer, although it was not always comfortable for me to pray out loud. It is ironic that fieldwork helped me to appreciate this style of prayer that perplexed me as a child in my grandmother's church. I felt confused by what felt like a chaotic practice to me then, and I often wondered why the women were crying and the men were shouting and pointing their fingers toward the sky. At Friendship Community Church, the women's Pentecostal prayers helped me to see the profoundly participatory nature of this type of worship. As Joyce began to pray, we all joined in, praying together for our families and for healing in our own lives. The voices spilled over one another, some loud and boisterous (like Pastor Meah's), and others quiet and reserved, like Pastor Jones, who knelt in front of a chair, bowing her head into its seat. Observing prayer as an ethnographer is difficult; I found myself immersed in these prayers, not only because of my work, but also for the sense of personal healing that I began to find through them. My eyes closed, and my thoughts and prayers drifted to my own issues—the places I needed support, my own family members who were hurting—and I prayed with the group for many of the same things for which they hoped: healing, forgiveness, support, and grace. We asked for forgiveness for the things we had done wrong, then asked for God's healing in relationships that needed mending. We prayed for our

---

19. "Count Your Blessings" was sung at many events. The words to the song reflect what was discussed in the last chapter, with Joyce's remarks about God's blessings being "more than the hair on your head." The chorus of the song is:
Count your blessings, name them one by one,
Count your blessings, see what God hath done!
Count your blessings, name them one by one,
And it will surprise you what the Lord hath done.

community and the world, and I heard prayers for Liberia (for peace, prosperity, and hope). Joyce concluded the prayer, which at this point had been going on for more than twenty minutes, with prayers for our visions and hopes for the future. Petitions for God's blessings—for ourselves, our families, our communities—reverberated through the sanctuary as we closed the communal prayer. As we said our final Amens, I looked around the room. Bodies had shifted in the course of this time together: some stood from kneeling; some returned to the front of the room from the back where they had been walking: others stood up, stretching their arms and legs a bit. It was only later that night that I realized how sparse my notes would be from this event; I didn't really know what anyone else had prayed about, as I'd heard only snippets of the prayers that were loud enough to carry over to me. What I was left with, instead, was a sense of the participatory nature of this practice. We did not come to the prayer meeting to listen and absorb a teaching (as the Pastor hoped we would during Bible study and her sermons). Instead, we came to participate, to share our own stories, to petition for our own healing, and to ask for hope to imagine a new future.

Prayer for This Life, for This World

The prayers at the women's prayer meeting were directed toward this world, to our families, communities, hopes and dreams. Although this practice is rooted deeply in evangelical traditions, it also speaks to the ways prayer is understood in African Religions. Although life extends after death through the participation of ancestors in the life of the community, "traditional African religions do not appear to be concerned about the kind of life that will be led by the immortal soul."[20] Instead, African religions are concerned with the promotion of life in *this* world. The practical role of prayer in African religions reflects this. "There is much evidence to indicate that should a deity fail to deliver on a request sought in prayer, that deity will be censured, treated with contempt, and ultimately abandoned by the people. This means that, as far as the followers of the religions are concerned, the deities exist, and are to be called upon, to supervise and enhance the well-being of human beings."[21] Theologian Laurenti Magesa echoes the significance of practical concerns in African religions, noting that a common element of African prayer is petition, or asking for help with "practical needs" like

---

20. Gyekye. *African Cultural Values*, 14.
21. Ibid., 16.

healing, shelter, sustenance, and fertility.[22] People perform prayer and rituals so that health and well-being are experienced in the created order as it exists in the present place and time; "religious faith is, thus, perceived as utilitarian and practical, rather than as a means for spiritual upliftment or the union of the human soul with God."[23] This practicality extends itself into the relationship of the divine and the human through rulers here on earth; relationships to the divinities and to their representatives on earth are predicated on the belief that intervention on the part of the divinity can bring about well-being in the created order. Hence in the prayer meetings we petitioned a God who was active in this world, not a God whose promises were limited to the afterlife. God's movement in this world, in our lives, reflected an African Religious cosmology in which God and the divinities had concrete effects on life here and now.[24]

In addition to being rooted in this world, these Pentecostal prayer practices also reflected the ways women were constantly reinventing and recreating the religious traditions of which they are a part. As Mercy Amba Oduyoye writes, women constantly take in elements from culture and the outside world, discard what is unhelpful or unjust, take in what is good and just, and recreate the world. Comparing this to beadwork, she writes that "All is flexible, all is renewable."[25] Transformation can, and does, occur out of pain because "where pain is felt, life is still present."[26] Both beadwork and weaving recall the fact that women are continuously working with and through traditions to create something of beauty and meaning. By taking what is meaningful, discarding that which is not, and weaving together disparate elements of experience and the various traditions and communities in which they live, Oduyoye argues that African women can and do cultivate understandings of healing and justice that are grounded in right relationship. This continued re-working and re-weaving of meaning that African women do resonates with the African symbol of the whorl. The whorl describes the spiraling motion of change, the movement of past into present, and the continual flow into the future that Oduyoye wants to position at the center of an African women's theology. This is a theology

---

22. Magesa, *African Religions*, 197.

23. Ibid.

24. Recall here what Joyce said about the prayer warrior's ability to petition God for women's fertility and for job success. God works in and through lives in this world.

25. Oduyoye, *Daughters of Anowa*, 209.

26. Ibid., 211.

that both learns from the past and tradition, while also taking it and creating something new. It begins with African women's analysis of their own material realities, traditions, and spiritual practices, taking what is most meaningful and life-giving from these, and moving toward something new and liberating, a new vision of interconnected humanity and justice.[27]

The prayer practices at FCC are, in many ways, emblematic of this type of chaotic, whirling theology. Voices blended on top of one another, creating layer upon layer of petition and hope. Like the narratives described in the previous chapter, they created a communal story that was aware of the difficulties of life—the illnesses that aren't being cured, the wounds that refuse to heal, the children who turned to a life of violence—and yet, they also moved toward and envisioned something new, something beautiful. We closed each prayer with our "visions and hopes" for the future in a move akin to Oduyoye's description of the whorl. The prayers moved up and through these moments of hardship; tears were shed, wounds were opened. And yet as the prayers continued to build, layer upon layer, something else emerged—some new story in which the women saw God working in and through this world to provide hope, survival, and reimagined possibilities. This was not an easy redemption story; it was woven through with tragedy and memories of loss and trauma.[28] It reflects the ways in which women draw on religious traditions and contemplative practices like prayer to encourage transformation and healing. Their practices thus craft a collage that reveals the "messiness" of our religious lives.

Robert Orsi notes that fieldwork allows religious studies scholars to see the work of religious history as it happens in real time. His observations of the shrine to Saint Jude at the Church of Our Lady of Guadalupe in Chicago:

> suggest there are aspects of people's lives and experiences within religious worlds that must be included in our vision and attended to beyond what is officially sanctioned. This is a call, then, for attention to religious messiness, to multiplicities, to seeing religious spaces as always, inevitably, and profoundly intersected by things brought in to them from outside, things that bear their

---

27. Ibid., 217.

28. As Marcia Mount Shoop writes, "Tragedy is an important aspect of human experience that allows us to attend to loss and harm in a way that is not focused on blame or even on justice. Feeling helps to tune us into the body's capacity for telling a story, for witnessing to harm, and for holding grief." Shoop, *Let the Bones Dance*, 9.

own histories, complexities, meanings different from those offered within the religious space.[29]

Religious spaces and practices, Orsi argues, are created from the inside-out and the outside-in. By bringing their lives, their cares, their worries into the worship space, the women of Friendship Community Church fundamentally changed the space and its theologies. Likewise, they offer a vision of transformation and healing as an emergent process, one that is layered with women's lives, stories, traditions, and practices. Through practices of prayer, women were able to recall memories of past and present harms; their voices echoed with the pain of the past and present losses. However, these practices, like Oduyoye's whorl, continued to build into a shared narrative of hope and transformation. We closed the prayer meeting by articulating our hopes for the future.

Like the memorial practices noted above, the spiritual practices of prayer represented one way in which women engaged the work of personal and communal transformation in and through everyday life. Despite practices of prayer and the empowerment group, which encouraged a certain performance of public acts of memory, there were many women and men at the church who did not want to talk about what they had endured during the war. In the next section, I explore the ways in which forgetting trauma happened in the community, and the positive and negative impacts that such forgetting had on communal life.

"Moving On": Going Beyond the Trauma

Many of the women with whom I worked expressed a strong desire to "move on" from the trauma they had endured. Trauma demonstrates that memory itself is "a roadway full of potholes, badly in need of repair, worked on day and night by revisionist crews . . . When encouraged to flesh it out, we readily engage in imaginative elaboration and confabulation and, once we have done this, the bare bones memory is lost forever within the animated story we have constructed."[30] Trauma theorists remind us that memory is

---

29. Orsi, *Between Heaven and Earth*, 167.

30. Laurence J. Kirmayer, "Landscapes of Memory, 176. Kirmayer argues that trauma narratives are accepted differently in different contexts, pointing to the dissociative narratives of childhood abuse (forgotten information, gaps in knowledge) and the collective remembering of traumas like the Holocaust (public retellings). For those whose narratives are perhaps too difficult to hear/speak in public (rape, childhood abuse, domestic

inherently flexible and shifting. Although we often think of memory as if our memories are "locked away" in a secret part of ourselves, able to be accessed and recalled at will, trauma demonstrates that memory itself is tenuous and fragmented. Indeed, as anthropologist Rosalind Shaw's work on the TRC in Sierra Leone demonstrates, forgetting and remembering can be conditioned by human beings who desire to actively control the effect that traumatic memory has on their daily life.[31] "Narratives do not merely represent suffering; they mold and shape it, recontextualizing intolerable experiences and producing new ways of remembering and forgetting."[32] As Shaw recounts, sometimes forgetting is not just a reaction to the trauma, but instead serves as an act of narrative agency in itself.

Trauma theorists note that there are several types of forgetting that can occur related to traumatic memory: 1) Forgetting at the moment of trauma. This is what Judith Herman describes as "dissociation," or the practice of separating oneself from the traumatic event, oftentimes by suppressing the memory. This type of forgetting usually occurs as a way for the person to survive the traumatic event.[33] Joyce's experience of forgetting what happened on the Caldwell Bridge reflects this type of forgetting trauma. 2) Forgetting in the aftermath of trauma. While this type of forgetting may initially be adaptive, it can become debilitating. This type of forgetting attempts to ward off the invasive memories that penetrate the presence, and can involve using alcohol or drugs to block out traumatic memory. As I noted earlier, Ruth's alcoholism might have been a symptom of this type of

---

violence), the memories become dissociated and sequestered "in a virtual space shaped by the social demand—and personal decision—to remain silent, or to speak the unspeakable only with a voice one can disown."

31. As Shaw writes, "In many communities, people sought to displace explicit verbal memories of this violence through a range of social and ritual practices—sacrifices, prayer, exorcism, funerals, ritual healing, church services—the purpose of which was to create 'cool hearts' that form the basis for life in a community . . . Directed forgetting, then is part of the post-war work of memory, continually practiced and therefore continually remembered in order to reach the' Archimedean point' with which one can transform one's world." Shaw, "Memory Frictions," 195.

32. Ibid.

33. As Judith Herman notes, at the time experienced, traumatic events enter a body that is prepared for survival only—a body that is in a primal "fight or flight" response. This can lead the survivor of trauma to feel that they are suspended from the event. They might block it from their consciousness, feel as if they are "floating" above the scene, or enact other forms of dissociation from the moment. Herman, *Trauma and Recovery*, 34–36.

traumatic "forgetting."³⁴ The experiences I have had with the Liberian community in North Carolina point to a third type of forgetting: 3) Forgetting, or "moving on," as an act of agency and self-creation.

In working with survivors of Sierra Leone's Civil War, Shaw found that young people actively sought to forget experiences of the war through practices of prayer, ritual, and drama in their Pentecostal church. This type of forgetting violence was "enabling" rather than disabling, and allowed the young people to envision a new life and world in which God's power vanquished the evil they experienced.³⁵ Thus forgetting itself was an act of agency rather than of repression, and led to healing.³⁶

This third type of forgetting was also present among the young people affiliated with Friendship Community Church and Laura's foundation. In our meetings over the course of several months to plan the trauma healing workshops and other events for young people scheduled for the summer of 2011, the issue of talking about trauma came up a lot. When we asked the young men and women gathered at one of the meetings about topics for speakers for a kick-off event, Laura's son Jacob spoke up, telling us that he would rather hear a "motivational speaker," not just someone who talks about trauma. He reasoned: "If you say trauma healing, it will hurt people's feelings . . . they will think that you are going to point them out for stuff." I learned later in a conversation with Laura that "pointing them out for stuff" meant talking about what people did during the war. When one young man in our group came to the United States, he got into a fight with another young guy, who had been a fighter during the conflict. Other young men were shot as a result of war-time conflicts that have transposed into gang

---

34. Herman notes that for those who are unable to "spontaneously dissociate" from the event, they may use drugs or alcohol to numb the pain. Ibid., 44.

35 As Shaw writes, "The displacement of harrowing experiences from the past into other, transmuted forms is often viewed as synonymous with repression or false consciousness. But just as the physical displacement of GP youth is not an entirely negative condition, their displacement of violent memory is enabling rather than constraining. From the silence surrounding the Civil War in their plays, they retrieve a different kind of memory and voice, creating a moral life course in which they are much more than weak dependents." Shaw, "Memory Frictions," 89.

36. Veena Das writes that to assume agency in speech is problematic, instead for some agency is seen in the "descent into the everyday." As she writes, "Even the idea that we should recover the narratives of violence becomes problematic when we realize that such narratives cannot be told unless we see the relation between pain and language that a culture has evolved . . . In the register of the imaginary, the pain of the other not only asks for a home in language, but also seeks a home in the body." Das, *Life and Words*, 57.

warfare here in North Carolina, both Laura and Samuel told me. For these young people, sometimes talking through what happened was not healing but dangerous. Additionally, like the young people with whom Shaw worked, the youth of FCC and of Laura's foundation wanted to hear about how they could rebuild their lives and create something new—how they could go to school, get a job, create a family. Such practical and forward-thinking concerns were also the focus of the church, as I heard in a conversation with Samuel Grigsby, one of the ministers at FCC.

Samuel and I were talking over lunch about a conversation that had occurred in one of the women's empowerment group meetings. In this session, we were discussing moments of which we are the most proud. Samuel told our group about his participation in the student movements that led to Samuel Doe's indigenous takeover of the Liberian government. While Samuel was proudly describing his role in this indigenous movement in Sinoe County, several of the older women present looked on and shook their heads, sucking in their teeth with displeasure. Despite this disapproval, Samuel continued to talk about how satisfied he was with this work and what he had done to move toward increased indigenous participation in the Liberian government. When I asked him about this apparent discord between him and the women at the empowerment group, he told me that they "just don't talk" about these sensitive political issues related to the Liberian Civil War in the church. Instead the leaders of the church are encouraged to put these differences behind them to work with young people who have come here from Liberia or refugee camps, particularly those young men and women who participated as "fighters." Samuel told me that his goal was to help young people to understand that they could have a new life, and that they didn't have to turn to drugs; instead they could "make something out of their lives." The church leaders did their best to assist these young people as they tried to create a new narrative of hope, one that could be layered over the horrific narratives of violence they had experienced and perpetrated during the war.

Although this was not something I intentionally explored in my fieldwork (since I did not interview other men for this project), there seemed to be both gendered and generational differences in these ways of forgetting trauma. Joyce and Evelyn, both members of the younger cohort of members (in their twenties and early thirties), had a much different perspective on talking about trauma than the young men who often spoke up at the weekly meetings between FCC and Laura's foundation. During the women's empowerment groups, these younger women wanted to recount what they had been through during the war. Comparing herself to the biblical Jonah, Joyce said she would no longer remain silent or ashamed about what she had gone through. In a parallel instance, when it came to responsibility for the war and rehashing political conversations, unlike the younger men the older women like Ruth, Pastor Meah, Ella, and Laura did not see the point in continuing to "talk politics." As Laura told me, this kind of "talk, talk, talk" can only breed more instability:

> I just feel that if we only dwell upon this we will never move forward. We will still be bitter. This is what happened to a lot of the men in Africa, the men in Liberia as a whole. They just think about what used to be . . .
>
> You will listen to a lot of the men, sometimes when you listen to the men they are always talking, "there will be another war in our country." You know . . . when they talk about stuff they will be like, "we're going to fight, again."

Ella echoed this when she told me that she hoped people could move forward and forgive, despite what they have been through. She wanted Liberians to return to the times when they took care of one another. Many women wanted to forget the "politics" that had driven a wedge through their country and had created instability and chaos, and instead focus on the rebuilding of the country and its citizens.

This response to the war represents this third type of forgetting. For some of the younger women, it was important to talk about what they had endured during the war in order to harness their strength to build a new future. For the young men, rehashing what had happened during the war was more difficult (in part because of the violent roles some of the young men might have played during the war). However, both groups elided particular traumas of the war, and focused instead on what they could do to create a new life and story. This forgetting, or "moving on" is another practice of narrative reweaving, where the story of the "stuff" that happened during the war was layered with positive and affirming stories of potential growth and transformation.

In her exposition of South Africa's Truth Commission, Catherine Cole names these paradoxes of the transition periods after conflict when people and communities live "between the desire to remember and the impulse in transitional societies to forget the past and move on, between the impossibility of forgetting and the need to forget, between the desire for justice and the impossibility of achieving justice for atrocities perpetrated on a massive scale."[37] This push and pull of forgetting and remembering was felt profoundly in Friendship Christian Church; whereas some of the women wanted space to talk about what they endured, some of the men wanted to talk about their role in the political process, some women and men couldn't bear to talk about the trauma at all because it was "too much," and still others didn't want to talk about the war because of the role that they had played in it.

In her work with market women after the Liberian Civil War, Jo-elle Cruz found that traumatic memories "are particularly potent on organizations."[38] Drawing on organizational and trauma theories, she identifies three ways that memories of the war shaped Liberian women's post-conflict marketing practices: 1) idealization, in which members emphasized that the "reinvented organization significantly differs from how it used to be during the traumatic era";[39] 2) amplification, which describes the "intensification of certain elements, which become the most important in the organizing process;" this can heighten harmful experiences, making them stand out more sharply among organization members;[40] and 3) contraction, or "the propensity of susu [market] groups to close themselves off from the outside world. This inward focus accentuates an already existing tendency toward secrecy."[41]

Cruz's work is helpful in identifying the ways that traumatic memories can lead to secrecy, and the tendency for an organization to distance itself from others. I saw this, to some degree, at the end of my fieldwork when relations between Laura's organization and the church became strained. Both organizations were seeking funding for their work—the church to pay off a loan and secure a permanent building, and Laura for programming work with refugees and others who experienced trauma. I received a small grant from Emory University to pursue this research, and I used those funds to help support the trauma healing groups (paying for snacks and art supplies for the group). Unfortunately, word got around that Laura's organization "had got some money" (which was not true) for the healing groups, whereas the church received none. Even though I sat down with both parties to

---

37. Cole, *Performing South Africa's Truth Commission*, 159.
38. Cruz, "Memories of Trauma and Organizing," 448.
39. Ibid., 453.
40. Ibid., 454.
41. Ibid., 456.

explain what had happened, the reaction of distrust and rumor-mongering from the church made Laura resentful of working with them and wish she could instead put her "good work" toward those who appreciated it. For a while, Laura stopped coming to church on Sundays; however, towards the end of my fieldwork, she came back again.

Much has been made of and written about secrecy in Liberia, and Stephen Ellis's seminal text about the civil war, *The Mask of Anarchy: The Destruction of Liberia and the Religious Dimensions of an African Civil War*, provides an historical argument for the ways religious traditions steeped in secrecy (namely, the Poro and Sande societies) provided an apt backdrop to develop a political system that was able to disregard democratic politics in favor of autocracy and violent suppression.[42] Cruz's work with women's susu [market] groups also names the "historical" tendency towards secrecy in Liberia, and provides a cautionary tale for how that type of secrecy can prohibit women's organizations from growing and expanding in a post-conflict market. I must admit that I felt extremely frustrated and hurt when the "money problem" happened; I had been transparent about being a graduate student with a small budget to support the project that the community requested; however, the wires got crossed somewhere, leading to hurt feelings, damaged relationships, and a severing of outside relationships.

Here I would like to offer two cautions regarding secrecy and its interpretation. The first comes from Melinda McGarrah Sharp, a pastoral theologian who draws on her fieldwork in Suriname and her experiences of cross-cultural misunderstandings to develop a postcolonial pastoral theology that emphasizes a practice of understanding that empowers, liberates, and resists. Sharp argues that "participating in this kind of justice-oriented work demands being willing to assess whether and to what extent one's participation is in fact contributing to mending with intercultural fluency."[43] Instead of blaming the rupture in relationship on a tendency towards "secrecy," I must examine my own role in this process: I came into a community with very limited resources, and I represented an organization (Emory) that had substantial financial and representative power. Although I went to great lengths to engage participatory research practices, shaped

---

42. Ellis, *The Mask of Anarchy*, xxxi. As Ellis writes, the text provides a "history of how spiritual beliefs have helped form the structure and ideology of power in Liberia over a long period."

43. Sharp, *Misunderstanding Stories*, 6.

perhaps most profoundly by Linda Tuhiwai Smith's work, I represented a foreign entity in this world, and a foreign entity that came with particular power and privilege. I was a white graduate student from an elite Southern university. My presence, then, was necessarily disruptive, and I must recognize my role in the breakdown in relationships that occurred.

My second caution regarding secrecy is with using the word itself. Ellis has argued that the Liberian civil war was understood and narrated using ideas about secrecy and sorcery that originate in the Poro and Sande religious societies in north-west and central Liberia. While I would agree that religious beliefs and practices can inform the ways that life and politics are understood, I would here call attention to Sylvia Boone's ethnography of the Sande society in Sierra Leone, in which she notes that secrecy is not necessarily related to political corruption and the solidification of power in a few individuals. Rather, she argues that secrecy developed as a part of Sande both to protect the sacrality of the tradition from outside interventions (anthropologists, missionaries) and as an inherent part of a tradition that values knowledge as a process of initiation and enlightenment.[44] Likewise, Mary Moran's ethnographic exploration of Liberian communities before (1990) and after (2006) the Liberian civil war reminds us that the secret societies that emerge from Mende-speaking people in Liberia and Sierra Leone are not the only religious or traditional political systems on which Liberians draw. Rather, she calls attention to dual-sex societies of the south-east that have generated what she calls "alternative democratic traditions" that are "designed to preserve the rights of all in a context in which strictly equal rights are not recognized."[45]

As Mary Moran rightly notes, drawing on reductionist explanations for conflict (cultural concepts like "secrecy") plays into the hands of "tribalist" accounts of violence (particularly those used to understand the Liberian Civil War) that depict African wars as caused by "ancient tribal" or religious hatreds instead of a result of the "interaction of numerous factors and local histories."[46] This type of "othering" of African cultures also fails to recognize what anthropologists have long proclaimed, that "*all human beings*, by definition, are rooted in culture."[47] If we follow Moran, Boone, and Sharp (and the field of anthropology more broadly) in recognizing that

44. Boone, *Radiance from the Waters*, xviii–xix.
45. Moran, *Liberia*, 50.
46. Ibid., 18.
47. Ibid., 19.

culture is local and contextual, then it is important to consider ideas like secrecy on their own terms.

Conclusions

In the Liberian community in North Carolina traumatic memories were "forgotten" in several ways. In some cases, traumatic memories were actually forgotten—like Joyce who couldn't remember how she got home from the Caldwell Bridge. This represents what others have called the "pot hole" nature of memory, particularly when impacted by trauma. Susan Brison argues this point as it relates to her own experiences of rape and trauma, noting that in the wake of the absurdity that violence visits upon a self, one realizes that the idea of a linear narrative is no longer real or possible. In fact, the reality of violence reminds us that the linear narrative of the subject—and any ideas about the linearity of memory at all—have been an imaginary fallacy all along (although one we buy into for the sake of the sense of control it offers to life).[48] Often in a desire to deal with the absurdity and horror of trauma, individuals rely on the second type of forgetting, which often include harmful coping mechanisms (like alcohol or overeating) that aim to help the survivor deal with all they have experienced. The final kind of forgetting represents the ability to "move on" that Ella named, or the "silencing" of violence evidenced by the youth group. This type of forgetting does not actually "forget" the traumatic memory; instead, it is an act of willful agency in which the memory is woven with other stories and practices of hope and repair in order to imagine and create a new future in which there can be good in the world. As Brison writes of her own recovery and the hope that she has for her son:

> What I wish most for my son is not the superhuman ability to avoid life-threatening disasters, but, rather, resilience, the capacity to carry on, alive in the present, unbound by dread or regret. Not the hard, flinty brittleness of rock, but the supple tenacity of the wind-rocked bough that bends, the bursting of desire of a new

---

48. As Susan Brison writes, "As I use the term, a 'narrative' does not need to have a beginning, middle and end, unless that is taken to mean, simply, that it starts and ends, with something in between . . . It is a social interaction—actual or imagined or anticipated or remembered—in which what gets told is shaped by the (perceived) interests of the listeners, by what the listeners want to know and also by what they cannot or will not hear." Brison, *Aftermath*, 102.

mown field that can't wait to grow back, the will to say, whatever comes, *Let's see what happens next.*[49]

Looking forward to what might happen next represents a faith that good can exist again, despite intense pain and trauma.

In this chapter, I have looked at the ways that memories shaped and were shaped by collective practices of transformation that took place at Friendship Christian Church. These practices of memorialization reveal several things. First, they allow us to see that memories of violence, while incredibly difficult, also offer opportunities for women to recognize their shared humanity and build on that relationality to envision a future of hope out of hardship. Second, we recognize that the process of memorialization is not always a verbal process, but instead often happens through a "descent into the everyday."[50] Third, we see the ways that contemplative practices, in which women are able to remember past and present losses and re-member a community through prayer, are apt examples of the ways that women draw on their rich spiritual resources in the face of the anxieties that our human, vulnerable condition exert upon us. And finally, we see that there are multiple kinds of forgetting trauma. It is important, then, to parse how and why forgetting trauma happens in particular communities and contexts. In the following chapter, I turn to women's leadership practices to understand the ways in which individual women make the moral, theological choice to respond to violence with peace in their work to rebuild and repair their communities at home and abroad.

---

49. Brison, *Aftermath*, 117.
50. Das, *Life and Words*, 57.

4

Women's Leadership from Local to Global

"When women speak, do we listen?"

I wrote this question in the margin of field notes that I recorded at a public symposium in New York on the implementation of the Liberia Truth and Reconciliation Commission's (TRC) final report in the fall of 2010.[1] During a panel discussion on the theme, "Why did things fall apart with the TRC and where can it go?" I was sitting with a prominent women's human rights activist from Liberia. When the panelists finished, she raised her hand, visibly frustrated that this conversation that was meant to address reconciliation broadly instead seemed focused narrowly on political and legal methods of redress. She reminded the group that, "there are other aspects of the TRC" besides prosecution, and called attention to the gender dialogues conducted by the Women's NGO Secretariat of Liberia (WONGOSOL) and UNIFEM. These dialogues brought together women after the civil war to talk about how they understood reconciliation and peace.[2] These women, this activist noted, were looking for ways to memorialize the thousands who had died during the war who had been piled in mass graves across the city and had not been properly buried.[3] They also were expressing a desire for healthcare for survivors of sexual violence, for

---

1. Held October 29–30, 2010, the Symposium on the Liberian TRC Process: Reform, Redress, Recovery, was co-sponsored by the New School, Columbia University and African Refuge, a non-profit in Staten Island.

2. See Republic of Liberia, "Women and the Conflict."

3. This is a key argument of Jenny Sharpe's work that the postcolonial task (often attended by women) is "unburial" and "proper reburial." I'm grateful to Melinda McGarrah Sharp for pointing this out for me. See Sharp, *Ghosts of Slavery*, xi.

scholarships for the children of widows, and for community-level reconciliation mechanisms. As she told the group, "the women are saying: Repair, restore us."

Although many in the audience applauded this speech, the official conversation quickly turned back to politics and the legal system, prompting my hastily scribbled note: *When women speak—particularly about peace and healing—do we listen?*[4] This woman's concern that the dead were not being memorialized, and the ways that later comments and panels glossed over such religious sensibilities, are examples of how human rights conversations about peace and healing often ignore the nuances of women's religious lives and the ways in which women are engaging religious and spiritual practices and sensibilities to restore and repair their selves and communities after conflict.

This chapter focuses on interviews with three leaders of the Liberian community in North Carolina to make visible a more nuanced understanding of religion and how religious traditions, practices, and beliefs impact the ways that women practice peace and negotiate leadership in post-conflict situations. In addition, I argue that careful listening to and learning from the ways women practice peace and negotiate leadership in post-conflict situations leads to a more nuanced understanding of those religious traditions, practices, and beliefs. After hearing three women's stories, the chapter reflects on the ways that international women's rights conversations about violence often discuss religion. The chapter concludes with a constructive turn: I suggest the need for a wider conception of what leadership means, particularly for women in post-conflict societies, in order to counter the ways in which global human rights discourse ignores or compartmentalizes women's peace practices—and, importantly, their religious lives.

What the Women Say

As civil society organizations have attested, women's participation in peacebuilding work and women's ideas about what peace is and how it is practiced often go unrecognized.[5] The invisibility of women's peacebuilding work and the lack of attention to the ways women think about peace and

---

4. See also International Civil Society Network and MIT Center for International Studies, "What the Women Say."

5. International Civil Society Network and MIT Center for International Studies, "What the Women Say."

healing, has had concrete implications for women's lives and for the future of peace processes worldwide. As Fionnuala Ní Aoláin, Dina Francesca Haynes, and Naomi Cahn argue in the introduction of their book *On the Frontlines: Gender, War, and the Post-Conflict Process*, attention to gender and women's perspectives on peace and conflict can ensure that the gender transformations harnessed during conflict are carried through in the post-conflict period. They write, "Women are the group most historically marginalized and excluded from the peacemaking and peace building process across all jurisdictions and conflicts. A gender-centered lens of analysis, followed by practice, enforcement and oversight, has the possibility for transformative effect on women's lives in post-conflict societies."[6] Meintjes, Pillay, and Turshen echo this, reflecting that "societies focus in the aftermath on finding the truth about atrocities and on the reconciliation process; this diverts women from looking at the advances they made during war and distracts them from creating new blueprints... the survival strategies that kept families alive and communities together—are erased from the historical record."[7]

Given this gap in peacebuilding literature, feminist scholars have recently noted the urgency of their addressing issues of post-conflict transformation and transitional justice.[8] So far, much of this work has focused on the role of the state in mediating justice for women. However, feminist historian Pamela Scully has argued that, "there is a fundamental conceptual misfit in terms of trying to secure women's rights in transitional justice in terms of the state and the law only."[9] In what follows, I explore the stories of three leaders in the Liberian community in an urban area of North Carolina in order to highlight women's peacebuilding work—the work that happens outside of the confines of the state and the law—asking the following questions: How and why do women harness the transformative possibilities

---

6. Ní Aoláin, Haynes, and Cahn, *On the Frontlines*, 5.

7. Sheila Meintjes, Anu Pillay, and Meredith Turshen, "There is No Aftermath for Women," 17.

8. Ibid. As the editors write in their introduction to this seminal volume on women and post-conflict transition, their aim is to "document and analyse women's survival strategies and post-war activities, enabling us to identify the seeds of transformation and showing us the important role of solidarity with women in conflict zones. In the aftermath it becomes incumbent upon us all to develop conscious strategies that help women build on their activities and find ways of incorporating new gender relations in democratic societies," 18.

9. Scully, "Feminist Theory, African Gender History, and Transitional Justice," 30.

of conflict to promote peace and healing? How do women make space for this kind of transformative leadership in broader peace and healing movements? We begin with the women's stories to hear "what the women say."

Laura's Story

Laura, a Liberian community organizer and director of a non-profit that works with Liberians in North Carolina and Liberia, echoed Scully's frustration at peacebuilding's selective focus only on politics and law. On a chilly winter afternoon, Laura and I met for lunch to talk about her organizing work and about some youth empowerment workshops she was planning for the Liberian community in partnership with Friendship Community Church. She hoped that these youth events focusing on the upcoming Liberian elections and political process would help young people to feel invested in the future of Liberia. She also wanted to organize events that addressed the concrete needs that young people had identified during the meetings: jobs, safety and security, and education. Laura noted that the young men often talked about politics in Liberia. She saw them regularly at parties, huddled together in corners, discussing the candidates and the future of their home country. Laura hoped to get women more engaged in the political process. As she told me, men often thought that their opinions were the ones that mattered while women were often the ones doing the actual work:

> [W]hen you talk to each and every Liberian woman who is doing the work I am doing . . . the first focus of these people [is] how can we protect our children . . . or how can we develop them, change their mindset, or help them to educate themselves? Those are the things we think about. We don't think about how much money can I make? Or who's going to be in power? I know myself I just want the work to be done.

She noted that for many men in her community, politics was the most important avenue for change. But to Laura, and women like her, sometimes this talk of politics was just that—talk. Instead, the work of actually repairing the community was her priority. That work was about getting beyond the "talk, talk, talk" of politics:

> I mean, really, I could [care] less about being in the Liberian government, about who will become President . . . I don't care,

it's just that those people should focus on the things that really need to be done—education for the Liberian children, therapy included in health [care] . . . those are the things that we really need to focus on.

At the time of our interview, Laura ran a non-profit organization in North Carolina that "focuses on the rehabilitation of immigrants who survived the brutality of Civil War in Liberia and surrounding African countries." Laura's work centered on healing the wounds in her community suffered as a result of what had happened to them during the war:

> But I never hear about any [trauma healing] program [here]. You know, these people came up from the war too! You know? Most of them just came up from the village and they were brought here [to North Carolina]. They have their own issues that have not been addressed. Nobody addressed those issues. Mentally [there are] a lot of things going on with their children. You know? And then some of them were abused. So many were in Liberia [during the war], and . . . no one has taken care of that. They are just put in the community to fend for themselves.

Working with FCC, the "pillar of the Liberian community here," Laura wanted to organize trauma healing programs—informal, small group discussions where men and women could talk about and process what they had been through. As she told me: "And those are the things I think, OK, how can I help these women? [I want to help them] to be able to move forward with their lives, mentally, to not think about the things. I know it is difficult, but we could help, there's a way that if they could talk about it, there's a way that would help them to move forward." As Laura was well aware, many women in Liberia found comfort in sharing their stories with other women during the community dialogues organized by WONGOSOL as part of the Truth and Reconciliation Commission Process.[10] Laura wanted to carry out a similar project in North Carolina, to help women begin to heal.

Laura's commitment grew out of her own experiences during the first Civil War in Liberia, specifically her experiences of being stranded with her family in the early 1990s that we heard about in Chapter two. Laura brought these horrific memories of war with her when she came to the United States in the mid-1990s. An undergraduate student at a local university, Laura began collecting money in 2003 to send back to Liberia through the Red

10. See, Republic of Liberia "Women and the Conflict."

Cross. The campus community quickly became involved, and a member of the staff there helped Laura to start a non-profit organization to increase her impact on Liberians back home in Liberia and in North Carolina. Although she raised thousands of dollars to send to the beauty school she started in Liberia and to support the children and widows in her hometown of Caldwell, the journey was not easy:

> It has been a difficult time. I don't want to lie to you. I have spent everything, including my own money that I don't have, you know. I have spent everything, but whenever I think about giving up, I think OK if I give up . . . But I just think that if I give up on these people, who's going to help them? That's what mentally I think about every day.

This work was happening on a small scale, with limited money and without international fanfare. Despite these limitations, it continued—because it must:

> And I think that's the role that I want to play to be able to help these people. From the children, the women, the men, some of the things they've been through. They have anger problems, and you know they are very angry. Some of the young guys, I'm not talking about these older men. And maybe because of what has happened in their life, they are just angry at everybody. You know? And that's the role I see myself playing. I'm not there to talk about politics all day, you know. I'm the kind of person [who likes] to see solutions. I don't like to talk, talk, talk, but let me see something going on. I've got to see something.

Laura saw the impact of violence on her community and set about the task of repair. Hearing these people's stories, visiting her home village of Caldwell, and responding to the local needs there—this was what Laura saw as her calling in life. At the time of our interview, Laura was working on a healthcare project to train young women in Caldwell on basic healthcare practices to prevent "senseless" deaths, like that of her nephew who drowned a few months before we talked. She was struggling to find money for the project, having been denied grant funding. She hosted house parties to raise funds, sent out donor letters, and was selling tickets for a local university's football games as part of a non-profit partnership. Laura's regular trips home to Liberia kept her connected to the needs and issues of the women with whom she worked there. These were her constituents, these women and their children, and it was to them she held herself accountable.

As she did in North Carolina so too in Liberia Laura went "around the villages [to] listen to these people's stories and think about the way how to help them." As Laura said, "I mean those [things] are the work that we need to be doing as women and the people of Liberia. This is the work that the women do."

Aletha's Story

I met Aletha Meah in January of 2011, between Sunday School and Worship Service at Friendship Community Church. Along with Assistant Pastors Jones, Samuel Grigsby, and Laura, we crowded into Pastor Meah's small office. The church worship space is a large rectangle, with enough room for about a hundred chairs. In the center of the rectangular space is the pastor's office, with three seemingly makeshift walls that jut out into in the center of the church's worship space. We could hear everything outside through the flimsy walls. The mood outside was picking up, thanks to the praise and worship music that had just begun. Pastor Meah and Laura were meeting to talk about whether they might collaborate on some programs for the Liberian community. Pastor Meah told Laura that it would be great to work together for the good of the community, and that we could all sit down to talk more next week after the worship service which she needed to prepare to lead. We prayed together, the sounds of the praise music swelling into the office space, and then we dispersed into the worship service.

The church's Assistant Pastor, Janet Jones, preached that day, and her sermon was on Psalm 51: David's prayer of forgiveness. She read the Psalm to us, expanding upon each line to offer some wisdom for the community. At the root of the sermon was the theme of forgiveness, which was illumined by David's pleads to God to "Have mercy on me, Oh God, according to your steadfast love; according to your abundant mercy, blot out my transgressions."[11] David was just like us, Pastor Jones intoned; he sinned repeatedly. Despite his sins, he continued to ask God for forgiveness for the ways he mistreated others. Heaven, warned Pastor Jones, would not be granted to those who "stepped all over" their sisters and brothers. Such disregard of one another happened in the church too, she noted, where members mistreated each other regularly. Pastor Jones reminded us that to serve God was to seek forgiveness for the wrongs we have done to each other. If others refuse to forgive, she admonished the congregation to keep

---

11. Psalm 51:1.

praying: pray to God that others will forgive and pray that God will also forgive us. Additionally, we must change our ways, doing all that we can to "make things right" with others we have wronged. Forgiveness without change, she warned, was empty. She closed the service by telling us that, "Repentance leads to forgiveness leads to unity which leads to peace."

Unity and peace: I heard these two words countless times during my fieldwork at Friendship Community Church. They formed the mission statement of this immigrant congregation, and achieving unity and peace among the community and for the world was the goal of the pastors of the church. Pastor Aletha Meah led the congregation of Liberians at Friendship Community Church. Back home in Liberia, in addition to her government job (see Chapter One), she served as an Assistant Pastor of her Baptist church. It therefore seemed natural, upon moving to North Carolina from Cote d'Ivoire where she was living as a refugee, to start an informal church for the growing Liberian population in her new home. Knowing that people's work schedules often prevented them from being at church on Sunday mornings, she and Pastor Janet Jones started a prayer meeting on Sunday evenings. During my fieldwork at the church, I watched as these two women worked together seamlessly, spending much of their time in and out of the sanctuary together. Their friendship dated back to these early church meetings, which lasted for several years in the mid-1990s.

The two women noticed that attendance at the Sunday night prayer meetings continued to grow, and they decided (as they often did before making any major decision) to fast and pray about what to do next. During that time, Pastor Meah felt God come upon her. "Get some paper, write this down," she told Pastor Jones, feeling that God was speaking to her about the future of this new church and community. The name, "Friendship Community Church," came to her during the prayer and she was enlightened as to what she felt as God's desire for the denominational standing of the church. "Although I am a Baptist," she said, this church would be for all people. As she told me, "If you love God, we all move together." She had a vision that she should build a church for her people. "The Lord said he would make a way" for this to happen she firmly believed.

The two women officially founded the church in 1999 in Pastor Jones's basement, which although "very big," soon became too small for the still growing congregation. Pastor Meah resigned herself to wait for God's will to be done and hoped that they would find a more permanent place for the church. As she recounted to me of this time, "The Bible says don't rush, you have to pray . . . let it be God's will." At Reverend Grigsby's wedding, however, things came to a head. There were so many people at the wedding that guests began parking on the neighbors' yards and across from neighbors' houses. These neighbors called the police on the Jones family, and presented them with a letter that said they could not host a place of worship in a residential neighborhood. Pastor Meah and the church members felt dejected, but the next day at her job at a convenience store Pastor Meah learned about an abandoned school building on a major street that was being rented out by the city. She took two hours off work to visit the site that would become the second home of Friendship Community Church. They stayed in this space for four years, but were forced to leave when a developer purchased the building and raised the rent.

During my fieldwork, the church was nestled in the tiny strip mall setting described earlier, in a building that used to house a cell phone store owned by a Liberian man. He negotiated the use of his space for the church after he moved away from the area. As Pastor Meah told me countless times, this small strip-mall setting was not the permanent home for Friendship Community Church. The church was seeking funds from members for a loan payment on a piece of property they had purchased several years ago. Pastor Meah wanted to build a sanctuary and community center, but she was having a good deal of trouble scraping together the funds to pay off the loan. Like her parishioners, Pastor Meah wondered when the new space would come into being but knew that "[God] has his time." Pastor Meah's ultimate goal was to return to Liberia, but she couldn't do that until this vision was fulfilled. She told me that if she left for home before the building was constructed, she would be "like Jonah, and you know what happened to Jonah when he tried to run from God." Knowing that she must stay in the area until God's vision was realized, Pastor Meah continued to recruit Liberians to help to pay for the new building. "The number of Liberians in the community," she told me, "if they all were to come, we would have built our church a long time ago, because there are many."

This church is the only Liberian congregation in this city, which meant that Pastor Meah and the ministerial staff were intimately aware of the issues facing this community. As she told me, one of the most difficult aspects of her ministry was working with Liberians who had come over here during and since the Civil War. These refugees and immigrants had homes, businesses, jobs in Liberia, but here it "is hard." Their families typically gave them space and help for a little while, but because they were also just getting by, they couldn't offer newcomers much assistance. She counseled people often, telling them that it was "God who sent you here, it was not a mistake ... God who has brought you here will make a way." As she told me:

> For me, I didn't really experience the war because I left when the war was getting worse, because we were the target. I was an official in the government, so we were a target. So when I left most of the government officials had left, I was one of the last! So when I left, the killing had started. Bodies were lying all in the street, but God lifted me up. But these people [at church], they went through the war. They went through bullets, walking on dead bodies, as by the grace of God, people were putting guns to them. They went through a lot. And the only person who can heal their wounds is God.

The church was a family for its members, many of whom had lost family and loved ones in the war, or who have had to leave these people behind in Liberia. Pastor Meah and the ministerial board tried to create a supportive environment for those who came here, helping them with both physical and spiritual needs, like this family who came to the United States from Liberia during my fieldwork:

> When they come into the ministry we pray[ed] with them. The last kids that came, the group that came, the husband and wife and the three kids, they come to church every Sunday. I told the church whatever we can do to show love, we should do it. And people are taking them things, taking things for the children, essential things that are needed. When they came, they didn't come with a lot of clothes.

Perhaps the most important guidance the Pastor offered was related to immigrants' "new" life in America:

> I've been a couple of times to encourage [this new family] to [teach] them what America is all about. America is how you want it and how you take it. There are good things here and there are bad things. A lot of our young people who came, they are deported. [They come] from different states because they come and they don't know their reasons for being here, [and] they come and join the wrong group. You came to America, you have been through war, and your parents brought you here from Liberia, then you are going to join the gang group, just to make quick money, to be involved in drugs and stuff like that? No. So when they come, we try to tell them what America is all about ... I know this country

is full of milk and honey... but you get what you want. The main thing you can do is to go to school and keep out of trouble. So those are the kind of things we are doing when they come.

The harsh realities of life in this city were not lost on Pastor Meah, who counseled members of her congregation who grieved over young lives lost to gang violence. The community center the church was hoping to build would be a safe space where young people could come after school to learn and experience the safety and support of a loving community.

For a community so wounded, knowing that they are loved and appreciated is critical, according to Pastor Meah. In this sense, the church was like a new family:

> Some came and they lost their children, some came and they lost their husbands. They had a program called resettlement, and that brought a lot of them. That's what we do, we encourage them... Most of them don't have a lot of relatives over here, so the church can serve as family over here. That's why we have the baby showers. The last one we had, she had a lot of gifts, a lot. So those are the things we do to encourage our people.

For Pastor Meah, much of what she did was "appreciate" the people in her church. She went to birthday parties, baby showers, funerals, and anything else that she was asked to do so that she could make her congregation feel special and loved. "Life is just happiness, you give it to God," she said. "To be healed, you have to change the mind. You need to make somebody feel that they are worth living"—by which she meant that a person needed to feel that their life itself was worth it. As she told me on a different occasion, "Human beings like to be treated like human beings." By attending important events in people's lives, Pastor Meah aimed to show her community the love of God: "That's what it's all about. Love. God is love."

Marie's Story

Marie and I met through a mutual friend at a domestic violence and sexual assault organization in North Carolina. I heard about her work for gender-based violence survivors in Liberia and set up a time for us to meet over breakfast at a local café. At our first meeting, Marie and I discussed her work with the shelter, but spent most of our time talking about how difficult it is to get funding for the work that she does.¹² She hoped to be able to partner with organizations like the domestic violence shelter to work with the Liberian community here, but also to have the funds for the domestic violence shelter staff travel to Liberia to help her to set up standardized shelter procedures. As she explained to me, the government and other NGOs in Liberia did not understand the need for confidentiality among shelter clients and consequently they asked Marie for information about her clients that she felt is unsafe to give. She hoped that the domestic violence shelter staff from North Carolina would be willing and able to travel to Liberia with her to train her staff there, along with government officials, about shelter protocol, confidentiality, legal issues, and safety for clients.

As Marie began to talk about these issues, however, her own story began to come out as well. A survivor of sexual assault who had fled the war in its early days only to become a refugee, Marie did the work that she did because she had "been there."

A few weeks after this meeting, I went to Marie's house for a more formal interview. Marie and her husband had moved from Maryland down to North Carolina about a year before our interview. They lived in a two-story house in the suburbs of Raleigh. During the course of our conversation, Marie's two daughters came home from school. Boisterous, adorable girls, they showed me the dance moves they had been practicing and told me about what they wanted to be when they grew up. Marie shooed the girls back upstairs, with a good deal of hugging and laughing along the way, and we settled down to talk.

We began by talking about how she had started the shelter, one of the only shelters for gender-based violence survivors in Liberia:

> The shelter actually, the organization . . . started in 2005, officially 2005, but like in the early 90's, you know, [I was] advocating as an individual, because at that time I was going through my own personal struggle you know as a survivor and also surviving the Civil

---

12. The lack of funding for the work that the three women highlighted in this chapter do is something that came up regularly in my conversations with all of them. I have some experience in grant writing through my former profession in public health, so I held a grant writing course for some of the members of Friendship Community Church. I also reviewed and helped to revise several grant applications for Laura's foundation. I connected Marie with other local organizations working on issues of women and violence, in the hopes that her work could gain a more public audience in the area, increasing her fundraising efforts. I saw these tasks as part of the reciprocal research relationship, but wish that I could have been more strategic in helping each of these women to pursue funding opportunities.

War. I planted the seeds in the early 90s that, you know, I wanted to open the shelter. Because [of what] I was going through, surviving, there wasn't a shelter at that time, so it was a seed I always had to get planted . . . It was important to open it because there was no shelter, and you had survivors who had been raped during the Civil War and also after the war . . . There was an alarming rate of children who were seven to thirteen who needed a place where they could go to because the community would you know, shun them, you know, so they needed a place.

This "place" that Marie created was not always a physical location. Instead, survivors were linked with volunteers via cell phones in several communities. Along with her all-volunteer staff, she educated several communities in Monrovia and beyond about the importance of breaking the silence about gender-based violence. By giving women in these communities the courage to speak about what they had been through, and then connecting them with the mobile number for the crisis center should they need it, Marie's organization was able to provide support for women who survived violence, and who were in some cases rejected by their communities. When a survivor called one of the ten to sixteen volunteers who work for the shelter, sometimes all that they needed was someone to talk to about what they have been through. Because of funding constraints, "we can't [always] provide the level of services we want to, [sometimes] all we can provide is that shoulder to cry on."

Despite this lack of funding for more broad-scale programming, the volunteers were able to:

> accompany [victims] to the court, or they need transportation, or they need to go to the hospital, or the clinic at MSF [Médicins Sans Frontières] . . . We've been a shoulder, we rescue them and take them out of their environment when there wasn't a place where they could go, when the community says we don't want to have them. They cannot stay with us for a long time, because we are not funded, but it is a place you can go whenever you need to.

Unlike shelter systems in the United States, which serve as its model, the location of the shelter was not confidential. In fact, just over two years ago there was a jailbreak in Monrovia that led to a serious emergency situation for the volunteers. One of the escaped prisoners had been imprisoned for raping one of the shelter clients, a ten year-old girl.[13] When volunteers

---

13. For more information on the jailbreak in May of 2009, see Dulleh, "Liberia:

heard about the jailbreak, they called Marie and began evacuating the clients: "When the jailbreak took place, everyone knew where we were, the whole community . . . So we had to take all those children and put them with our women in places. So that's how vulnerable the situation is." Because of the lack of confidentiality, Marie had to create "underground" shelters located in the homes of volunteers, friends, and even Marie's family members:

> Well they cannot stay with us for a long time, because we are not funded, but it is a place you can go whenever you need to get away from home . . . there are special cases where we put them with someone, or they will stay with one of the women, or they will even stay with my parents. We had a little girl who was so traumatized, wherever she went after her trial, she would run away, you know she would just go off to a place. Or sometimes she would get so violent in school and she would take knife, and in school she was being teased. You know, [with kids saying,] "You are a woman now, because you were raped" . . . and then a couple of months ago, the Justice Department had a case, it is so bad where you can't even protect what you call it witnesses or what you call it vulnerable victims, and you do that underground shelter. So we do have underground shelters, we started that a couple of years ago. That actually worked, when the justice ministry came to us, there are big organizations on the ground, but they came to us to protect one of their victims. Here they call it witness protection, we provided witness protection.

Although organizations and government agencies were beginning to understand the importance of confidential safe spaces for victims of violence, Marie reminded me that "this shelter thing is a new idea for Liberia. People thought that anyone could just come, but no, not anyone can just come [into the shelter.]" She hoped that one day the shelter would be housed in a confidential location, saying "that's my dream that in the next five years, [that] we will have a place where people can come . . . we will get there."

In addition to the challenges of this lack of confidentiality, Marie's organization also struggled financially. She had not received any grant funding for the program, instead relying on donor funds, her own

---

Another Jailbreak—New Batch of Central Prison Inmates Escape," *New Democrat*, Online http://allafrica.com/stories/200905181369.html. For more on why development and human rights practices that rely solely on the state and the law are not effective in women's human rights work see Pamela Scully, "Should We Give Up on the State"; and Scully, "Expanding the Concept of Gender-based Violence in Peacebuilding and Development."

contributions, and an all-volunteer staff. At the time of our interview, she had recently completed a three-hundred-mile run across Liberia, coinciding with Liberia's first marathon, to raise money and awareness of the issues of gender-based violence survivors. She was increasingly working with the Ivorian refugee population at the border between Liberia and Cote d'Ivoire, providing support to the women who escaped the Ivorian conflict that erupted in 2010 after the elections in that country. According to a report by Amnesty International, titled "We Want to Go Home, but We Can't: Cote d'Ivoire's Continuing Crisis of Displacement and Insecurity," the peak of the Ivorian crisis saw between 700,000 and 1,000,000 people displaced from Cote d'Ivoire, with most migrating to Liberia.[14] Some of these women were forced into sex work because they lacked money to buy food and supplies for their children. One woman who was raped by three men in Cote D'Ivore stated:

> I have five children to look after and the food here makes them ill. I have to make money for other food. During sex with men in Toe Town, they ask me to do things I don't want to do and say they won't pay me if I don't agree. I need the money so I have no choice and I do what they say.[15]

In refugee camps, Marie worked with the UN High Commission on Refugees (UNHCR) to address the needs of "double flight" refugee women, who have moved across borders twice to flee from violence.

Despite the difficulties of doing this work, Marie worked with these women in large part because of her own life story. Sexually abused by a family member she was sent to live with during the Civil War in Liberia, Marie worked up the courage to leave his house despite the fact that there were "flying bullets. It was war." She went out on her own, fleeing the country with only her faith:

> I said you know what, let me stay and go through this, I didn't know where my meal was coming from. It was an act of faith that I took, you know, because there was fighting, I could have said, let me stay: I will still have food to eat, a roof over my head. It was a decision that myself and God made. I told him, sometimes you just have to have to let him take control. And I went, you know, I went perfectly crazy. But I still held on. I hated him, I hated God, until I came to the realization that I was going through this and since

---

14. See Amnesty International, "We Want to Go Home, but We Can't."
15. Human Rights Watch, "Liberia: Protect Refugees Against Sexual Abuse."

> I said that I was going, you know he would be there to take care of me, and you know he just started working, he started working.

Marie saw the presence of God in her eventual escape and healing process. At the time, however, Marie "hated God" for what she had been through. Like the survivors of gender-based violence with whom she worked in Liberia and in Liberian immigrant communities in the United States, Marie felt isolated—from God, from friends, and from her family:

> I was an outcast by my own society, my own family being [not sure], being from an [family] it was a taboo to say you were raped or molested or that your uncle wanted to speak with you. Relating my personal story, I had everything . . . If I could walk and turn out the person I became, they also could have that hope . . . It doesn't take much, just showing that you are there and you care for them . . . And just let people know. They don't always come out like me. I had to come out. I had to explain my story. Some people came to rescue me. Some people did not know that I have been sexually molested, [but] you want to get out of that situation and you want a better future. Most of the time, you know, [the women we work with] are strong. You know, they are strong. Sometimes I see them as stronger than I am. Because at the time for me [the abuse] was a shock because I had everything. For them, with the little they have, [coming from a] community in poverty, to shun them. And [still they] just had the courage to come out.

During "Breaking the Silence" events that she held in over thirty-five communities in 2006, Marie was able to stand with other women who had survived sexual and gender-based violence. As she continued to do work on prevention, hosting events in schools and community organizations in Liberian and refugee communities, Marie saw this as healing work not only for the survivors with whom she worked, but also for herself: "I think when they hear what you've gone through, I think that's why we've been so successful, and we've connected a lot in these communities with mothers and just the children. [We're saying] 'Hey, I've been there, you are not alone.' It's one thing when they hear, you know, 'I've been there.'" By telling her story and breaking the silence around gender-based violence, Marie and her volunteers were able to support the women and children with whom they worked: "Where we are right now, I just keep hoping that we can help them find true healing, you know, helping them concentrate and do well in school. We've done the advocacy part. We still live our nightmares, I still live mine sometimes. But everyday I'm getting better, I'm healing."

Even though it is brief, this discussion of the work that these women were doing to heal and restore their communities offers a glimpse of what they prioritized in terms of peace work as a reaction against the violence they experienced both in Liberia and here in the United States. These priorities included helping people to talk about what they had been through in an effort to heal, offering material and spiritual support to those without family or connections in the United States, and perhaps most importantly, restoring the sense of humanity among community members who, it is important to note, were affected by the war in different ways (perpetrating, experiencing, and witnessing violence). These everyday leadership practices reflected the ways that women were helping to rebuild their communities after the conflict. Laura, Pastor Meah, and Marie found themselves in situations they neither desired nor planned for—post-conflict refugee/immigrant life. This situation demanded a response, and they made what they considered to be moral, theological choices to respond in ways that promoted healing, peace, and unity in their community. These choices were made in and through the course of their everyday lives and emerged out of their religious practices and beliefs. Their leadership was profoundly shaped by experiences of violence and trauma. It was, in this way, not naïve, but instead reflected an intimate knowledge of the intense pain—and promise—of human vulnerability. It harnessed the transformative aspects of conflict and war.

Their lives were fragmented by conflict—they lost family members and loved ones—but they used these transitional moments that conflict afforded in order to create new leadership roles for themselves and other women in their community. While conflict and violence impaired and impeded social and individual life for these refugees, they also provided opportunities for this community to re-imagine what it meant to reconcile, heal, and thrive.

These women leaders often talked about unity and peace, but not in a naïve way. Instead, the women who led this post-conflict community used the congregation and their status among the Liberian community to create change and empower others in their community, particularly the future generation of youth. In the next section, I put these women's practices in conversation with international human rights frameworks, which, to the credit of hardworking feminist activists, is now much more attentive to women's voices and needs. However, I argue that sometimes these broader more global conversations overlook the day-to-day transformative leadership practices of women like Marie, Laura, and Pastor Meah.

Women and Conflict: A Human Rights Approach

International conventions and treaties like the 1981 United Nations Convention on the Elimination of Discrimination Against Women (CEDAW) have provided local and transnational women's rights activists with a powerful language and orienting framework from which to launch a critique of practices, policies, and laws that hinder the full flourishing of women.[16] Human rights policies and conventions emerged on the international stage in the 1940s and 1950s to address the harsh violations of the state of its own people, through practices of genocide, colonialism, and torture. Initially the focus on war, genocide, and torture in the language and policies of international human rights practice neglected the position and experiences of violence against women in war or in "peace" times. However, feminist theorists like Rhonda Copelon and Catherine MacKinnon were instrumental in expanding the discourse to include an analysis of the ways that human rights frameworks themselves discriminate against women by ignoring "private" acts like rape and domestic violence.[17] This expansion led to greater attention to women's issues in international treaty bodies like the UN, increased monitoring of violence against women by non-governmental organizations (NGOs) like Amnesty International, and a wider adoption of a human rights framework as a means of explaining and countering violence against women in both international and local contexts.

In the international women's movement, particularly movements dedicated to women, war, and conflict, international human rights treaty and consensus documents play a large part in the dissemination of programs and practices across the world. In particular, local peace activists in Liberia have used the following four United Nations Security Council Resolutions: 1325, passed in 2000, which calls for countries to include women in peacebuilding negotiations, post-conflict peacebuilding, and governance; 1820, passed in 2008, which establishes the links between ending sexual violence and sustainable peace; 1888, passed in 2009, which deals with the implementation of 1820; and 1889, likewise passed in 2009, which addresses

---

16. The full text of the convention is available from http://www.un.org/womenwatch/daw/cedaw/

17. See MacKinnon, *Are Women Human?*; and Copelon, "Surfacing Gender."

the lack of implementation of 1325, prioritizing international funding to ensure women's participation in peace processes.[18]

As Sally Engle Merry describes in her work *Human Rights and Gender Violence: Translating International Law into Local Justice*, the success of these orienting frameworks depends in large part on whether or not they are able to adapt and thrive in the everyday contexts in which people live. As she writes, "human rights are appropriated when they draw on transnational ideas but present them in familiar cultural terms."[19] In other words, the human rights frame must be translated and make a home for itself within local contexts; it must be found useful and productive by local actors. Merry examines the ways that global human rights discourse is cultivated at the transnational level (through international consensus), translated to local contexts, and situated within the lives of everyday individuals. As she notes, this process does not significantly alter the frame or content of human rights itself, positing instead that human rights language and orienting frameworks, through practices of translation, are re-written and lived out in the vernacular language and context of the communities in which they are placed.[20]

Merry's ethnography of the creation and translation of human rights discourse examines both international processes of deliberation and monitoring at the United Nations, and the ways that this consensus is localized by violence against women organizations in the US, Fiji, Hong Kong, China, and India. She describes the ways that international conventions, like CEDAW, are created through a process of consensus building, in which each nation can contribute to the wording of the documents yet can refuse to sign on to them once the process is complete (as the United States has done with CEDAW).[21] Additionally, these documents are crafted with the (sometimes peripheral) participation of NGO actors, who caucus with one another to draft language around issues that they then pass on to their national delegates, contributing to the sense that this global consensus reflects

---

18. See Gbowee, *Mighty Be Our Powers*; also Republic of Liberia, "Women and the Conflict."

19. Merry, *Human Rights and Gender Violence*, 178.

20. Merry writes that, "Human rights must become part of local legal consciousness in order to fulfill their emancipatory potential," but in her work with local gender violence advocates she found that "the knowledge of human rights within village communities was quite limited." Merry, *Human Rights and Gender Violence*, 179.

21. For a list of all states that have ratified CEDAW, visit http://www.un.org/womenwatch/daw/cedaw/states.htm.

on-the-ground issues and concerns. Yet in this attempt to cultivate international consensus, the resulting documents are often general and rely on language that is allegedly "agreed upon" and crafted in previous documents, conventions, or meetings. These documents often describe and name in general ways particularly contested issues like women's role in marriage, childbearing, or specific practices of violence so that the broadest possible consensus on document creation can be reached (despite the frustration of NGO actors, who often want more specificity in the documents).[22] While this process of generalization might be seen as a significant compromise in that it is too ambiguous to carry any clout, this lack of specificity actually contributes to these documents' transformative power at the state and local level. Because these documents rely and build on such a broad level of agreement, they carry both educative and cultural power; they are referenced as evidence of a global consensus around eliminating discrimination against women. As Merry writes, "A critical feature of the CEDAW process is its cultural and educational role: its capacity to coalesce and express a particular understanding of gender. Like more conventional legal processes, its significance lies in its capacity to share cultural understandings and to articulate and expand a vision of rights."[23] Although the CSW's actual power in monitoring state's compliance to CEDAW is persuasive, not coercive (they have no official sanctioning power), these documents do become a part of international consensus around good governance and states' responsibilities for upholding human rights.

This sense of international consensus and responsibility gives these documents a particular sort of power for local women's rights organizations. As Leymah Gbowee writes, the passing of UN Security Council Resolution 1325 helped to bolster the women's movement in Liberia and West Africa, and encouraged the founding of the Women in Peacebuilding Network (WIPNET): "It was an audacious, perfectly timed idea. Internationally, there was a growing recognition that women were being left out of peace and negotiating processes." The momentum around the resolution's passage, in addition to the international attention on the lack of women's participation in peace processes gave a certain legitimacy to the growing women's movement for peace in Liberia. In an effort to include women in the process, women who worked for Liberia's Truth and Reconciliation

---

22. Merry, *Human Rights and Gender Violence*, 72–109.
23. Ibid., 89.

Commission harnessed this international momentum around women, conflict, and peace.[24]

In the case of Liberia, human rights frameworks like SCR 1325 were able to provide some momentum, and some national and international attention for including women in the process of the TRC. This led to increased participation by women in the TRC process (51% of statements taken were by women), and the creation of transitional justice mechanisms like the Community Dialogue Process. Increased attention to the women's peacebuilding movement in Liberia and the awarding of the Nobel Peace Prize in 2011 to Leymah Gbowee and Ellen Johnson Sirleaf signaled that something had changed in terms of international women's rights work: women are finally being recognized as leaders in peace work. But this begs the question of how much this has has actually changed the way that this international work is structured and disseminated? Gbowee has this response:

> In September 2006 . . . I travelled to New York to address the UN. It was the fifth anniversary of the passage of Resolution 1325, which called for bringing more women into UN peace and security efforts, and for warring countries to take special measures to protect women and girls from gender-based violence. There wasn't anything new to say: the resolution still hadn't been widely implemented. Today, after another five years, the story's the same. Every time there's a conflict, the resolution is dusted off and everyone shouts, "We need to do something!" Then nothing happens."[25]

While human rights instruments and frameworks carry a great deal of power (especially if they are implemented!) and are able to harness a certain global critique of injustice to women, in their overarching view they can nevertheless neglect to recognize the ways in which women's religious lives affect the ways they understand and practice peace and healing.[26] As Veena Das points out, women's strategies of resisting, speaking, or embodying violence might emerge far from the expected contexts of truth commissions or the halls of the United Nations. Indeed, she argues for a turn

---

24. As the authors of the "Women and the Conflict" report note, during the Liberian National Conference for Women, held to discuss the TRC report and outcomes, "Strategic interventions and recommendations for the promotion of conventions, protocol, national laws and policies on women, including the UN Resolution 1325, and other international instruments were called for" in response to women's experiences of the war. Republic of Liberia, "Women and the Conflict," 21.

25. Gbowee, *Mighty Be Our Powers*, 197.

26. Asad, *Formations of the Secular*, 201.

to the "everyday" to chronicle and understand the ways that violence and recovery happen in real life.[27]

An expansive view of what constitutes human rights work and women's leadership in peace processes might not only provide a useful corrective to how we think about violence itself, but might also enlarge our views of practices and strategies of healing as well. As we heard from the work of Laura, Marie, and Pastor Meah, although this "everyday" work happened beyond international fanfare and outside of the scope of international women's rights meetings, these practices help to shape post-conflict societies in West Africa and the United States. These women were making the moral, theological choice to respond to violence with hope and love; they were offering a shoulder to cry on, and sometimes "just a word" in an effort to sustain and re-build their communities.

Healing and the Everyday

What is clear from hearing these women's stories and contrasting them with the international rights frameworks is that we need to pay more attention to the ways that women navigate leadership positions in post-conflict communities. Doing so allows for a more expansive view of what "counts" as religious in human rights work, and it validates the moral, theological work women are doing in their daily lives to restore communities affected by trauma and war. This type of healing work emerges out of these women's own experiences with violence and trauma, and therefore serves as a self-healing practice as well.

Indeed, a unifying theme in these women's stories is the ways their own recovery is tied intimately to their work on behalf of other survivors of violence. As Laura told me, "I get my healing from helping people." For Marie too, "reaking the silence came about because I had to explain my story in order for me to heal. The more I talked about it, the more I cried, the more I got it out, [the more] I became a better person." Pastor Meah regularly told her story of escaping the Civil War in her sermons at church, letting her congregants know that despite hardships, "God will make a way." Judith Herman writes about the importance of such recovery practices, naming this the "survivor mission." As she writes,

---

27. Das, "Violence, Gender and Subjectivity," 283–99.

> A significant minority, as a result of the trauma, feel[s] called upon to engage in a wider world. These survivors recognize a political or religious dimension in their misfortune and discover that they can transform the meaning of their personal tragedy by making it the basis for social action. While there is no way to compensate for an atrocity, there is a way to transcend it, by making it a gift to others. The trauma is redeemed only when it becomes the source of a survivor['s] mission.[28]

The survivor, by doing for others, is able to transform the trauma she has experienced. She might even see this transformation as part of a divine order, as Pastor Meah did, who said of working with trauma survivors in her church, "Yea, it is difficult, but as the Word of God says, with God all things are possible." Agnes Kamara-Umunna, who wrote of her work with former Liberian Civil War fighters, echoes this feeling of transformation: "Our lives have a plan for us, even if we can't see it for a while. We search for our path, push and pull away from our destinies, either because they are too big or too incomprehensible or scary or simply don't make sense."[29] These women were able to see their lives and work as part of something bigger than what they had been through. The traumatic experiences that Agnes, Pastor Meah, Marie, and Laura endured were transformed by their becoming a part—albeit a painful one—of a larger reality that transcended the evils they experienced. The women were then able to understand the violence as a part of a larger narrative in which evil no longer has the final say.

The leadership these women demonstrated was a moral, theological choice to confront evil and violence in a way that foregrounds the solidarity we share as human beings. This was evident when Marie reminded survivors, "you are not alone." It also, importantly, reflects that this understanding of human relationships and transformation was born out of an unfortunately intimate knowledge of the promises and perils of such relations. These women's leadership practices were profoundly shaped by loss, and could be seen, then, as practices of mourning. As Judith Butler writes,

> When we lose certain people, or when we are dispossessed from a place, or a community, we may simply feel that we are undergoing something temporary, that mourning will be over and some restoration of prior order will be achieved. But maybe when we

---

28. Herman, *Trauma and Recovery*, 207.
29. Kamara-Umunna and Holland, *And Still Peace Did Not Come*, 238.

undergo what we do, something about who we are is revealed, something that delineates the ties we have to others, that shows us that these ties constitute what we are, ties or bonds that compose us.[30]

It is precisely *because* their work emerged out of their own traumatic experiences that these women's work was not naïve. As Herman writes, survivors who take on a "mission" in their own healing process must do so with the awareness that there is no "inevitability of victory."[31] They have faced evil and know its power. Despite this, survivors carry on, "based not on the illusion that evil has been overcome, but rather on the knowledge that it has not entirely prevailed."[32] Like the mothers I describe in the next chapter, this reparative work was done not only in an effort to repair the self, but also to restore the other, in an effort to rebuild a community fractured by violence. As Laura stated about the importance of healing work in the Liberian community, "We are all connected in so many different ways." As Das writes, "In regions of the imaginary, violence creates divisions and connections that point to the tremendous dangers that human beings pose to each other . . . Human beings, however, not only pose dangers to each other, they also hold hope for each other."[33] Hope and promise. Risk and repair.

Conclusions

These women's leadership practices help us to see the ways that everyday women were making moral, theological choices to repair their post-conflict communities. This work happened in and through their everyday lives, and it served as a reminder of the connections we all share as human beings. Laura, Marie, and Pastor Meah undertook this work because they saw that the repair of the other was often integral to the repair of the self. Hearing their stories helps us to understand *why* and *how* women are willing to undertake the risky work of post-conflict transformation, and it widens the lens to see a broader picture of the things that "count" as human rights work and the ways in which their sense of a God who moves in and through them in an effort to restore life after violence affects that work.

30. Butler, *Precarious Life*, 22.
31. Herman, *Trauma and Recovery*, 209.
32. Ibid.
33. Das, *Life and Words*, 14–15.

Women's Leadership from Local to Global

Laura, Pastor Meah, and Marie's leadership practices demonstrate that while human rights instruments and frameworks carry a great deal of power and are able to harness a certain global critique of injustice to women, this expansiveness can fail to see the nuanced ways that women serve as everyday leaders in the rebuilding of their selves, their families, and their communities after conflict. These frameworks also do not help us to see why or how women take such courageous leadership positions. In this chapter, I have demonstrated that some of these leadership practices emerge because women remember the violence they—or their communities—endured. Memories of violence can be profoundly debilitating; however, these women were able to tell their stories and develop a "survivor mission" that recognized their own healing as intimately bound to another. In this way, their leadership practices were built out of their sense that we are all connected to one another, and that healing for one promotes healing for all. As Pastor Meah put it, "human beings like to be treated like human beings."

As Veena Das points out, women's strategies of resisting, speaking, or embodying violence might emerge far from the expected contexts of truth commissions or the halls of the United Nations, as they do in this Liberian community. The women described here were confronted with a world that was not as it should be; they made a decision to do something about it, in order to transform and heal self and community. They did so out of their everyday lives and drawing on deep spiritual practices and sensibilities.

As feminist theorist Tina Sideris argues, "Healing requires reconciliation and reconstruction within communities at a grassroots level. It is at this level that women are most often involved, although their efforts and the value of this kind of reconciliation are usually neither recognized or acknowledged."[34] Although international frameworks and meetings like the United Nations CSW no doubt shape the stories that are told about war and peace, based on my fieldwork with Liberian women in North Carolina I argue for a focus on local contexts, including women's religious realities and narratives, in order to answer in the affirmative the question from my fieldnotes, "*When women speak, do we listen?*"

---

34. Sideris, "Problems of Identity," 59.

5

Mothering Practices

As was chronicled in the documentary *Pray the Devil Back to Hell*, and in Leymah Gbowee's memoir, *Mighty Be Our Powers: How Sisterhood, Prayer, and Sex Changed a Nation at War*, the Women in Peacebuilding Network (WIPNET) in Liberia was a vital force in helping to bring peace to the country. As Gbowee describes, when the women learned that Liberians United for Reconciliation and Democracy (LURD) had shown some signals of being willing to meet with representatives from Charles Taylor's government in the final days of the war, they sprang into action. Gbowee recounts the conversation that followed when three of these women, Asatu, Grace, and Sugars, met with LURD representatives:

> "You are our children!" Grace rebuked the young men. "We've borne you! We are *tired*! We want you to go to Ghana for peace talks! People are dying and you must listen to us!"
>
> To her surprise, Asatu recognized an old schoolmate. "What are you doing here?" he demanded of her. "Don't say anything to me."
>
> Asatu never backed down. "Are you not happy to see me? Your mothers, your sisters have come this far to talk to you! If you don't go to [the] peace talks, don't you know people will die in Monrovia? And don't you think you'll be guilty for their deaths?
>
> Sugars just played to their egos. *You're such important men! . . . Everyone depends on you to save Liberia.* By the time the meeting ended, the LURD leaders had agreed to participate in the peace talks.

Mothering Practices

"Our mothers came all the way from Liberia to talk to us," the men told Asatu, Grace, and Sugars. "Well, mothers, because of you, we will go."[1]

The women in the peace protests drew on their authority as mothers to work for peace. As Mary Moran and Veronika Fuest have noted, although the women's peace protests did not in themselves cause the end of the war, they were successful in forging a 'collective identity politics' capable of attracting significant support and funding from outside sources.[2]

Most of the women with whom I worked experienced serious hardships related to motherhood during and after the conflict: they lost children during the war, their children were killed as a result of violence when they came to North Carolina or they dealt with and grieved their children's scars from the war. The paradoxical fragility and power of motherhood were incredibly apparent in stories I heard from women at Friendship Community Church. Despite these losses (or perhaps because of them), the women at Friendship Community Church emphasized that motherhood was one of the most important parts of their lives. This was reflected in the stories they told me, the prayers they prayed, the sermons that were preached, and their practices. Motherhood, despite its inherent tragedies, was one way that women repaired and restored life post-conflict.

In their attempts to transform life after experiences of violence, the women I worked with focused on rebuilding their selves, families, and communities by caring for the next generation. These everyday practices of mothering are often neglected in post-conflict transformation theory and practice; however, the women with whom I worked had found that these everyday practices of mothering were some of the most successful ways they found for "mak[ing[a way out of no way." In this chapter, I begin by enumerating transformative examples of mothering that emerged during the women's narratives and in the practices of the church in order to

---

1. Gbowee, *Mighty Be Our Powers*, 143.
2. Moran, "Our Mothers Have Spoken," 60. Moran and Fuest have both pointed out the subsequent fractures in this movement, which can be attributed, at least in part, to the presence of these international donors. As Moran writes, "These powerful outside agents, including multilateral organizations like the United Nations as well as the numerous NGOs, may have overlooked internal divisions within the movement, based on class, ethnicity, religion and generation, in their willingness to reinforce familiar assumptions about women's "natural" peacemaking abilities. In the post-war period, these divisions have again risen to the surface as numerous organizations compete for the steadily declining funds allocated to Liberia's reconstruction." See also, Fuest, "This Is the Time to Get Out Front."

demonstrate the importance that women placed on these practices of care in their personal and communal healing.

Baby Dedications and the Blessings of New Life

The desire for new life in a post-conflict community was profoundly reflected at Friendship Community Church in the continued references to the importance of motherhood and children, and was illustrated during a baby dedication that I attended one spring Sunday. Two children were being dedicated, both beautiful baby girls. One was the daughter of two prominent young members of the congregation (the husband, Othello, is the president of the local Liberian young people's association). The other baby girl was the daughter of a young couple who had been recently engaged. The sermon reflected the theme of the service, and was titled "Good Training Shall Guarantee Children not to Rebel." Although this was the title of the sermon, Pastor Meah focused in her remarks on women's empowerment, in large part probably because both of the children being dedicated were girls.

The sermon began with a story about the "old days" in Liberia, when, as Pastor Meah told the congregation, many people regarded male children more favorably than female children. Mothers hoped for sons, and young men were given opportunities to go to school and to do work that young women often did not have. Pastor Meah forcefully reiterated to all of us that now "things are changing. African culture is changing. Women are doing things that men can't do." She drew our attention to Liberia's female president, Ellen Johnson Sirleaf, noting that, "It's a different world." Recalling her own path to ministry, the pastor talked with us about how the Missionary Baptist denomination to which she belonged as a young girl refused to acknowledge women as leaders. Yet already as a child, she knew that God had ordained her to be a minister, teacher, and preacher. So as a young woman, she joined a Liberian Baptist denomination that allowed and encouraged women in the ordination process. "That's why I love God. God loves us all the same," the pastor reminded us. God sees beyond gender to call people based on their gifts and talents. Because of this radical love, "Christians need to love one another." As God loves us, she went on to say, we should love each other.

The pastor's talk about women's roles led into a discussion of motherhood and the assumptions people make about women's biological functions. She told us a story about a young woman from her village who was assumed to be infertile. This woman's husband left her to find a new wife because of her supposed inability to produce children. The community, like the woman's husband, assumed that she was "to blame" for the couple's infertility. At this point in the story, the pastor let out a huge guffaw, moving down in front of the pulpit to come closer to the congregation. Shaking her head and laughing at the man's misfortune, the pastor let us know that when this man remarried, his new wife was also unable to have children. However, the first wife, who was assumed to be "barren" and infertile, went on to birth several children with a new husband. "They used to blame it on the women," she told us, reminding the congregation of the burden placed on women to bear children (and subsequent gender-based shaming of barrenness), when in fact sometimes it is the man whose body does not cooperate.[3]

For Liberian women, she argued, a new day had arrived. Women were no longer blamed for whatever goes wrong in the family, and they were now being encouraged to be ministers, educators, leaders, and even presidents. In the context of a sermon for a baby dedication, the pastor's message was meant to open the congregation's eyes to the ways in which girls and young women are a valued part of society, and as such, their parents should bring them up in a way that honors the gifts they bring to our world. Parents—and the church community—should be involved in the lives of children, which means being in contact with their teachers, knowing what they are studying in school, and ensuring that someone is home with them after school is done. The United States is not like Liberia, she reminded us, where there were aunts and relatives around to care for children while parents were at work. In the United States, parents must make sure that their children are supervised. If you leave them and "do not raise them," the pastor chided, you are heading for a disaster. Raising them includes not only helping them with schoolwork, but also being sure that they are brought up in the ways of the church—that they come to Sunday school and worship. "If you do not show them the right way," she admonished, "they will rebel."[4]

---

3. The concept of barrenness and infertility came up numerous times at the church, in sermons, testimonies, prayers, and informal conversations. On Mother's Day, for example, Pastor Jackson Jones preached about how all women are mothers, even those who are unable to have children.

4. Pastor Meah was here demonstrating what Melinda McGarrah Sharp names as "cross contextual fluency," or "meaningful translation" across cultures, in her attempt to help the Liberian community to understand the differences in parenting practices in

What went unmentioned in the pastor's sermon was the arrest that had happened just months before of a young man, a member of the church, who was involved in selling drugs. Nonetheless, that morning the congregation got the message that the new life that members of the church find in the United States was not easy or without violence and harm. As both Pastor Meah and Reverend Grigsby told me, much of their work at the church consisted of helping young people to reject the life of crime and violence that the U.S. offers in favor of a new life where they could, as Reverend Grigsby told me, take advantage of the "second chance" they had been given at life. In addition to the young man mentioned above, the pastor's own son had died in a gun shooting, and another young male member of the church was shot the same year of my fieldwork. As Reverend Grigsby related, the gang lifestyle seemed easy to step into "when you are coming from violence." The leaders in the church were concerned about this issue as it affected their community in North Carolina and in Liberia. When these young men and women "get into trouble" here in the United States, they are often deported back home (because they are here with temporary status or with no documentation). The gang life then is transported back to Liberia, contributing to instability there.

This environment was remembered at events like this baby dedication, where opportunities to talk about raising children "so they will not rebel" took on a new meaning. In his book *Little Liberia: An African Odyssey in New York City*, Jonny Steinberg cites Rufus Arkoi, a community leader in Staten Island's Liberian community on this issue:

> The African-American kids in this neighborhood were in for a shock... They see these African refugees arrive, washed up from a civil war, and the American kids think exploitation... But the Liberian kids, they are soldiers. They have been shooting automatic weapons. They are fresh from the battlefield. They are too hardened for the local kids. They start getting a reputation. Many, many get incarcerated. Many others are deported. And so the cops on the street, they learn who is Liberian and who isn't, and they start picking on the Liberians... and I think, no man, this is going to end badly.[5]

The sermon, reminding the congregation to raise young women with an eye toward becoming who they were meant to be and offering some

---

Liberia and the United States. See Sharp, *Misunderstanding Stories*, 5.

5. Steinberg, *Little Liberia*, 28.

pointed advice on caring for children in the new (harsh) surroundings in North Carolina was followed by the actual dedication. The couples came forward with their baby girls, with a flock of godparents. One baby, Adeline, had one male and one female godparent, while the other girl, Hannah, had seventeen godparents, meaning that much of the church congregation made their way to the front of the pulpit, crowding around the two little girls. The small space in front of the pulpit was densely populated with parents, godparents, and relatives, many with cameras and phones pointed over their heads in an effort to photograph the action at the front of the mass of people. Pastor Meah offered a blessing over each child, and asked the godparents to commit to helping the parents to bring up the children in the community and to do their part in helping to raise them. As the service closed, we all went forward to congratulate the parents, cooing over the adorable baby girls who were dressed to the nines in frilly dresses and bows. We broke to join together in a lunch after church, with talk of the joys of children permeating most conversations.

This brief vignette illustrates some of the key messages regarding children and mothering that I heard at Friendship Community Church. On the one hand, children played a major role in helping women to restore life; children were another type of "second chance," an opportunity to make this world a better place by creating a new generation. I heard time and again, from women like Evelyn, Joyce, and Ruth that the work they did to become better women (by getting an education, in the case of Joyce and Evelyn or helping the community, like Ruth) was premised on their role as mothers. They worked outside the home, or committed themselves to community projects, so that their children could enjoy a life that was better than the one they lived. In this way, children were the "blessing" that I heard them described as in countless sermons and talks from the pulpit at church. Children provided a sense that life was worth living; indeed it was a "blessing" from God. On the other hand, the women at Friendship Christian Church were also profoundly aware of the losses that paradoxically accompanied this sense of maternal blessing.

She's with a "Bad Man": Mothering and Risk

The concept of being a mother was incredibly broad, in large part due to the effects of the war on this community. As Reverend Grigsby told me when I first came to Friendship Community Church, many families in the church were created during the immigration process, when one family member would make it to the United States, then bring relatives (sometimes very distant or of no biological relation at all) to live with them. For one woman I met, the death of her sister during the war meant that her sister's children became her own. Very few members of the Liberian community know that her son and one of her daughters are not in fact her biological children. Families were created and blended, forming bonds that enrich both the parents and children, creating something beautiful out of the horror of war, but also drawing on older patterns of fictive kinship in Liberia.[6]

Despite the ways that motherhood was able to provide a sense of new life and love, the women I worked with were also painfully aware of the fact that motherhood itself contained elements of the tragic. To be a mother (or, for some, the inability and/or choice not to become a mother) was a process that was fraught with both pain and promise, as I heard in a conversation with Marlene at Pastor Meah's graduation.[7] On the Saturday of the graduation, a hot day in early June, I walked alone into the sanctuary of a very large local church.[8] I sat on the left side of the sanctuary, thinking that I would catch up with the members of FCC after the service was over. It was then that I saw a couple of hands waving at me, motioning for me to come and join the group situated in the center of the sanctuary, in the middle pews. As I apologized to my seatmates and made my way across the room, I wondered how I could have missed the two rows of bright African dresses and head wraps. The two and a half rows that made up the FCC congregation was a colorful picture in the midst of a sea of more drab colors.

A little more than a dozen members of FCC had shown up for the Pastor's graduation, and some of the women there pulled me into the middle of the aisle to sit with them. After a few minutes of chitchat, Marlene turned

---

6. As Mary Moran has noted, the idea of fictive genealogies is not foreign to Liberians. She writes of how native Liberians used their Western education to rewrite their genealogical history, refuting their native origins. Moran, *Liberia*, 81. Additionally, in her dissertation, Maura Busch Nsonwu writes of how the Liberian women she interviewed did not distinguish between the children they birthed and the children they cared for. See Nsonwu, "God-Talk and Kin-Talk," 114.

7. In addition to the mothering pains that I describe here, I would also point out that the inability to bear children marks their participation in society, straining marriages and community ties. The loss of a child, whether through miscarriage, stillbirth, or death (recall the young men who have died in the last year due to gun violence) reveals starkly the intense pains of being a mother.

8. Pastor Meah was graduating with a bachelor's degree from a local Bible college, which was housed in one of the larger evangelical churches in town.

to me and asked where my friend (and church member) Laura was. When I told Marlene that Laura was in Liberia, she replied that she always asks people who are going to Liberia to look for her daughter Joanna when they go. Marlene then began to tell me about her estranged relationship with Joanna, caused by their separation in the 1990s, during the early stages of the Civil War.

When the war started, Marlene remembers Joanna going to school like any normal day. However, that afternoon, rebels entered her town, destroying properties, homes, and lives in their wake. Marlene's family told her that the rebels had already taken over the school, so she needed to leave immediately to ensure her safety. Afraid for her daughter, but also afraid for her own life, Marlene left with her family. She and Joanna were separated for over ten years, each never knowing if the other one was alive. Marlene went across the border with her family to Ivory Coast, where she eventually landed in a refugee camp. Mother and daughter should have been reunited in 2005, when Marlene's family went back to Liberia to find Joanna. Marlene was leaving to come to America and wanted to see if her daughter was alive, and if so, if she would come with her. Marlene had won the elusive "American lottery,"[9] and could bring family along with her to the United States. Marlene's uncles were able to find Joanna, alive, who now had four children and was living "in the bush" with a "bad man" who had done horrible things during the war.[10] Joanna, who has children with her partner (the "bad man"), did not want to leave him to come to America. In anguish, Marlene left for the US with her three other children.

After she told me this story, Marlene explained in her stilted English that she always asks for people who are going to Liberia to look for Joanna, to see how she is doing. Joanna sold produce at a market in Monrovia, and then returned "to the bush with that bad man." Marlene held my hand for a second, remembering, I guessed, the daughter she had not seen for over twenty years. I promised to let Marlene know if I went to Liberia again, so that I could look for Joanna and try to play a part in making sure she was doing alright.[11]

---

9. As I heard from Joe, Evelyn's husband, and Reverend Grigsby, being accepted for admittance to the United States under the protective status afforded to Liberians during and after the Civil War was like winning the lottery, a rare and amazing feat.

10. While Marlene did not say this, her tone led me to believe that the "bad man" was one of the rebels that Marlene and her family fled during the war.

11. Agnes M. Fallah Kamara-Umunna tells a similar story in her memoir, of a woman whose daughter married the man who killed her family members. Kamara-Umunna

It was at this point that the graduation ceremony started, and Marlene and I turned our attention to the front. A few hours into the service, the graduation speaker asked us if there were people in our past who we left behind, only to find ourselves uncomfortably reminded of their existence by social networks like Facebook and Twitter. Hearing knowing laughs from the congregation, the speaker went on to read Mark 16:24, when Jesus tells his disciples to "take up their cross" and follow him. Unlike awkward re-connections with old acquaintances over Facebook, to follow Jesus meant to leave the past in the past—to move forward to new beginnings, new possibilities, and new prosperity. As I sat next to Marlene, I wondered how this speech resonated with her. For Marlene, and other mothers I talked with, the pain they endured during the Civil War was compounded by the experiences of their children. To forget the past, this past where one's children were harmed, killed, or taken in by "bad men," was impossible. As Ruth told me, "When my children came [to live with me in the United States], they tell me how they treated people, killing all these pregnant women, then taking their babies from their stomach. Then, let me see, they would go to the stream where they went to take a bath, [and] they got to put the body aside before they can even drink the water." Knowing what their children endured, and in Marlene's case, continuing to feel the effects of what happened in the dissolution of relationships, was a stark reminder that in the process of transformation, hardship and suffering could not always be avoided.

Mothering as a Practice of Peacebuilding

These two stories about motherhood—the joys of a baby dedication and the pain of losing a child to war—reflected the ways that hope and hardship existed side by side in practices of mothering that attempted to knit a life and a community back together in a Liberian community. Pastor Meah and the leaders of Friendship Community Church often focused on children as the center of the family. Children provided a reason to persevere despite the fact that it sometimes seemed as if everything in life was going the wrong

interviewed her on her radio program, "Straight from the Heart," where she recounted, "What am I to do? Tell my only child her husband whom she loves killed her father and three sisters? Tell her the truth even if it destroys her marriage? I can't . . . She was too young to know, too young to realize. But also, not telling her will cause me to carry the guilt all my life. I don't know what to do. I don't know how things like this happen in the world." Kamara-Umunna and Holland, *And Still Peace Did Not Come*, 102.

direction. As Evelyn recounted to me several times, the difficulties of life were worth it if they might offer some hope that her children could live in a better world, one without war and violence. In so many ways, children were seen as a "blessing," and they brought joy into the home. And yet, as the sermons named (if implicitly) and as women recounted, the joy that came with bringing new life into the world was always tempered with pain and loss.

Indeed it was this relationality, felt in and through motherhood, that led many women to work for peace during the Liberian Civil War. As Gbowee recounts in her memoir, the final days of the Civil War were some of the bloodiest. Gbowee and her colleagues were watching the destruction, shelling, and looting of Monrovia on the television and Internet, as they attended the peace talks being held in Accra, Ghana. She writes:

> I sat there feeling sick to my soul. How could I have been so stupid as to think a handful of women could stop a war? You fooled me, God.
>
> There was a video on the [web]site: Two little boys had been brushing their teeth outdoors when the missiles hit, and all that was left of them was their slippers. The camera shifted to an old woman holding a baby who had been born the night before. The baby's mother had come outside to hang up diapers. She had been standing next to the boys and she, too, was dead.
>
> I looked at the baby; I thought about the dead children—their slippers were the same size that Arthur would be wearing now—and my despair was so deep that crying couldn't begin to ease it.[12]

Gbowee's anger, lament, and frustration led her to take a final stand—along with the other women protesters—at the peace talks. She encouraged her colleagues to gather as many women as they could and go to the hotel where the talks were being held. At this hotel, the warlords had been enjoying several weeks of easy times, sunshine, delicious food, and poolside drinks. Gbowee looped arms with the other women outside the wide glass doors of the negotiating room and sent a note to the Nigerian President, General Abubakar, saying that they were taking the hall hostage until a peace agreement was reached. As security guards came outside to find out what the fuss was about, Gbowee began taking off her clothes, drawing on a powerful traditional practice that was meant to convey her incredible anger and impatience:

---

12. Gbowee, *Mighty Be Our Powers*, 160.

> These negotiations had been my last hope, but they were crashing too. But in threatening to strip, I had summoned up a traditional power. In Africa, it's a terrible curse to see a married or elderly woman deliberately bare herself. If a mother is really, really upset with a child, she might take out her breast and slap it, and he's cursed. For this group of men to see a woman naked would be almost like a death sentence. Men are born through women's vaginas, and it's as if by exposing ourselves, we say, 'We now take back the life we gave you.' Fear passed through the hall.[13]

When the warlords began to shout back at Gbowee and her comrades, they were silenced by General Abubakar, who met with the women and negotiated an agreement that led to a different, more somber feeling process at the peace talks (in contrast to the lackadaisical way that many of the warlords had been treating the talks) and that marked "the beginning of the end" of the war.[14]

Maternality was a vital source of power for women who were a part of the Liberian women's peace movements. As Gbowee notes, many of their practices drew on "traditional authority" to resist oppression and violence that includes practices that might seem antithetical to the ways mothering is interpreted in the West, including significant resources related to economic and political power. As Mary Moran writes, "African constructions of women as 'mothers' have been sources of power for women to use to protect their own interests as women as well as to protect their children."[15] In fact, Moran found that in interviews with over eighty men who did not participate in violence during the Civil War that, "My mother wouldn't let me" was one of the most prevalent explanations for their refusal to fight. She writes:

> Many of my informants attributed their survival during the war years to the patronage and protection of older female kin, who hid them at home, kept them off the streets when armed factions were known to be recruiting, or ransomed them from the factions when they were forcibly taken. One informant who told me he had wanted to go along with his friends from school who were lured by the opportunities for looting but, "you can't disobey your mother." Another young man's grandmother threatened to disown him from the family if he joined the fighters. Such statements echo

---

13. Ibid., 163.
14. Ibid.
15. Moran, "Our Mothers Have Spoken," 58.

those of the faction leaders and warlords who responded to talks called by the women's peace movement in the 1990's saying, "when your mother calls you, you must show up."[16]

As Moran has illustrated in her exposition of the Liberian Civil War, although Western conceptions of equality and democracy do not neatly map into Western conceptions of either, Liberian understandings of human life and citizenship do reveal practices in which individuals who are viewed as unequal can be provided opportunities to protest and air grievances. She describes women's marches she witnessed during her fieldwork in Southeastern Liberia that demonstrate this point; although women were never seen as equal to ("older than") men, they could—and did—band together to resist political practices that they deemed unjust.[17]

She describes one instance in which the Market Women's Association banded together to support students at the University of Liberia who were being jailed and persecuted during the military government of Samuel Doe. One of the student leaders told Moran in an interview, "Without these women, we would be dead. They called us their children, you know? They said to the government, 'What? We go in the market and work so hard to keep our children in school and you want to kill them?'" Moran attributes this to Liberian indigenous practices of democracy; however, I point to it here to mark yet another instance in which women harnessed their maternal power to resist violence and oppression. Moran also draws on these examples to point to the ways that these practices were and are practices of alternative democracy, "not the actions of people who are fatalistic, clientalistic, mystified by hierarchies of secrecy, or utterly dominated by 'religious thinking.'"[18] I note that religious and political practices were not and are not necessarily antithetical to one another. In other words, the women's peace protests were grounded in their maternal authority and indigenous practices of democracy, whereby the women drew on their shared status as women/mothers in order to protest injustice. Their protests were *also* grounded in their religious sensibilities, practices, and beliefs, as noted above in Gbowee's text and throughout the narratives and fieldwork I have explored here. In what follows, I turn to feminist theory in order to explore the gaps and overlaps that occur when we overlay theory and practice.

16. Ibid.
17. Moran, *Liberia*, 28.
18. Ibid., 52.

Mothering as Religious Practice

Feminist political theory emerged as a discipline in response to the marginalization or absence of women in political theory and discourse. Key to the emergence of the field was the recognition that issues women face, like domestic violence, rape, and sexual assault, had been defined by the law as "private" issues in which the state could not legitimately intervene.[19] As feminist theorists began to challenge these public/private divides, their analyses and strategies for recourse began to diverge along several lines. These included liberal feminist theorists who sought an extension of formal equality to women, radical feminists, who argued that women's inequality could not be understood without analysis and dismantling of patriarchal structures of universal sexism, and feminists who urged a widening of political participation. Despite these varied approaches to women's rights and violence against women, theorists IfiAmadiume and Martha Nussbaum have argued that religion has often been a disparaged topic in the discourse of feminist theory.[20] As Nussbaum writes, this is most likely because "there is no doubt that the world's major religions, in their actual historical form, have been unjust to women both theoretically and practically."[21] This extends also to human rights work that addresses gender-based violence.[22] There has been sustained research on women's interactions with various legal and political systems.[23] Less is known about the spiritual or religious navigations that activists and survivors make.

As has been noted throughout this text, the Liberian women's peace movement demonstrated the significance of international human rights documents, like United Nations Security Council Resolution (SCR) 1325, which calls for countries to include women in peacebuilding negotiations, post-conflict peacebuilding, and governance. However, it was not only international human rights frameworks that grounded the work of the Women in Peacebuilding Network (WIPNET) in Liberia. Harnessing religious assets brought a significant contingent of leadership and support

---

19. See MacKinnon, *Are Women Human?*

20. See Amadiume, *Male Daughters, Female Husbands*, and Nussbaum, *Women and Human Development*.

21. Nussbaum, *Women and Human Development*, 177.

22. See Merry, *Human Rights and Gender Violence*.

23. Meintjes, Pillay and Turshen, "There is No Aftermath for Women." See also Meintjes, Pillay and Turshen, eds., *The Aftermath*; Merry, *Human Rights and Gender Violence*.

MOTHERING PRACTICES

for the peace movement among the people and leaders of Liberia, drawing upon accepted avenues of redress and representation, including mediation, prayer, and the women's status as mothers.[24] Through songs, prayer, and mediation, the women of WIPNET were able to draw upon the resources of their congregations as well as indigenous traditions of women's ritual, maternal, and political authority to work for peace.[25]

As we have explored throughout this book, in women's human rights discourse, religion is often talked about in terms of its institutional or organizational functions. The maternal practices highlighted in this chapter show that religion also matters for women in more everyday, ordinary ways. As sociologist of religion Courtney Bender writes:

> Sociologists have abandoned the idea that people subjectively carry religion or other culture internally in ways that do not change much from setting to setting. They have also laid aside the simplistic notion that action in a single institution is shaped purely by the contingencies and rules of that setting. These unsettled currents in cultural sociology surrounding the relation between individuals' discursive styles and practices, and the contexts where they live and work, talk and play point toward the need to better understand the creative forces set in motion through unrelenting encounters with multiple others, multiple ways of responding, and a lack of stock certainty about how to respond.[26]

Rather than assuming that individuals are formed and created by their religious traditions, taking these dogmatic truths with them into each situation, these women's maternal practices are a reminder that religion matters throughout the course of life—in the ways women parent, in the ways they tell their stories, in the ways they interact with political systems, and in the ordinary course of their days. We must be willing to examine the ways that religion matters in women's lives, as they describe and practice it. Parenting, I argue, is a significant religious practice for the women with whom I worked, although mothering and parenting practices are not often thought of as specific ministerial practices of the Christian church.[27] For the women of Friendship Community Church,

24. Moran and Pitcher, "The 'Basket Case' and the 'Poster Child,'" 506–7.

25. See Moran, *Liberia*; Moran, *Civilized Women*; Amadiume, *Male Daughters, Female Husbands*; Boone, *Radiance from the Waters*.

26. Bender, *Heaven's Kitchen*, 140.

27. Feminist and womanist theologians have rightly pointed out that many "women's practices" have been left out of the theological canon in terms of what counts as religious

and the women of WIPNET, mothering practices were a central way that women experienced and narrated transformation, in their desire to create and sustain a new generation. As they were also aware, mothering carried with it great pains as well. A nuanced view of religious practices as they exist beyond formal institutions or doctrines is necessary for work on women, violence, and peace. As the women I worked with demonstrate, looking to mothering and parenting as religious practices that reveal the ways women heal would be one apt place to start.

Motherhood and Vulnerability: Toward a Language of Transformation

Theologian Elizabeth Gandolfo provides a powerful language of maternal subjectivity that speaks to the ways that the women highlighted above drew on their maternity in order to heal and transform self and community. Gandolfo develops a theological anthropology that is based in vulnerability, which she names as our "fundamental and unavoidable feature of the human condition."[28] She argues that resistance to oppression and injustice ought to be grounded in this awareness of our fragile human connection, and she illumines several spiritual practices that provide "assets for living courageously, peacefully, and compassionately both with the pain of the past and with present forms of vulnerability and suffering that cannot be changed."[29] To build this anthropology and illumine these practices, Gandolfo turns to maternality, acknowledging the pitfalls that come with drawing on these experiences.[30] Gandolfo outlines a triadic structure that

---

practice. They work to reclaim these practices as vital spiritual resources for women's lives. See, for example, Cheryl A. Kirk-Duggan's essay, "African-American Spirituals: Confronting and Exorcising Evil through Song," in which she draws on spirituals as a source for doing womanist theology. In Townes, ed. *A Troubling in My Soul*, 150–71. Also, Mary McClintock Fulkerson draws on "homemaking" practices in her theological ethnography *Places of Redemption*. Bonnie Miller-McLemore's seminal text, *Also a Mother*, is a striking counterpoint to the absence of maternal practice and reflection in theological scholarship.

28. Gandolfo, *The Power and Vulnerability of Love*, 8.

29. Ibid., 7–8.

30. These include the dangers of essentializing women as mothers, leaving out those who are not parents/mothers, romanticizing motherhood, and eliding differences among and between mothers. See Gandolfo, *The Power and Vulnerability of Love*, 13–18. This is also a particularly apt warning for post-conflict communities. As Meintjes, Pillay, and Turshen argue, "In reaction to the fearsome dangers of battle and the unrelieved

shapes maternal practices of resistance, including of practices of "memory, contemplation, and solidarity." I outline this structure as a way of conceptualizing the ways the women highlighted in this text experience and narrate transformation through motherhood. As has been discussed in previous chapters, the profound experience of remembering trauma has shaped the ways that the women from Friendship Christian Church (as well as Liberian activists from WIPNET) were able to survive and thrive during and after violence.

The memory of suffering has the capacity to wound—mortally; however, it also has the capacity to empower "human beings to inhabit the vulnerability of our basic condition with greater love and justice for ourselves and for others."[31] Memories of trauma allow us to experience—painfully—our relation to others. The women chronicled here were also able to draw on these memories to enact peace and healing; the memories and memorialization practices enacted for loved ones lost enabled them to imagine a new future and to create a new world in which transformation and healing could happen.

Second, Gandolfo looks to contemplative practices to understand how resistance to injustice can be fueled through our vulnerability to others (not despite it). As she writes, "in Christian language, the contemplative chooses to be defined and transformed by her status as God-bearer, temple of the Holy Spirit, and the body of Christ, as opposed to being defined by the actions of those who have harmed or seek to harm her."[32] We have seen in previous chapters, and in this chapter, how contemplative practices like prayer and biblical reading has provided sustenance to mothers who grieve.

Finally, Gandolfo recognizes that through memory and contemplation we might finally enter into practices of solidarity and resistance that allow us to "lighten the burden of vulnerability" for others, particularly those most vulnerable to risk and harm.[33] Gbowee's account of holding the peace process hostage and Pastor Meah's sermon extolling the empowerment of

---

machismo of military life, men romanticize the mothers and wife they left at home; they construct stereotypes of femininity bearing little or no relation to the masculine roles that circumstances have forced on women. The clash between reality and the idealized vision of womanhood may be bitter in the aftermath, especially if women like and want to retain their new identities and men want to preserve the pre-war prerogatives of domination." Meintjes, Pillay, and Turshen, "There Is no Aftermath for Women," 13–14.

31. Gandolfo, *The Power and Vulnerability of Love*, 275.
32. Ibid., 290.
33. Ibid., 300.

girls reflect this kind of resistance and solidarity. In the face of a world that was telling women and girls "no"—and in which they represented communities plagued by violence—both women drew on their memories of harm and their practices of prayer and contemplative sustenance in order to empower others to seek healing and peace.

For the women at Friendship Community Church, motherhood played a vital role in the healing process. For many of the women who formed the Liberian women's peace movement, motherhood was at the center of their struggle to bring an end to the violent conflict that killed almost a quarter of a million people. As Gandolfo's poetic theological language extols, maternality is a reminder of our fundamental human condition: vulnerability. Connection and love in relationship with the other are (often) a profound part of the maternal experience; however, that love means that we feel the other's loss more acutely when it is experienced. This led the women of Friendship Community Church to grieve for what they had lost, but it also transformed their practices of self and community post-conflict. They sought to re-build families in North Carolina and to nurture the next generation in an effort to heal self, neighbor, and community.

These practices of creating and sustaining families—of caring for children in the community and in the family—were, for the women I worked with, part of a spiritual, faith-filled life. However, much of the history of the Christian tradition has presented a marked preference for celibacy as a higher form of religious life, something that has unfortunately crept into Christian ideas about an "authentic life of faith." To illustrate this, Bonnie Miller-McLemore (whose work on mothering and theology is a rare exception to the lack of literature on the topic) recounts her experiences of a systematic theology conference where one participant remarked that she was forced to give up her "discipline of prayer" when she became a mother.[34] Miller-McLemore, like the women I worked with, claims caring for children as a vital, nourishing religious practice. She refutes assumptions that busy parents are "Christians on idle," taking some years off from their faith journey while others "seek God on their behalf."[35] Miller-McLemore and feminist theologian Janet Soskice look to parenting itself as a practice of faith, one in which women can connect to God through the daily practices of life, like breastfeeding.[36] The women I worked with are doing the

---

34. Miller-McLemore, *In the Midst of Chaos*, 3.
35. Ibid., 4.
36. See Soskice, *The Kindness of God*.

same reclaiming work for the Christian tradition that these theologians are demonstrating. Their everyday religious practices of parenting—painfully aware of both the joys and hardships it implies—help us to see the ways that religion matters as women navigate post-conflict transformation for self and community, in the course of everyday life.

As we think about new theological languages of transformation, we would do well to remember these everyday practices like mothering and caring for children that some women draw on in their attempts to heal post-conflict. They also, as Gandolfo makes us aware, remind us that we are all vulnerable; this vulnerability can bring with it great harm but also great promise for healing and peace.

Conclusions

These everyday faith practices of caring for the next generation allow us to see that with transformation comes an element of the tragic. The loss and pain that came before was never erased; however, out of this hardship the women I worked with were able to craft and create lives that were worth living. By meeting weekly to pray for the church, their families, their communities, and the world, and by focusing on creating and sustaining old and new family ties, the lives they created were crafted from both pain and hope.

A language of transformation, one that is attentive to everyday practices like mothering, must acknowledge this co-mingling of tragedy and hope, pain and love, so brilliantly felt by women at the Liberian church who attempt to create new life after civil war. This paradox is part and parcel of our human condition: we are relational beings, and as such, we offer hope and harm to one another, risk and repair.

These practices of faith are, I argue, one way that women piece together a life and hope out of harm and difficulty. They provide a complicated understanding of the types of self and community transformations that women undergo post-conflict. These transformations through women's everyday religious practices are not naïve, but instead acknowledge the tragic elements of life. In other words, although the women with whom I worked were able to "count their blessings" and see the presence of God in and through their children and in the practices of resistance and care that aimed to protect current and future generations, they also acknowledged that blessings were not always easy to find. There was not always a happy ending to the story, as I was reminded by Marlene's story of losing her daughter to a "bad man" who killed people during the war, or the prayers I heard for the young men who have committed suicide or killed one another because of their wartime experiences.

The vision of transformation presented by the mothers here is not naïve. It does not seek simple answers or try to find meaning to contain senseless violence. It emerges out of what is and reacts to a world that is not as it was intended to be. Recall pastor Meah's words: Jesus wept. As the women I worked with in the Liberian community demonstrate, healing can be felt, described, and lived through the joy and pain of bringing new life into the world, through shared stories and gestures, and in the ways in which communities are rebuilt after experiences of war and violence. In order to discern new vocabularies for healing and to identify limitations of linear narratives that often accompany it, I conclude, we must start by being attentive to the ways women cobble together the fragments and scraps of belief, practice, narrative, and interpersonal relationships to create a life that is worth living (and mothering) in the aftermath of violence.

6

Practices of Transformation: Making a Way

After church one Sunday, I went with Reverend Grigsby to visit one of the older women in the congregation who had not been in church for several months because of her glaucoma and advanced diabetes. As Reverend Grigsby told me on the drive over, one of the ministers of the church visits shut-in members whenever the larger congregation celebrated Communion, in order to ensure their continued participation in the life of the church. We arrived at the woman's small house in a relatively new neighborhood a few miles away from downtown. Mrs. Taylor lived with her daughter, who answered the door when we got there, and invited us to the formal sitting room, which was darkened by heavy curtains over the windows. Mrs. Taylor came into the sitting room, assisted by her daughter, and sat in a chair across from the couch upon which Reverend Grigsby and I sat. Reverend Grigsby then brought out a small box that held the Communion set that the members of Friendship Community Church used during Communion, a small plastic cup of grape juice, covered with another sealed container that contained the communion wafer. We talked with Mrs. Taylor for a while, asking about her health and updating her on some of the goings-on of members of the church.

Reverend Grigsby started Communion with a prayer, which focused on Mrs. Taylor's health. Healing, he told us, does not always come quickly or easily. Instead, it comes in God's time. Because of her eye condition, Mrs. Taylor's milky eyes teared up as he talked, and she softly repeated, "Yes, Yes," after each of Reverend Grigsby's sentences. We prayed for healing in Mrs. Taylor's life, and Reverend Grigsby reminded her that God was always present. "Oh yes," Mrs. Taylor remarked, "[God] has not forgotten me." Reverend Grigsby administered the Communion, opening the little pouch with the wafer that sat above the small cup that held the grape juice. As she ate and drank what was offered, Mrs. Taylor thanked us for being with her. After some smalltalk, Reverend Grigsby and I left.

Practices and stories of faith reveal the ways that religion matters in the lives of the women from Liberia at Friendship Community Church. As Mrs. Taylor told us, these practices of faith helped women to know that God and their community "has not forgotten" them. As the memories of God being present in violence highlighted in previous chapters or the work of the women's empowerment group, these faith practices created new narratives in which women who survived the Liberian Civil War could live. As Reverend Grigsby told me the afternoon that we left Mrs. Taylor, the members of Faith Community Church knew they had been given a "second chance" at life. They had lived through immense hardships both in Liberia and in the United States, and aimed to live into that second chance, to reimagine life out of fear and death.

Worship practices at Friendship Community Church helped the women to create new narratives of hope and life out of hardship and harm. As Marcia Mount Shoop writes, "Transformation is the core promise of Christian life. And transformation is an actual change in form, not simply a new outlook on life or a welcomed assurance of an eternal reward. Our bodies change in an incarnational faith—our individual bodies and our corporate bodies."[1] In other words, transformation is not only spoken; it is lived and enacted in the body. This chapter explores such bodily practices, arguing that it was not only through narrative and story that women experienced the healing impacts of faith in their lives. Practices, gestures, and bodies—like narratives and stories—revealed the ways that religion matters in women's post-conflict transformation. In the chapter that follows, I begin with an exploration of religious practices and how they have been studied in both anthropology and theology. Second, I look at worship practices at Friendship Community church and there find a rich description of how worship is one way in which women transformed life or attempted to "make a way" after war and conflict. Finally, I unpack that term, "making a way," noting both its indigenous uses in the church and its theological

---

1. Shoop, *Let the Bones Dance*, 129. As Mount Shoop writes, these transformative changes themselves take practice. She notes that, "like a creek bed slowly changing course, practice is the trickling current that creates transformation in time. Practice is the wind, the push in the current."

overtones in womanist theology. The languages and practices of "making a way," I concur, were some of the everyday ways that women from Friendship Community Church sought healing and transformation. As such, this phrase, as it was used both in the Liberian community and as it is illumined in womanist thought, provides valuable insight as to what transformation is and how it is lived in one post-conflict community.

Religious Practices: Setting the Terms

Throughout this text, I have put women's voices and practices in conversation with international human rights frameworks and theories in order to explore the gaps and overlaps and build a better understanding of how post-conflict transformation happens, and the role of religion in bringing it to bear in one local context. In addition to offering a way to glimpse of the practices and gestures that reveal the ways healing emerges as a process of everyday life, I argue that ethnographic, particularly feminist ethnographic methods, can encourage this work. These methods, which I explore in more detail below, can prompt a certain reflexivity that can shift and transform our theoretical and theological categories—if we let them. Here, I draw briefly on the work of two feminist anthropologists—Saba Mahmood and Joyce Burkhalter Flueckiger—and two womanist scholars of religion—Monica Coleman and Tracy Hucks, to argue for a mode of encountering practice that not only aims to understand transformation as it occurs in everyday life but that aims to *be* transformative in terms of how it envisions research and praxis.

For anthropologist Saba Mahmood, suspending the lens of secular feminist political theory (and its assumptions about what it means to be a political subject) while working with women who are part of the Mosque movement in Egypt led her to adopt a "mode of encountering the Other which does not assume that in the process of culturally translating other lifeworlds one's own certainty about how the world should proceed can remain stable."[2] She turns to the bodily practices women adopted in order to cultivate a particular form of pious subjectivity, arguing that these are forms of agency that must be understood in and on their own terms.[3] Arguing that our assumptions about what is meant by the political, agency, or a subject might change given our particular encounters with others, she

2. Mahmood, *Politics of Piety*, 199.
3. Ibid., 34.

pushes her readers to "embark upon an inquiry in which we do not assume that the political positions we hold will necessarily be vindicated, or provide the ground for our theoretical analysis, but instead hold open the possibility that we may come to ask of politics that a whole series of questions that seemed settled when we first embarked upon the inquiry."[4] Mahmood's research asks us what might happen if we began our work by paying attention to—and allowing our theoretical assumptions to be changed by—the ways the women with whom we work actually speak and practice.

For my work, this has meant women's understandings of transformation and healing—and the bodily practices they inhabit in order to bring these about—have formed the starting point for research. Womanist theologian Monica Coleman echoes this focus on the ways embodied movements reveal our faith:

> Not only can practices be shared but, for many, religiosity is located in the practices; it is sacramental. To be religious is to *practice* one's religion. In this sense, we are not born into a faith, nor do we adjust our beliefs in order to belong to a particular faith; nor might we know our faith by our justice-ethics. Instead—or more aptly—in addition . . . our activities reveal our faith.[5]

Drawing on work with a women's "womb circle"—a group of women who gathered together to address reproductive health issues using African traditional religious practices—Coleman finds that women's religious identities are multiple and complex, and their healing practices draw from multiple traditions. Because this is the case, she argues that "activity is primary, with meaning ascribed *after* practice."[6] Like Coleman, I argue that it is helpful to develop an understanding of women's religious lives that is born out of their own practices and narratives. For many women, religious identity is not a fixed category. Instead, multiple religious practices and traditions inform what we come to understand as a person's religious life. Tracy Hucks defines this as women's "multiple religious allegiance," whereby women blend together traditions and practices "for accessing spiritual power and for obtaining alternative modes of healing and recovery."[7] She comes to this understanding based on her ethnographic work and interviews with African-American women who practice African-derived religions. As she

4. Mahmood, *Politics of Piety*, 39.
5. Monica Coleman, "The Womb Circle."
6. Ibid.
7. Hucks, "Burning with a Flame in America," 90.

Practices of Transformation: Making a Way

found, often practices and traditions focused around particular issues, like "healing" or "empowerment" were more important to the women than a sense of orthodoxy of belief.[8] They created a bricolage of healing practices and beliefs that allowed them to experience healing in their lives. As Hucks notes, the women saw no conflict between practices derived from various religious traditions; each, instead, helped them to feel closer to God. A fixed sense of boundaries for African-American women's religious lives precludes an actual understanding of their religious lives, which are defined by fluidity.[9]

This understanding of practice and context in keeping with anthropologists of religion like Joyce Burkhalter Flueckiger, who argue for an indigenous understanding of religious practice. As Flueckiger found in her work with Amma, a Muslim healer in Hyderabad, India, rather than understanding Amma's work in terms of some conception of "real Islam," a more nuanced understanding of the particularities of a religious tradition (and the blendings women make between and among traditions) can be found when this claim to authenticity is set aside.[10] Before placing an analytic or theological lens on a practice or belief, we might listen to and observe how women narrate and practice their sense of what it is to be religious, to experience transformation, and to find healing.

It is important to ground this discussion as well in the broader context of the study of religious practices. First, what are religious practices? Alasdair MacIntyre defines them as:

> any coherent and complex form of socially established cooperative human activity through which goods internal to that form of activity are realized in the course of trying to achieve those standards of excellence that are appropriate to, and partially definitive of, that form of activity, with the result that human powers to achieve excellence, and human conceptions of the ends and goods involved, are systematically extended.[11]

This definition of practice seems to fit with Pastor Meah's desire for her church congregation to be formed in the ways of faith through participating in worship, Sunday School, and Bible Study at the church. As I noted in chapter four, she believed that it is through "teaching that people get

---

8. Ibid.
9. Ibid., 105.
10. Flueckiger, *In Amma's Healing Room*, 2.
11. MacIntyre, *After Virtue*, 204–5; quoted in Fulkerson, *Places of Redemption*, 39.

healed. Without knowledge, people perish." Pastor Meah told me this as she was explaining why it is important for people to participate in the life of the church; she saw her ministry as a pedagogical intervention, encouraging right thought and behavior in the life of her parishioners through the practices of the church.[12] Particularly around worship and parenting practices, ministerial staff focused on developing practices that taught their members how to be strong in their faith, to believe that "God will make a way," and to focus on a future of hope and prosperity. In this sense, they were practices of the form that MacIntyre describes, aimed at cultivating "standards of excellence" among the Friendship Community Church members as Christian believers.

However, practices of faith often do not align with the particular goals and aims that either tradition or leadership might desire.[13] As Hucks, Coleman, and Flueckiger emphasize, practices can be as discontinuous or chaotic as the people who participate in them. It is important to recognize, in addition to the pedagogical impetus inherent in some religious practices, that there are practices that in fact shift or even contradict the standards and ideals compelled by a tradition of faith. Additionally, as we have seen in previous chapters, transformation and healing are not so much a destination (an end moral goal), but instead are understood by women as a process, wherein the self that emerges is just that: emergent. As such, I now follow with a description of the worship practices at Friendship Christian Church to show how religion matters for women who survived violence. These practices also encourage us, as theologians and scholars, to imagine ways that these practices might shift how we imagine and describe healing and transformation.

Worship and Praise: Making a Way

Over the course of nine months, I attended worship at Friendship Community Church, where I heard sermons from Pastor Meah, Pastors Felicia

---

12. This reflects the Aristotelian notion of habitus that Saba Mahmood draws on in her work with the women's mosque movement in Egypt. As Mahmood describes it, the women who participate in the mosque movement do so in order to train their bodies—and by effect, their minds—to achieve piety. See Mahmood, *Politics of Piety*, 139.

13. As Fulkerson writes, "While it is in some sense the ends of Christian tradition that open up the possibility of discerning its inadequacies, my point is that the very definition of faithfulness and tradition must include a way to think about continuity as more than the repetition of tradition," McClintock Fulkerson, *Places of Redemption*, 42.

Practices of Transformation: Making a Way

and Jackson Jones, Reverend Grigsby, Reverend Gaye, and various guest preachers. We sang hymns, took Communion, read scripture, and offered songs of praise and worship. The services lasted anywhere from an hour and a half to three hours, sometimes spilling over into a late lunch in honor of one of the events at the church. I came to know many of the members of the congregation, which swelled and contracted depending on who was preaching and who was traveling that weekend.[14] Babies were dedicated, weddings were celebrated, and graduations (including Pastor Meah's) were honored. These practices created a community, a community that many members valued as family. One such Sunday, Pastor Meah encouraged her congregation to "have hope for tomorrow."[15] Her sermon that day was focused on the belief that "God will make a way" despite all that the community had been through.

A Sunday Service: A Thick Description

On a sunny June morning, I arrived at church a little after eleven, late for me, but at the point in the service when the praise and worship team was getting the congregation ready for the service. Songs of praise resonated through the small, L-shaped worship space, and from outside the church I could hear the sounds of drums and tambourines. Always trying to be a bit more inconspicuous (although that was nearly impossible in this church because I was often the only white person there), I tried to sit in my usual spot in the middle of the sanctuary, just across from the door to the pastor's office. As happened from time to time, one of the ushers spotted me and moved me to the front, in a spot of high honor for the ministers, but not great for an ethnographer who wants to observe the whole congregation. The seats reserved for special guests at Friendship Community Church

---

14. About once every two months, the pastors would travel to other churches in Philadelphia or neighboring cities in North Carolina. On these days, the congregation was always a bit smaller.

15. As anthropologist Clifford Geertz writes in his seminal essay, "Thick Description: Toward an Interpretive Theory of Culture," "if anthropological interpretation is constructing a reading of what happens, then to divorce it from what happens—from what, in this time or that place, specific people say, what they do, what is done to them, from the whole vast business of the world—is to divorce it from its applications and render it vacant. A good interpretation of anything—a poem, a person, a history, a ritual, an institution, a society—takes us into the heart of that of which it is the interpretation." Geertz, *The Interpretation of Cultures*, 18.

were just in front of the jutted-out space in the sanctuary in front of the pastor's office. They afford a front row view of the ministers, pulpit, and choir; however, much of the congregation is hidden behind the walls of the pastor's office. As I made my way up to these seats, shaking hands and hugging the men and women I knew along the way, I noticed two white college students sitting in the front row. Eric and Emily, I later learned, were both students at anearby university. Emily met Pastor Meah while she was working on campus (Pastor Meah worked as a security guard there), where the two became friends. Emily's friend Eric spent last summer in Sierra Leone and planned to go to Liberia this coming summer to help start a rice farming co-op with some former fighters just outside of Monrovia.

As we said our hellos, the praise songs slowed down, shifting to more reverential worship music in preparation for the service that followed. Reverend Grigsby was leading the service, and was dressed for the occasion in long, flowing robes. He read the Call to Worship, Psalm 118:24,[16] and led the call to worship from the used Baptist Hymnals that ushers distributed throughout the church. Seeing these hymnals reminded me of growing up in my Southern Baptist Church in Raleigh, North Carolina, where these maroon hymnals sat in the back of each chair every Sunday. Mid-way through the service, Sister Clemmons stepped forward to make the announcements, as she did each week as church secretary.[17] This week the big announcement concerned the upcoming Women's Workshop, and she distributed envelopes for each of the women in the congregation. We were each instructed to offer $25 to help pay for the event, which would include a weekend-long schedule of speakers, prayer, praise, and workshops. After the regular announcements, Pastor Meah took the pulpit for her weekly pastoral announcements, where she reiterated the importance of the upcoming women's event and encouraged the church to support that work. The usher then came forward to collect the weekly offering, and we all joined in for the hymn, "The Solid Rock." Once the offering was completed, the choir sang a selection in preparation for the Pastor's message, which served as the central part of the service and the time when most members

---

16. The Psalm reads, "This is the day that the Lord has made; let us rejoice and be glad in it." Psalm 118:24, NRSV.

17. As I was editing this chapter, I learned that Sister Clemmons passed away. While I was attending FCC, her husband had been seriously ill and recovered. I describe my experiences at her funeral in the conclusion. I was on the listserv for the Liberian Association in the Triangle, where Sister Clemmons's passing was marked over an email exchange that included several songs and poems.

of the church were in attendance (people continued to trickle in during the earlier parts of the service, so by the time Pastor Meah spoke, the entire congregation numbered close to 60 or 70 people).

The message for the sermon was, "I have hope for tomorrow." As she had done several months before, Pastor Meah related this message to the Civil War in Liberia and the struggles that Liberians went through both back home and here in the United States. She said that Liberians suffered, but that they still maintained hope for tomorrow, "Thanks to God." At the time, Ivory Coast was going through a brutal power struggle between supporters of past-president Laurent Gbagbo and the winner of the November 2010 elections (by international observers and standards) Alassane Ouattara.[18] Pastor Meah denounced the violence, preaching that it reflected a "problem in Africa" with leaders refusing to hand over power democratically, instead being "greedy." This, she said, is "wickedness" and evil. Despite the presence of leaders who refused to give up power and the harsh conditions that emerge out of such conflicts, she reminded the congregation that people still had hope to go on. They still hoped that things would change for the better.

Pastor Meah began to talk about her own hope, and the hope of other elders in the community, to be able to go home to Liberia. However, for Pastor Meah this hope was tempered by her sense of God's injunction that she firmly establish the church here in North Carolina before she left. This included building a permanent church on the land that was owned by Friendship Community Church, a plot of land located away from downtown in a more residential area.[19] Once this was accomplished, Pastor Meah

18. At the time of this service, in May of 2011, forces loyal to newly elected President Ouattara were narrowing in on Abidjan. From an NPR report on April 3, 2011, "And while there is still continued fighting, we hear the explosions of mortars and the sort of rat-tat-tat of automatic gunfire. The city's still being fought neighborhood-by-neighborhood, and I guess most importantly, the President, Laurent Gbagbo still controls the television and both the presidential palaces." National Public Radio, "Ivory Coast Violence Turns to Massacre," www.npr.org/2011/04/03/135087144/ivory-coast-violence-turns-to-massacre.

19. This is something that I have heard the Pastor say almost every time she and I talk, her desire for there to be a permanent home for Friendship Community Church, one that is not at the whim of landlords and limited to the small worship space they now have. Instead, she and other leaders of the church want a church home, a place where young people can come after school for homework help, or where children can come each summer for camp (this camp happens once a week in their current location, but there is nowhere for the children to play outside in the gritty industrial complex the church now resides in), and a place where funerals and weddings can be held (because the current sanctuary is so small, they often have to hold these events at other local

would leave the United States, feeling that her mission for God was fulfilled. She would not stop ministering; instead, as she told us that Sunday, God had given her a vision that Friendship Community church was to expand to Liberia. Pastor Meah would be its Bishop, presiding over the two churches. The office of Bishop requires multiple congregations, she shared with us, laughingly telling the congregation that, "You go to some churches and the man says, I am the bishop of this church . . . and he only got one church!" Pastor Meah told her gathered parishioners that when she goes home to Liberia she could just return to the work she did before the war and "drive around in a big car."[20] However, this would not serve her people or fulfill God's mission for the church and for her life. She could take the easy way out, leave her people here at FCC, work in the government, and make money, but instead she was choosing to be at the church where God called her because she has "hope for tomorrow."

The pastor closed her sermon by asking us all to have hope, like the Children of Israel, as she read from Jeremiah 29:1–14. She reminded us that God told the Children of Israel that they would be in exile for seventy years, during which time they should increase their families and prepare for the prosperity that God ordained for them. "Seventy years!" she said, looking around in amazement, shaking her head. She laughed, exclaiming that she hoped that it wouldn't be that long until she was able to go home again. Although it took seventy years to fulfill God's promise to the children of Israel, Pastor Meah reiterated to us that they maintained their hope all those years. As she closed her sermon, she reminded us that "we all have hope because God will make a way. God will lead us out of the wilderness."

After her message, Pastor Meah invited the children forward for their weekly blessing. As we sang a hymn together "I Surrender All," more than twenty children stood, waiting for her to rub their foreheads with oil and offer a blessing upon them. Their parents gathered them back in their arms after the song was over, and we closed the service with a prayer.

---

churches).

20. As I noted in chapter four, this is something that Laura also expressed. Rather than getting a government job, she wanted to serve her people, even though that would not guarantee any money.

Practices of Transformation: Making a Way

Living into Narratives of "Making a Way"

The worship practices outlined above demonstrate the fluidity and even chaotic nature of religious practices. At the outset, what was described might seem like a "traditional" Christian worship service—singing hymns, reading scripture, collecting offering, hearing sermons and announcements. However, the worship space—as has been noted in previous chapters—was continuously interrupted by memories of past and present (Cote d'Ivoire) violence that shifted how and why the practices were performed. Pastor Meah and the other ministers continuously took the pulse of the community and addressed their concerns in the worship space. Like on this Sunday, this often included talk of politics. This might be seen to reflect African religious sensibilities that religion is about healing in this life and in this world, and that appeals to divine beings are rooted in that assumption. However, I would also argue that it reflects the ways that the situation—in this case the messiness—of life shapes and transforms religious practices.[21]

Throughout my fieldwork, one phrase kept emerging in some iteration: "making a way." This one phrase represents an indigenous description of the messy, complicated ways that transformation is lived and narrated in this post-conflict immigrant community. In the sermon above, Pastor Meah compared the members of Friendship Community Church to the Children of Israel. Both were communities in exile. Both desired to return home.[22] Yet as Pastor Meah elaborated in the sermon, God had and continued to "make a way" for those who were lost. In what follows, I explore how congregants at FCC employed this term "making a way" to narrate and perform transformation. This concept, I argue, might be one way to name transformation as it occurred in this community and context. In other words, "making a way" speaks to the indigenous ways women at FCC recognized that God did not always deliver them from difficult circumstances, but instead offered resources of survival and sustenance for hard times. The concept, as articulated by womanist theologians, also offers us a rich analytical description of practices and experiences of transformation, and as such has much to offer our understandings of how healing emerges in post-conflict communities.

---

21. See Fulkerson, *Places of Redemption*, also Orsi, *Between Heaven and Earth*.

22. It is important to note that this desire to return home was, it seems, stronger among the older women with whom I talked. For many in the younger generation, the opportunities in the United States were alluring. They wanted to stay to raise their families, start or finish school, start a business, etc.

In her preface to *Sisters in the Wilderness: The Challenge of Womanist God-talk*, Delores Williams describes the experience of growing up as a young girl in church, where she would hear women testify about "their belief that God was involved in their history, that God helped them make a way out of no way."[23] Williams turns to the biblical story of Hagar to understand God's salvific work for African-American women through survival, not only liberation. Hagar's story is recounted in two places in Genesis: Genesis 16:1–16 and Genesis 21:9–21. Williams reads these stories together with "the slave women Hagar as the center of attention" to illustrate the fact that "the slave woman's story is and unavoidably has been shaped by the problems and desires of her owners."[24] Williams points out that although there is a great deal of courage in Hagar's actions, we must not forget that Hagar's position is extremely precarious. As a young pregnant woman alone, she is "without family support or protection. Courageous though her liberation action may be, Hagar is without the support and physical sustenance a pregnant woman needs."[25] It is at this point in the story that Williams identifies God's involvement in Hagar's life. As Hagar travels alone, she is met by the angel of God, who is present with her "in the midst of her personal suffering and destitution."[26] In this passage, God is not a liberator. Instead, God offers Hagar "survival and quality of life" by telling her to go back to live with Abram and Sarai. God offers a blessing over Ishmael, which promises "survival" and "forecasts the strategy that will be necessary for survival and for obtaining a quality of life."[27] Although leaving the wilderness and returning to Sarai and Abram means that Hagar will once again be controlled by her slave owners, God promises through the blessing that in the future Hagar's family will be free and protected. To ensure her survival in the present, however, Hagar must return to Sarai and Abram.

The story of Hagar continues in Genesis after Ishmael has become a young man and Sarah has given birth in her old age to Isaac. Sarah worries that because he was the first born, Ishmael will receive Abraham's inheritance instead of her son Isaac. God enters the story at this point, promising that Isaac will receive the blessings of being Abraham's son while Ishmael

23. Williams, *Sisters in the Wilderness*, ix.
24. Ibid., 15.
25. Ibid., 20.
26. Ibid.
27. Ibid., 22.

will be the leader of his own "great nation." Hagar and Ishmael are sent out of Abraham and Sarah's house with only bread and water; Hagar is, once again, homeless.

Hagar finds herself "not only without economic resources," but also "without protection in a nomadic culture where men ruled the families, tribes and clans."[28] In this dire and precarious situation, Williams points out that once again God does not provide liberation for Hagar and her son Ishmael, but rather offers a "vision to see survival resources where she had seen none before." Survival is offered by God, liberation, by contrast, "finds its source in human initiative."[29] This wilderness desert is, as Williams points out, "hardly a place where a lone woman and child ought to be wandering" without food or shelter. However, God gives Hagar "new vision" so that Hagar and Ishmael are able to gain autonomy over their own situation and live on their own. As Williams notes, Hagar finds a wife for Ishmael, establishes her own house, and possibly, founds her own tribe. Williams retells this story of motherhood, slavery, and autonomy from the perspective of Hagar because these "narratives reveal the faith, hope and struggle with which an African slave woman worked through issues of survival, surrogacy, motherhood, rape, homelessness and economic and sexual oppression."[30] As Williams writes:

> Hagar has "spoken" to generation after generation of black women because her story has been validated as true by suffering black people. She and Ishmael together, as family, model many black American families in which a lone woman/mother struggles to hold the family together in spite of the poverty to which ruling class economies consigns it. Hagar, like many black women, goes into the wide world to make a living for herself and her child, with only God at her side.[31]

I bring Williams's understanding of "making a way out of no way" to the forefront here, drawing on the story of Hagar and Ishmael to note the parallels with Pastor Meah's sermon on the Liberian community living in North Carolina.

Like Hagar, most members of the community came to the United States because they were fleeing violence and fearing for their lives. Also

28. Ibid., 30.
29. Ibid.
30. Ibid., 33.
31. Ibid.

like Hagar, they were not immediately liberated by God. Instead, they faced an American life where gang violence, systemic poverty, and immigration barriers at times seemed insurmountable.

This narrative stream of "making a way out of no way" that I heard so often in the church reflects Williams's contention that God's work guides and sustains even when it doesn't save us. Pastor Meah's work to create a church home in North Carolina is indicative of this. As she told the women's empowerment group, she remembered being a young girl, meeting missionaries who traveled from the United States to Liberia to plant churches and preach the gospel. She remembered that along with the other children in her village, she would "run to go see the white people because they were different." As a young woman, she felt the calling to serve God, and that knowledge sustained her. "To have a gospel ministry," she recounted, "that is very empowering." She went on to tell us that it was high time for Liberians to minister to Americans because "this place needs the gospel too. America needs God!" Pastor Meah saw herself as a missionary in the United States, like the missionaries she experienced in Liberia as a young girl. Despite the fact that she felt God ordained this work, finding money to pay for it was immensely difficult. In the fall of 2011, the church's loan on the land was coming due, and despite massive fundraising efforts (letter-writing, pledge drives in the church, fundraising dinners and events), the pastors were unsure of whether they would pay off their loans. Despite these hardships and the fact that God did not miraculously step in and solve these budget problems, the work continued, with a faith in God's ability to help them "make a way" where once there was none.

As Monica Coleman describes it, a "making a way out of no way" womanist theology of salvation "is not always liberation or freedom from all pain and suffering . . . Salvation is also survival and quality of life, and it requires the cooperation of the world in which we live. While God offers salvific resources, humanity must take advantage of these resources to effect salvation."[32] Coleman explores womanist and process theologies of salvation in critical correlation to determine a "postmodern womanist theology" that is able to speak to both the "problem of evil" and "declarations about survival, healing and salvation."[33] Salvation, here "literally means health and wholeness."[34] This postmodern womanist theology begins

---

32. Coleman, *Making a Way Out of no Way*, 32.
33. Ibid., 8.
34. Ibid., 11.

with the concerns of everyday, focusing on the "attainment of health and wholeness . . . as an activity that happens in particular contexts throughout the entire world."[35] She begins her text with an exploration of womanist conceptions of salvation, naming these as "making a way out of no way." Through examinations of the work of Joanne Terrell, Karen Baker Fletcher, Kelly Jones Douglas, and Delores Williams, Coleman is able to discern certain commonalities among these theologians in the ways that they discuss salvation. She writes that perhaps the most important contribution of these theologies is that they bring a "metaphorical language to a constructive womanist theology." This helps us to

> discuss salvation in concrete images: survival, quality of life and discipleship. Womanist theologians use the ministry of Jesus to provide action verbs to the process of salvation: teaching, healing, praying, welcoming, suffering-with. In this way, they give pictures of what salvation looks like and how it is achieved. They expand understandings of salvation such that we can see salvation in black women, poor people, those marginalized because of their sexual orientations, and even blood and other natural elements.[36]

By grounding salvation in the lives of black women, Coleman posits that womanist theologians allow us to see and conceptually grasp the ways that salvation is lived and experienced in everyday life. Coleman's postmodern womanist theology likewise seeks to speak to women's experiences, recognizing that "we are all theologians—people who think about God."[37] Where Coleman differs from the womanist scholars with whom she begins her text is primarily in her process theological framework, which helps her to address religious practices outside the Christian tradition and provides a metaphysical framework for understanding change, evil, and the presence of God in the world.[38] As Coleman outlines it, a postmodern framework is built on five assumptions:

---

35. Ibid., 86.
36. Ibid., 32.
37. Ibid., 2.

38. Karen Baker-Fletcher also draws upon a process theological framework in her work, but unlike Coleman, she works specifically out of Christian theologies and communities. Coleman is here using process theology to build a framework that will allow her to speak about women's experiences beyond the Christian tradition (African traditional religions, etc.). For a description of Baker-Fletcher's uses and perceived limitations of process theology, see Baker-Fletcher, *Dancing with God*.

1. the ongoing processes of life,
2. individual ability to exercise power
3. the inevitability of relationship at all levels of reality
4. the eternal vision of God, and
5. opportunities for immortality in the midst of pervasive loss.[39]

Building on a Whiteheadean process metaphysic, Coleman demonstrates that God works in the midst of suffering, and argues that people can transcend that evil by heeding the call of God. She writes that, "moving forward into newness—into what God desires for us and calls us to—can rid the world of some evils. It's a bit of a conundrum. The same freedom that destroys can be used to create. The same loss that causes us suffering can also leave evil behind and alleviate some of our suffering."[40] Coleman's understanding of God and the world in process takes seriously the reality of evil in the world.[41]

As she works within a process framework to mold and create a postmodern womanist theology, she finds that Whitehead's process thought can address injustice and oppression in the world, but in a different way than has been done by black liberation theologians. For Whitehead, God is not only on the side of the oppressed, as liberation theologians espouse; "God is, rather, the God of all. God is the God of all people, and the nonhuman communities of the world as well."[42] This does not mean that God does not desire justice and wholeness for all people. Instead, this postmodern womanist God resists oppression by calling "each party to justice in their future actions. God calls the world around these people to enact justice in their lives."[43] In this way, the presence of God in our lives allows us to feel the suffering of our past, while also being called beyond evil and oppression in the future. This understanding of process allows Coleman to name her postmodern womanist theology as "an activity. It is a verb, a gerund. Health

---

39. Ibid., 73.

40. Ibid., 77.

41. Although she provides an apt critique of Whiteheads developmental-evolutionist leanings and imperialist language (his reliance on "kingdom of God" language), Coleman finds that speaking of God and the world as in process is the most helpful way to account for the presence of both evil and good in the world. Coleman, *Making a Way*, 45–47.

42. Ibid., 82.

43. Ibid.

Practices of Transformation: Making a Way

and wholeness come through teach*ing*, heal*ing*, remember*ing*, honor*ing*, possess*ing*, adopt*ing*, conform*ing*, and creatively transform*ing*. Sav*ing*. It is mak*ing* a way."[44] Coleman expands upon womanist conceptions of making a way by emphasizing the "doing-ness" of this theological stance. It is not something that is ever finished. Rather, making a way reflects the ways that the world and God live into justice and wholeness in the "gritty, localized and contextual" places we inhabit.

Coleman's exploration of "making a way out of no way" as a process is particularly compelling when placed in conversation with the narratives and practices of the women with whom I have worked. As these women talked about their lives, they did not see the past as all that they were. Rather, they saw themselves as works in progress, seeking wholeness and growth. By placing Delores Williams and Monica Coleman's conceptions of "making a way out of no way" in conversation with the experiences and narratives of Liberian women in North Carolina, I illuminate the fact that these women see themselves as survivors *and* visionaries. While clearly the past does have a hold on who they were, their ability to envision a new future arose out of their belief that God would "make a way," something that we discussed in the women's empowerment group that focused on strengths and visioning. Pastor Meah talked once again about her "hopes for the enlargement of [our] ministry" and her desire to "have a large building that can serve as a community center" and church home. Laura acknowledged that she "[hopes] to get funds to work in other areas" and with other communities facing trauma and poverty. Joanna told us that like some of the other older women in the church, she hoped to return to Liberia. "When I go home," she told us, she hopes "to be able to work with children, to have a place where they can come in and learn to read the Bible." These visions for the future rest in a faith that goodness and healing are possible out of trauma and hardship. Like Coleman and Williams's work, these visions also point to the importance of human agency in the work of healing in the world. The women of FCC did not, as the building fund example demonstrates, live in a world where God swooped in to liberate them. Instead, they saw themselves as working in partnership with God to create a new world where peace and healing could emerge. The work is a process. The project of healing is never finished.

The concept of "making a way out of no way" is an important lens for understanding worship as a practice of transformation at Friendship

---

44. Ibid., 169.

Community Church. The pastor and other members of the ministerial staff aimed to provide a narrative that spoke to the suffering experienced by the community while also helping them to live into a new narrative of continued hope. It is important to note that being able to envision a new future is always tempered by the knowledge that there is no easy path; salvation is not about immediate change. Instead, languages and practices of "making a way" demonstrate that post-conflict transformation is not naïve. It acknowledges that life at times can seem impossible to live. Despite this, however, women at FCC were able to draw on their sense of spirituality and divine connection in order to hope—and work—for a new future.

Finally, language of "making a way" helps us to see that despite feeling disparaged (recall Evelyn's statement that "we all die"), this realistic view of the world does not imply fatalism. Instead, it speaks to these women's conception that although God works in the world, that work was not always done to save. Sometimes God's work was done in order to sustain, or even to aid in survival. Womanist theologians, whose deft attention to African-American women's lives (and for Coleman, the ways many women's religious lives are multiple and draw on a wide range of resources, including African religious traditions and practices) offer a language of transformation that speaks to the ways the women describe it. In other words, it reflects these indigenous descriptions of transformation, providing an apt analytical category with which to understand the concept and its practice. As such, to better conceptualize what healing and transformation mean after violent encounters, and the ways religion matters in those transitions, language of "making a way" deserves our utmost attention.

Conclusions

For the women with whom I worked, most of whom were members of Friendship Community Church, their stories and practices of transformation were imbued with elements of faith and redemption: as Pastor Meah's sermon identified, they were able to relate a story of salvation in which God saved God's people from hardship and affliction. This is not to say that they believed that God allowed them to live while others did not survive (that they were special or more faithful than family and friends who died). Rather, I would argue, placing faith in God's saving powers gave them a sense of control over the narrative itself. They were able to survive, to make a way, despite their intense hardships. As Monica

Practices of Transformation: Making a Way

Coleman writes, " 'Making a way out of no way' is sometimes experienced as release and joy; other times it is experienced as resources in the midst of oppression without release. Either way, it disrupts the past from continuing on as it would without the possibilities offered by God."[45] The practices of faith the women engaged helped to weave a narrative of life and hope out of harm and difficulty. Sermons about "making a way out of no way" provided performative scripts into which women could begin to imagine themselves and create life anew. Prayers that layered multiple voices of concern and praise helped to create a communal imagination out of which hope for the future could emerge. These embodied practices and gestures help us to see that it is not only the words that we speak but also the ways our bodies move that form and transform us as human beings. These practices are as much a part of our story as the words that we speak to one another about who we are. Language of "making a way" is then both an indigenous description of the ways these processes happen and an apt analytical tool to understand the role of transformation in the lives of a particular community of Liberian women.

---

45. Coleman, *Making a Way*, 35.

7

Transformation Is

As I finished up my fieldwork, Sister Clemmons, one of the women leaders of Friendship Community Church passed away. I went to the funeral, held a couple of weeks after her death at a large church in the city where I conducted fieldwork. Pastor Meah and the ministerial board of FCC officiated at the service, which was attended by almost two hundred people. The service was particularly poignant for me because when I started attending FCC in January of 2011, Sister Clemmons's husband had been seriously ill. I remember going to the front of the church during the final blessing, where we all prayed for his recovery. He lived, and every Sunday after he got out of the hospital, the couple would come to church and sit in the second row (I often sat behind them and we chatted almost every Sunday). Sister Clemmons was the church secretary, the person who would read the church announcements and welcome visitors to the congregation. She told us during those announcements each Sunday, "Come to Friendship Community Church and be blessed." When her husband survived his illness, the pastor and other members of the ministerial board sent praises to God during service, marveling at God's ability to bring someone back from the grave.

    I remembered these moments as I watched Sister Clemmons's funeral and as I talked with Pastor Meah on the phone a couple of days before. She sounded so haggard and tired. It was obvious she had been crying. At the funeral, Pastor Meah talked about her grief, telling each of us that it is okay to cry; she said that God acknowledged and heard our cries of lament and mourning. These two snapshots of a life given

(Brother Clemmons) and a life taken away (Sister Clemmons) reflect, for me, the ways that the women I worked with experience, narrate, and practice healing. For them, God is present at both moments—in the joys of celebrating new life and salvation and hope and in the pains of death and despair. God is there. By tracing the ways that women experienced this divine presence through their narratives and practices, I aimed to provide a language of transformation and healing that speaks to the relational, everyday-ness of this work to repair self and other.

Looking back at the women's words, practices, and theories presented here, a vision of transformation emerges with the following crucial elements: 1) Transformation is often remarkably everyday; 2) Transformation is a process; 3) Transformation is relational; and 4) Transformation acknowledges the tragic and mourns loss. In what follows, I cultivate a language for this work that is cobbled together much like the peace flag that we created in the final empowerment group was brought together by each of these themes that emerged in and through women's narratives and practices. Although more elusive to grasp and impossible to quantify or measure, this vision of transformation reflects an effort to pay close attention to the ways in which religion matters in particular women's lives.

Transformation Is

Everyday

The women with whom I worked were able to cultivate healing in and through the practices of everyday life. They participated in their community of faith, finding narratives of "making a way out of no way" that offered a performative script out of which they could create new stories of hope and promise. They also cared for children in an effort to develop a new future. They supported their families, friends, and communities by hearing their stories, providing, as Marie told us, a "shoulder to cry on." Laura echoed this when she says that she often just listens. "I'm somebody they can talk to," when no one else will. As these chapters have illustrated, transformations like this often happen outside of the often cited legal and political arenas, instead emerging in and through the course of everyday life.

I have drawn heavily on the work of Veena Das in an effort to understand the everyday processes of healing that I have seen in this Liberian community. As Das writes, the retrieval of the self after experiences of violence is remarkable in its ordinary-ness:

> There is no pretense here at some grand project of recovery, but simply the question of how everyday tasks of surviving—having a roof over your head, being able to send your children to school, being able to do the work of the everyday without constant fear of being attacked—could be accomplished. I found that the making of the self was located, not in the shadow of some ghostly past, but in the context of making the everyday inhabitable.[1]

This reflection on her anthropological work in India resonates with the ways that women I worked with were rebuilding their lives after experiences of the Liberian Civil War. They were not always willing or able to talk about what they had endured. Instead they sometimes focused on the more practical aspects of life (much like those Das describes above) and drew on the resources of their faith to create a life that was livable.

Transformation can also be seen in the ways women were helping their communities to survive and thrive despite the hardships of conflict and the harsh experiences of immigrant life. Leymah Gbowee reflects on the need for this kind of "ordinary" peace work when she states:

> Donor communities invest billions in funding peace talks and disarmament. Then they stop. The most important part of postwar help is missing: providing basic social services to people. Not having those resources might have been a reason men went to war in the first place; they crossed the border and joined an armed group because they didn't have jobs. In Liberia right now, there are hundreds of thousands of unemployed young people, and they're ready made mercenaries for war in West Africa. You'd think the international community would be sensible enough to know they should work to change this. But they aren't.[2]

As Pastor Meah told me, much of the work that she did to help her community was in both providing their spiritual guidance *and* providing them with the material resources they needed to survive. Laura echoed this when she told me about how her work got started, during her time as a student at a local university:

---

1. Das, *Life and Words*, 216.
2. Gbowee, *Mighty Be Our Powers*, 174.

Transformation Is

> That really broke my heart. I didn't know where my own family were, but just, I didn't know where my family were, but all I knew was, look at these children dying from starvation, from not having food to eat! I started to think what can I do to help these children. So I wanted, my main reason was to collect money, maybe dollar, [one] dollar and send it through the Red Cross . . . So I started collecting [a] dollar, quarter from everyone I met on campus. I started talking to them [about the Civil War in Liberia] . . . the first time I collected about $600. So I started going around, [and then] somebody came up to me, the Director of Community Services . . . She said you know what, Laura, I see you asking for quarters and dollars, and you know we could help you. I could help you. That's when we started raising money on campus and that's when other people got started.

Laura's work, like Marie's, like Pastor Meah's started small, working through the resources each woman had at her disposal. In this way, women's work for transformation and healing can be remarkably ordinary. It does not always consist in retelling and revisiting the wounds of the past, but instead might also be concerned with the practicalities of the present and the possibilities for the future.

A Process

Transformation is not something that happens overnight. Instead, it emerges in lives and communities in a non-linear way. This process involves the repair of self, of family, of community. It involves telling new stories out of the scraps and fragments of life and the past that was gathered up. As Lederach writes:

> Peacebuilding requires respect for the center and the edges of time and space, where the deep past and the horizon of our future are sewn together, creating a circle of time. The circle of time, constantly in motion, moves around our biggest inquiries: Who are we? Where do we belong? Where are we going? How will we journey together?[3]

These questions are not answered overnight or even in the course of a truth and reconciliation commission. They are instead worked out in community, and emerge gradually, over time. As Marie, Pastor Meah, and

---

3. Lederach, *The Moral Imagination*, 147.

Laura affirmed, they did not always receive funding or recognition for this work, making it difficult to continue. However, they persevered. As Marie recalled of her time living with her uncle who sexually abused her, "I slept in the kitchen, you know, nobody wanted to have anything to do with me pretty much. I lived in three African countries, you know, trying to find that light. It's a step." Marie's statement that finding the light is a journey taken step by step is a reminder of the continued work for transformation and healing that these women engage. That work is never finished.

Relational

As I have discussed throughout this text, healing is realized in and through relationships. As Ella and Marie shared with me, talking through the horrible things you endured in the past was healing. As Marie stated, "Breaking the Silence came about because I had to explain my story in order for me to heal. The more I talked about it, the more I cried, the more I got it out, [and] I became a better person." This was also reflected in the women's empowerment group, where women related that talking with others about what they had been through allowed them to see hope for the future. Sharing their stories helped them know they were "not alone," while also creating a shared narrative of survival and resilience within you they could live. This healing work also happened through practices of faith, where women's everyday theologies, parenting, and communal prayer practices helped to find healing in a world that was still marked by violence. As Serene Jones writes, "healing lies as much, if not more, in the stories we tell and the gestures we offer as in the doctrines we preach."[4] The everyday practices and gestures women embodied as they sought out healing speak to the ways transformation happens on a local level, in and through the healing of self and other.

Leymah Gbowee's understanding of peacebuilding resonates with this sense of the transformation through relationship. She writes that:

> Peacebuilding to me isn't ending a fight by standing between two opposing forces. It's healing those victimized by war, making them strong again, and bringing them back to the people they once were. It's helping victimizers rediscover their humanity so they can once again become productive members of their communities. Peace-building is teaching people that resolving conflict can

---

4. Jones, *Trauma and Grace*, 2.

be done without picking up a gun. It's repairing societies in which the guns have been used, and not only making them whole, but better.[5]

Peace, for Gbowee and for the women with whom I worked, does not live in the international treaty documents that mandate it. It happens as women repair the wounds in their own lives, reweaving narratives of hope and healing out of tragedy as they recognize the presence of God in their moments of hardship. Through storytelling, artwork, and ritual practice women restore peace—a peace that existed not only in and for the world, but in and for the self. As Ella told me, this is often where peace begins. You "have to start with your own self, in our hearts to see how we can work towards peace." Theologian Wendy Farley argues this point as well in her text *The Wounding and Healing of Desire: Weaving Heaven and Earth*. For Farley, much of feminist and liberation theology has started with structural change, neglecting the changes of heart and mind that can actually fuel large scale social justice work for the world. As she writes:

> Attention to the interior landscape of human beings is not a rejection of the claims of justice. To the contrary, attention to our interiority deepens our capacity for justice. Or rather, it roots justice in the well-spring of compassion . . . Attention to interiority can resuscitate our capacities for relationship and ignite in us the desire for compassion and delight in life. In this sense it is integral to the desire for justice.[6]

As Farley and Ella argue, starting with the self is a helpful corrective to the often overwhelming large-scale focus on structural, governmental, and political changes in international peace-building work. Gbowee reminds us that peace starts with healing the people who are damaged by war—individual selves included.

Susan Brison writes that,

> If we are socially constructed, as I believe we are, in large part through our group-based narratives, the self is not a single, unified, coherent entity. Its structure is more chaotic, with harmonious and contradictory aspects, like the particles of an atom,

---

5. Gbowee, *Mighty Be Our Powers*, 82.
6. Farley, *The Wounding and Healing of Desire*, xviii.

attracting and repelling each other, hanging together in a whirling, ever-changing dance that any attempt at observation—or narration—alters.[7]

Understanding the self as relational helps us to see why the practices of healing that have been described here are so powerful; we are created in and through our relationships with others. Through violence, others have the power to tear us down and apart. And yet, paradoxically, it is also through others that we find healing and recovery, through the gestures and practices of love and friendship that enable us to see love and light in each other.

Attentive to Tragedy

The processes of healing and transformation that I have described were realized to a greater and lesser extent. In other words, although the women with whom I worked talked of ways they could "count their blessings" and see the presence of God in and through their narratives of hardship, they also acknowledged that blessings were not always easy to find. There was not always a happy ending to the story, as Marlene's remembrances of her daughter, or the stories of the young men who have committed suicide or killed one another because of past wartime experiences highlight.

Both life and death are always encompassed in the experience of trauma. As pastoral theologian Michael Wilson writes, "There is an infinite gradation of losses upon which to forge our willingness to die that we may live, as we discover the faithfulness of the life which so constantly wells up to renew us. We become acquainted with the pattern of life-through-death."[8] These experiences of death and tragedy require of us a creative response. They painfully teach us what it means to be human, and they need to be understood, not overcome—although our impulse might be to overcome the tragedy through a theological exposition of it.[9] Shelly Rambo notes that this is not possible. She writes that, "While theodicies might provide explanation, the degree to which explanations are helpful to the healing process is unclear."[10] While there can be no meaning made in the senseless-

---

7. Brison, *Aftermath*, 95.
8. Wilson, *Health is for People*, 120.
9. Ibid.
10. Rambo, *Spirit and Trauma*, 5. This echoes Robert Orsi's contention that the saints of Catholicism might not provide a helpful sense of meaning for survivors of trauma.

ness of trauma, the narratives and practices presented here help us to see that there is always the potential for something new to emerge from it. I recall Pastor Meah's words in our final women's empowerment group that we are living in a world that is not what it was intended to be. Although this is the case, something good can be made from it.

Based on my work with the women from one particular Liberian community, I argue for a way of understanding healing and transformation as the repair of everyday life that happens in and through the rebuilding of the self and community. This vision of healing is not naïve. It does not seek simple answers or try to find meaning to contain senseless violence. It emerges out of what is, and reacts to a world that is not as it was intended to be. Out of this, peace is the faith that this wounded world can be more.

Women cultivated healing from the ground up, picking up scraps from their life and world that they found helpful and sustaining. This included elements of their faith journey, their own narratives, the feeling of God in the moment of trauma, the support they find in one another, and doing work to restore their communities. Healing is a process, much like the collages that we made in the women's empowerment classes. And transformation happened in the ways that women made something good and beautiful out of the scraps and fragments they found in their lives and in their worlds. In this process of collage work, their sense of a divine presence and reliance on spiritual and religious practices that encouraged this demonstrates just some of the ways that religion matters for women who have survived violence. Their faith offered a way to frame what they went through, and it provided a way to find hope where once there was only suffering and hardship. In this way, practical theology offers a compelling contribution to conversations about women, violence and peace, in that practical theologians are attuned to the ways religion emerges in and through daily life. Before we do so, however, I offer some caveats about engaging in such participatory scholarship.

Instead, he notes that what they might "have offered [is] companionship on a bitter and confusing journey . . . in between a life and the meanings that may be made in it, for and against that life is the wound. Meaning making begins in wounding, and the process of meaning making is wounding," Orsi, *Between Heaven and Earth*, 145.

Working with/in Religious Communities: Some Considerations

I offer here a few considerations for individuals and organizations who would like to work with faith communities around issues of violence, peace, and healing. As I have noted throughout this work, religion matters to women and it is time for the international community to take this fact seriously. It is also time for us to have a more complicated picture of the ways religion matters to women than the instrumentalized or formal ways that it is often presented. The women's empowerment group is one example of a way to partner with religious organizations in this sort of work.

First, I would note that this work takes time. I spent several months with the community before we even began to plan the women's empowerment workshops. They were held at the end of my fieldwork, in August and September of 2011.

Second, I believe that it is important to be attentive to the need for ritual and practice-based responses to violence. As I have noted throughout this text, healing from violence does not only happen through speech. Instead, for those for whom speaking about violence is "just too much," attention should be paid to ritual and practice-based ways to create new narratives that promote healing and recovery. As Elaine Ramshaw notes in her article "Making (Ritual) Sense of our Own Lives," in the United States, "the challenge of empowering the community" and creating "ritual empowerment" is often our cultural "individualism."[11] Ramshaw suggests that ritual be dispersed from a clerical model to a more communal ("midwifery") model in order to facilitate healing and empowerment from oppression and prejudice in society. She suggests we encourage "ritual agency" in our faith communities so that individuals will develop the skills and confidence to make use of ritual in the community and for their own lives.[12] In the women's empowerment group, we did this by creating memory boxes, something that resonated with the women's ideas about memorialization (as many of the boxes were decorated like Liberian tombs), while also providing a way to continue to experience the healing effects, through prayer and remembrance, at home.

Third, when working with religious communities, be aware of cultural contexts and restraints. Often women's rights programs are disseminated

---

11. Ramshaw, "Making (Ritual) Sense of Our Own Lives," 299.
12. Ibid., 303.

in different countries without much of a change in their actual structure and style from that used in their country of origin.[13] The ineffectiveness of such approaches was demonstrated to me during the group sessions and as we planned them. As I have noted, for some, talking through their experiences was helpful. Joyce, Ruth and Evelyn particularly described how important it was for them to be able to tell their stories in such a supportive environment. However, for others, like Joanna, who created the picture of a fish in our first meeting, artistic practices allowed women to memorialize, remember, and mourn what they have lost without always having to talk it through. When working with faith communities—or any community—on issues of violence, it is important to be attentive to the ways the community wants, or doesn't want, to deal with it. This takes time, but it leads to programs better attuned to a community's own indigenous ways of healing. Given these caveats, I would like to offer some ideas for the implications of this work and suggestions for continued scholarship in both post-conflict transformation and for religion and health more generally.

Implications and Future Scholarship

This work demonstrates that to understand the ways religion matters for women who have experienced violence, researchers and theologians must first pay attention to what women say and the ways women practice and live. This type of work necessitates increased attention to the complexity of women's lives and to the fluid ways that they build and construct both narratives and practices. In what follows, I offer two reflections on future research on women's religious lives, particularly as it relates to research on violence and peace: 1) that such research should endeavor to be participatory, working with communities rather than working for communities; and 2) that practical theologians, given their significant expertise in respectfully studying the complexity of faithful people's religious lives, should claim their place at the table of women's human rights discourse and practice.

---

13. As Sally Engle Merry writes, "As a legal system, human rights law endeavors to apply universal principles to all situations uniformly. It does not tailor interventions to specific political and social situations, even when these might suggest different approaches to social justice. Local context is ignored in order to establish global principles." Merry, *Human Rights and Gender Violence*, 103.

Participatory Research

As I have argued, working with religious communities necessitates participatory research methods that allow communities to tell them how they experience healing. As Gbowee writes, there is a particular sort of arrogance that comes from those outside of a country telling those on the inside how to find peace. She writes, "Organizations like the UN do a lot of good, but there are certain basic realities they never seem to grasp . . . Maybe the most important truth that eludes these organizations is that it's insulting when outsiders come in and tell a traumatized people what it takes for them to heal."[14] What would it look like if researchers and practitioners instead took a participatory approach to working with communities that have been through conflict and war?

While I don't have the answer to this question, I posit that community-based participatory methodologies like those utilized by the International Religious Health Assets Programme (IRHAP) could significantly impact the shape of programmatic and research-based responses peace work. Through mapping projects, where researchers spend time with/in communities, encouraging these community members to describe and define the ways they live into and seek out healing, IRHAP researchers are able to align "the health assets of religion and religious entities in Africa with those of the public health system, thus contributing to the livelihoods of the people of the continent by widening Universal Access."[15] IRHAP researchers have focused on "making these assets—which are generally known to the religious community—visible to the public health community."[16] Research models like these ask local communities to identify the places and people they seek out for healing. Research practices like these could transform peace and healing work as it happens at local and global levels. They could encourage a widened space for participation in women's rights work and provide a place for local communities to name the resources, practices, and traditions they turn to for peace and healing. Rather than assuming that individuals seek out peace and healing through more traditional arenas of politics or the law, researchers and practitioners might help community members to chart and build upon their own religious, healing, and justice assets to develop comprehensive and effective programs and policies.

---

14. Gbowee, *Mighty Be Our Powers*, 171.
15. De Gruchy, "Re-Learning Our Mother Tongue?," 47.
16. Ibid.

TRANSFORMATION IS

Practical Theology's Place at the Table

Second, as I have noted, being attentive to life and practice is central to the practical theological task. Looking specifically at pastoral care, I believe that understanding how peace and healing emerge in the context of everyday life can help us to continue to expand beyond current models of care (individual, communal-contextual) to think about pastoral care on a global scale.[17] This is an apt place for practical theologians in women's human rights work, and I believe that practical theologians have constructive contributions to make to such conversations that build on expertise in care-based work like storytelling, narrative theories, empowerment strategies, and liberation praxis. Religion matters, as this work demonstrates, and it does so in complex ways. It is time for practical theology to enter women's rights conversations in an effort to speak to this fact. There is much work to be done in this area, and it is my hope that this project is one step in encouraging such interdisciplinary conversations about women, violence and healing.

This project has been an effort to learn from the ways women cobble together the fragments and scraps of belief, practice, narrative, and interpersonal relationships to create a life that is worth living in the aftermath of violence. This process of healing collage work is not unique to Liberian women in North Carolina. Instead, this is the task of being human. We are all collage makers, artists weaving life and hope out of the hardships and traumas we endure. We do this, as Laura reiterated to me, because we must. Laura's work has grown and flourished over the years that I have known her, and as I was finishing up my fieldwork, an anonymous donor approached her (through some contacts at a local university) with a matching pledge of $15,000 for her work. I cried with Laura over the phone the day she told me about it. So much had changed, and yet so much seemed to stay the same—she is still plugging away, trying to find the matching funds so that she can start a healthcare program for women in her native home of Caldwell, Liberia. As our conversation on that day drew to an end, Laura

---

17. See Lartey's description of the four paradigms of pastoral theology, including the "classical-clerical" (focused on ordained clergy), "clinical-pastoral" (informed by psychotherapy), "communal-contextual" (widened lenses to focus on the church and faith community), and "intercultural" models (expanded to the "global nexus"). As Lartey writes, "pastoral theology is currently engaged within a global context in which all four paradigms are operative. Each has strengths and weaknesses. The challenge is to draw appropriately and contextually on them in the midst of a world of tensions, ambiguities and complexities." Lartey, *Pastoral Theology in an Intercultural World*, 122–25.

reiterated to me that while she might not always be the "best Christian," she "[knows] that God has put me in this position for a reason. It's right in front of you, but you just can't see it."

For Laura, healing is "right in front of you." But we can't always see it, perhaps because we are looking for it in the wrong places—in the international frameworks, documents, treaties, and meetings. When we look at the ways healing is "right in front" of us, we see a vision of healing that is a much messier entity. It isn't easily measured or explained. It isn't quantifiable or contained as an objective. However, as the women I have learned from in the Liberian community demonstrate, healing can be felt and described and lived through the layered practices of prayer, through the joy and pain of bringing new life into the world, from the narratives of "making a way" into which women can live, through shared stories and gestures, and through the ways communities are rebuilt after experiences of war and violence. I hope that these women's words and practices encourage all of us to look for transformation in these ordinary contexts. Let us continue to look at the ways religion matters as women negotiate what it means to heal in light of their experiences of violence, conflict, and war.

Appendix A

Interview Participants and Research Methods

Research Methods

Each of these interviews evolved in a unique way, in part due to the open-ended interview style I utilized. In each interview, I opened with a general question related to a concrete event that connected me to the women, whether that was the women's empowerment workshops (both Evelyn and Joyce were interviewed after the workshop), an experience at church, or a conversation that we had at an event. I then delved more deeply into the women's stories, allowing them to guide the interview by providing information that they thought was pertinent to my questions about healing or peace. Women were interviewed in their homes, for the most part, with the exception of Pastor Meah, who spoke to me twice at the church.[1] Interviewing is a delicate skill, one that takes a good deal of patience and care. It also, I believe, requires significant investment in the community, building relationships and helping people to feel comfortable talking about the intimate details of their lives. I built these relationships by attending community

---

1. This research was approved by Emory University's Institutional Review Board on August 5, 2011. Written informed consent was obtained by each woman who was interviewed. As per the IRB protocol, I obtained verbal consent for the participant observation research that I conducted in the women's empowerment group. Additionally, both Laura's organization and Friendship Community Church provided written documentation approving my participant observation research with their organizations.

meetings, being present at weekly services and events, and by engaging people in conversations about their everyday lives. Below, I provide a brief biography (current at the time of the interview) of each of the participants who consented to an interview for this project.

Interview Participants

Aletha Meah

Pastor Meah is sixty-five years old and the Senior Pastor of Friendship Community Church. She moved to North Carolina in 1992, after spending two years in Ivory Coast as a refugee. She knew as a young woman that she was destined for leadership. She remembers the white Baptist missionaries in her town in Grand Gedeh county where she grew up, and told me that it was this Baptist influence that led her to join that denomination (albeit a Liberian Baptist denomination) as a young woman. She soon became Assistant Pastor of a Liberian Baptist Church in Monrovia, where she moved as a young woman. After Samuel Doe established himself as President in 1980, later bringing other Grand Gedeh residents into his political circle, Pastor Meah became an Assistant Deputy Minister in his government, a position she held until she was forced to leave Liberia in 1990 at the start of the Civil War. She eventually settled in North Carolina because she had some family members there (although most were in Philadelphia) and because she liked that she could drive her car, rather than relying on public transportation. Along with Felicia Jones, she founded Friendship Community Church in 1999. Her dream is to build a sanctuary for the church on some land they own outside of downtown, providing a worship space and community center for the growing Liberian community. Until this vision is fulfilled, she feels she cannot return home to Liberia. Her two interviews focused on her role as pastor and leader of this community, including the ways she helps community members to heal, given the trauma they have been through.

Laura Paynes

Laura is fifty years old and came to the United States in 1992, after working at the U.S. Embassy in Monrovia. She is from Caldwell, Liberia, a small town outside of Monrovia. Laura has three children, two in their

Interview Participants and Research Methods

mid-twenties and one in high school. She first lived in Atlanta after moving to the United States, where she met her husband. Laura started a community foundation in the mid-1990s, at the height of Liberia's Civil War, while she was a student at a university in North Carolina. The organization, which raised money for food and medical supplies for Liberians, eventually caught the attention of the school's administration. With support from staff, Laura developed this fledgling effort into a non-profit organization that now provides healthcare training, basic services, and a beauty school for young women in Liberia. She also partners with Friendship Community Church on youth empowerment events for Liberian and other African youth. Laura's interview discussed her experiences of the Civil War (some of which were highlighted in Chapter one) and her work in Liberia and in the Liberian community in North Carolina.

Ella

Ella is in her mid-fifties and resides in an apartment in an urban city in North Carolina. She is recently divorced and has two children, a middle-school-aged boy and a son who is in his early twenties and currently in the U.S. Navy. She came to the United States in 1985, first moving to Texas. Ella grew up in Monrovia, the daughter of "Congo people" (descendants of the settlers of Liberia). She was in nursing school when Samuel Doe took power in Liberia through a coup, and she watched her mother get arrested during this tumultuous time. She currently attends a Baptist church (not Friendship Community Church) because she grew up Baptist in Liberia and feels most comfortable there. Ella's interview discussed her views of peace, which she describes as "like a baby," and her memories of the family and friendship ties that were broken due to the war in Liberia.

Marie

Marie is in her late thirties and came to the United States in 1999 from a United Nations refugee camp in Ghana. Marie's family was able to leave Liberia in the early 1990s, but she was not able to join them on the flight out, so she was forced to stay behind with her uncle, a man who sexually molested her. She left her uncle's home in the mid 1990s, fleeing to Ivory Coast and then Ghana, where she was able to come to the United States. Marie lived in Maryland until just a few years ago when she moved to

North Carolina. A city planner by training, she started a shelter for abused women and children in Liberia in 2005. In addition to this work in Liberia, she has worked with the Liberian community in Arizona, where in July of 2009 a young girl was sexually assaulted by four young boys.[2] Marie has two young daughters, both in elementary school. She and her husband live in a suburb of a major city in North Carolina. Her interview focused on her work with the women's shelter and her own experiences of "breaking the silence" about sexual assault and rape.

Evelyn

Evelyn is a twenty-nine-year old mother of three young boys. She sings in the church choir at Friendship Community Church along with her husband. She told me that the other women at church call her "Mother Theresa" because she acts so old for her age. Evelyn came to the United States in 1991, following her mother, who came first, fleeing both the war and an abusive partner. They moved to Boston, along with Evelyn's sister and brother (another sister stayed behind in Liberia). Evelyn went back and forth between her mother's homes in the northeastern part of the United States (between Boston and Philadelphia) and her aunt's home in Ghana. She was alone a lot as a child because her mother worked two jobs to support her family. Evelyn is close with her family members, although she thinks of herself as something of a "black sheep" among her siblings because she is so focused and determined. Her sister passed away in Liberia just after our interview, and the fact that she was unable to go home for her burial compounded her grief. Evelyn and I met at Friendship Community Church. Her interview focused on her struggles to provide for her children and get an education herself, while also enduring all she has been through in her life.

Joyce

Joyce, like Evelyn, is one of the younger generation of women who participates in and leads events at Friendship Community Church. She is a prayer warrior, a member of a select team of women who pray with the ministerial staff by phone each night for concerns in the congregation. She is also a

2. Doug Gross, "Arizona Girl's Attack Sheds Light on Rape in Liberia," CNN, http://articles.cnn.com/2009-07-29/world/liberia.sex.crimes_1_sexual-violence-liberia-boys?_s=PM:WORLD.

Interview Participants and Research Methods

leader in the women's ministry and regularly leads the praise and worship time before Sunday church services at Friendship Community Church. Joyce found much comfort in the women's empowerment workshop conducted at the church because it gave her an outlet to grieve for her father. She lived through the entire Civil War in Liberia, although there are parts of the war that she can't remember. Joyce has six children and lives in an apartment close to the church. Joyce's interview focused on her experiences of the women's empowerment group and her desire for more story-sharing sessions among the women of Friendship Community Church. Her interview is not given prominent focus in chapter two, but her story is told in more detail through her participation in the women's empowerment group in Chapter five.

Ruth

Ruth is in her mid-sixties and is one of the missionaries at the church. The women and men designated as missionaries sit at the front of the church during each service, and are responsible for its leadership and guidance. They are the elders of the church community. Ruth moved to the United States in the early 1990s, living first in Staten Island. We began our conversation by talking about the large Liberian community there, but it soon moved into her remembrances of how difficult it was to live in the United States at that time while her children were still in Liberia or scattered in refugee camps in West Africa. Although Ruth did not discuss much about her journey to the United States, much of her interview was about her religious faith has helped her to get through the toughest parts of her life. A recovering alcoholic, Ruth credits God for her miraculous cure from addiction. Her interview discussed her views on healing and peace, in addition to the role that her Christian faith plays in overcoming struggles.

Appendix B

Interview Protocol

Interview Questions—Participants
Note: These interviews are semi-structured open-ended interviews.

1. I'd like to find out about your life history. Could you tell me about it? Describe it to me as if you were telling me your life story.

    Follow up: And then what happened?

    Follow up: How did you feel about that?

    Follow up: What did you do after that?

2. Were you or your family religious growing up?
3. How did you come to be here at _____ organization?
4. What have been some of the formative/important events in your life?

    Follow up: Why were these events important to you?

5. Given your experiences, what do you think that it means to heal? What does healing mean to you?
6. Does religion play a part in your healing process?

Bibliography

Amadiume, Ifi. *Male Daughters, Female Husbands: Gender and Sex in an African Society.* New York: Zed, 1987.

Amnesty International, "We Want to Go Home, but We Can't: Cote d'Ivoire's Continuing Crisis of Displacement and Insecurity." http://www.amnesty.org/en/library/info/AFR31/007/2011/en.

Asad, Talal. *Formations of the Secular: Christianity, Islam, Modernity.* Stanford: Stanford University Press, 2003.

AWID. "Shared Insights: Women's Rights Activists Define Religious Fundamentalisms." Online: http://www.awid.org/publications/shared-insights-womens-rights-activists-define-religious-fundamentalisms.

Baker-Fletcher, Karen. *Dancing With God: The Trinity from a Womanist Perspective.* St. Louis: Chalice, 2006.

Brison, Susan. *Aftermath: Violence and the Remaking of a Self.* Princeton: Princeton University Press, 2002.

Bell, Catherine, and Evelyn O'Rourke. "Does Feminism Need a Theory of Transitional Justice? An Introductory Essay." *International Journal of Transitional Justice* 1 (2007) 23–44

Bender, Courtney. *Heaven's Kitchen: Living Religion at God's Love We Deliver.* Chicago: University of Chicago Press, 2000.

Boone, Sylvia. *Radiance from the Waters: Ideals of Feminine Beauty in Mende Art.* New Haven: Yale University Press, 1986.

Bop, Codou, "Women in Conflicts: Their Gains and Their Losses." In *The Aftermath: Women in Post-Conflict Transformation*, edited by Sheila Meintjes, Anu Pillay, and Meredith Turshen, 19–34. New York: Zed, 2001.

Cabrera-Balleza, Mavic, and Nicola Popovic, "Costing and Financing Implementation of United Nations Security Council Resolution 1325." Cordaid and the Global Network of Women Peacebuilders. http://peacewomen.org/sites/default/files/1325_costingandfinanacing1325_gnwp_oct2010.pdf

Cole, Catherine. *Performing South Africa's Truth Commission: Stages of Transition.* Bloomington: Indiana University Press, 2010

Coleman, Monica. *Making a Way out of no Way: A Womanist Theology.* Minneapolis: Fortress, 2008.

———. "The Womb Circle: A Womanist Practice of Multi-Religious Belonging." *Practical Matters: A Transdisciplinary Journal of Religious Practices and Practical Theology* 4

Bibliography

(Spring 2011). http://practicalmattersjournal.org/2011/03/01/the-womb-circle-a-womanist-practice-of-multi-religious-belonging/.

Cooper, Helene. *The House at Sugar Beach: In Search of a Lost African Childhood.* New York: Simon & Schuster, 2008.

Cooper-White, Pamela. *The Cry of Tamar: Violence against Women and the Church's Response.* Minne-apolis: Fortress, 1995.

———. "Opening the Eyes: Understanding the Impact of Trauma on Development." In *In Her Own Time: Women and Developmental Issues in Pastoral Care,* edited by Jeanne Stevenson-Moessner, 87–102. Minneapolis: Fortress, 2000.

Copelon, Rhonda. "Surfacing Gender: Re-Engraving Crimes against Women in Humanitarian Law." In *Mass Rape: The War against Women in Bosnia-Herzegovena,* edited by Andrea Stiglmayer, 197–218. Lincoln: University of Nebraska Press, 1994.

Cruz, Joelle. "Memories of Trauma and Organizing: Market Women's Susu Groups in Postconflict Liberia." *Organization* 21 (2014) 447–62.

Das, Veena. *Life and Words: Violence and the Descent into the Ordinary.* Berkeley: University of California Press, 2007.

———. "Violence, Gender and Subjectivity." *Annual Review of Anthropology* 37 (2008) 283–99.

De Gruchy, Steve. "Re-Learning Our Mother Tongue? Theology in Dialogue with Public Health." *Religion and Theology* 14 (2007) 47–67.

Ellis, Stephen. *The Mask of Anarchy: The Destruction of Liberia and the Religious Dimensions of an African Civil War.* 2nd ed. New York: New York University Press, 2007.

Farley, Wendy. *The Wounding and Healing of Desire: Weaving Heaven and Earth.* Louisville: Westminster John Knox, 2005.

Fineman, Martha. "The Vulnerable Subject: Anchoring Equality in the Human Condition." *Yale Journal of Law and Feminism* 20 (2008) 23pp.

Flueckiger, Joyce Burkhalter. *In Amma's Healing Room: Gender and Vernacular Islam in South India.* Bloomington: Indiana University Press, 2006.

Freire, Paulo. *Pedagogy of the Oppressed.* 30th ann. ed. Translated by Myra Bergman Ramos. New York: Continuum, 2003.

Fuest, Veronika. "Liberia's Women Acting for Peace." In *Movers and Shakers: Social Movements in Africa,* edited by Stephen Ellis and Ineke van Kessel, 114–37. African Dynamics 8. Leiden: Brill, 2009.

———. "This Is the Time to Get out Front: Changing Roles and Opportunities for Women in Liberia." *African Affairs,* 2008.

Fulkerson, Mary McClintock. *Places of Redemption: Theology for a Worldly Church.* New York: Oxford University Press, 2007.

Gandolfo, Elizabeth. *The Power and Vulnerability of Love: A Theological Anthropology.* Minneapolis: Fortress, 2015.

Gbowee, Leymah. *Mighty Be Our Powers: How Sisterhood, Prayer and Sex Changed a Nation at War.* New York: Beast Books, 2011.

Geertz, Clifford. *The Interpretation of Cultures.* New York: Basic Books, 1973.

Germond, Paul and Sepetla Molapo. "In Search of Bophelo in a Time of AIDS: Seeking A Coherence of Economies of Health and Economies of Salvation." *Journal of Theology for Southern Africa* 126 (2006) 27–47.

Gyekye, Kwame. *African Cultural Values: An Introduction.* Accra, Ghana: Sankofa, 1996.

Hardison-Moody, Annie. "Getting This off My Chest: Ethnography as Disruptive Theological Practice." *Practical Matters: A Transdisciplinary Multimedia Journal of Religious*

Bibliography

Practices and Practical Theology 3 (2011). www.practicalmattersjournal.org/issue/3/analyzing-matters/getting-this-off-my-chest/.

Herman, Judith. *Trauma and Recovery: The Aftermath of Violence—From Domestic Abuse to Political Terror*. New York: Basic Books, 1997.

Horton, Robin. *Patterns of Thought in Africa and the West: Essays on Magic, Religion and Science*. Cambridge: Cambridge University Press, 1993.

Hucks, Tracy. "Burning with a Flame in America: African-American Women in African-Derived Religions." *Journal of Feminist Studies in Religion* 17.2 (2001) 89–106.

Human Rights Watch. "Liberia: Protect Refugees Against Sexual Abuse." https://www.hrw.org/news/2011/04/20/liberia-protect-refugees-against-sexual-abuse.

International Civil Society Network and MIT Center for International Studies. "What the Women Say: Participation and UNSCR 1325." http://www.usip.org/sites/default/files/Gender/What_the_Women_Say.pdf.

Jones, Serene. *Feminist Theory and Christian Theology: Cartographies of Grace*. Guides to Theological Inquiry. Minneapolis: Fortress, 2000.

———. "Transnationalism and the Rhetoric of Religion." In *A Just and True Love: Feminism at the Frontiers of Theological Ethics: Essays in Honor of Margaret A. Farley*, edited by Maura A. Ryan and Brian F. Linnane, 75–108. Notre Dame: University of Notre Dame Press, 2007.

———. *Trauma and Grace: Theology in a Ruptured World*. Louisville: Westminster John Knox, 2009.

Kamara-Umunna, Agnes M. Fallah, and Emily Holland. *And Still Peace Did not Come: A Memoir of Reconciliation*. New York: Hyperion, 2011.

Kirmayer, Laurence J. "Landscapes of Memory: Trauma, Narrative and Dissociation." *Tense Past: Cultural Essays in Trauma and Memory*, edited by Paul Antze and Michael Lambek, 173–98. New York: Routledge, 1996.

Kujawa-Holbrook, Sheryl and Karen B. Montagno, eds. *Injustice and the Care of Souls: Taking Oppression Seriously in Pastoral Care*. Minneapolis: Fortress, 2009.

Lartey, Emmanuel. *In Living Color: An Intercultural Approach to Pastoral Care and Counseling*. 2nd ed. London: Kingsley, 2003.

———. *Pastoral Theology in an Intercultural World*. Cleveland: Pilgrim, 2006.

Lassiter, Katherine. *Recognizing Other Subjects: Feminist Pastoral Theology and the Challenge of Identity*. Eugene, OR: Pickwick Publications, 2015.

Lederach, John Paul. *The Moral Imagination: The Art and Soul of Building Peace*. New York: Oxford University Press, 2005.

MacKinnon, Catharine. *Are Women Human? And Other International Dialogues*. Cambridge: Harvard University Press, 2006.

Magesa, Laurenti. *African Religion: The Moral Traditions of Abundant Life*. Maryknoll, NY: Orbis, 1997.

Mahmood, Saba. *Politics of Piety: The Islamic Revival and the Feminist Subject*. Princeton: Princeton University Press, 2005.

Meintjes, Sheila. "War and Post-War Shifts in Gender Relations." In *The Aftermath: Women in Post-Conflict Transformation*, edited by Sheila Meintjes, Anu Pillay, and Meredith Turshen, 63–77. New York: Zed, 2001.

Meintjes, Sheila, Anu Pillay, and Meredith Turshen. "There Is no Aftermath for Women." In *The Aftermath: Women in Post-Conflict Transformation*, edited by Sheila Meintjes, Anu Pillay, and Meredith Turshen, 3–18. New York: Zed, 2001.

Bibliography

Merry, Sally Engle. *Human Rights and Gender Violence: Translating International Law into Local Justice*. Chicago Series in Law and Society. Chicago: University of Chicago Press, 2006.

Miller-McLemore, Bonnie J. *Also a Mother: Work and Family as Theological Dilemma*. Nashville: Abingdon, 1994.

———. *In the Midst of Chaos: Caring for Children as Spiritual Practice*. The Practices of Faith Series. San Francisco: Jossey-Bass, 2006.

Miller-McLemore, Bonnie J., and Brita L. Gill-Austern, eds. *Feminist and Womanist Pastoral Theology*. Nashville: Abingdon, 1999.

Moon, Hellena. "Transforming the Paradigm of Wo/men's Human Rights through Intercultural Pastoral Care." *Journal of Pastoral Theology* 20 (2010) 47–66.

Moran, Mary. *Liberia: The Violence of Democracy*. The Ethnography of Political Violence. Philadelphia: University of Pennsylvania Press, 2006.

———. "Our Mothers Have Spoken: Synthesizing Old and New Forms of Women's Political Authority in Liberia." *Journal of International Women's Studies* 13.4 (2012) 51–66.

Moran, Mary, and M. Anne Pitcher. "The 'Basket Case' and the 'Poster Child': Explaining the End of Conflicts in Liberia and Mozambique." *Third World Quarterly* 25 (2004) 501–19.

Moschella, Mary Clark. *Ethnography as Pastoral Practice: An Introduction*. Cleveland: Pilgrim, 2008.

Neuger, Christie Cozad. *Counseling Women: A Narrative, Pastoral Approach*. Minneapolis: Fortress, 2001.

———. "Narratives of Harm: Setting the Developmental Context for Intimate Violence." In *In Her Own Time: Women and Developmental Issues in Pastoral Care*, edited by Jeanne Stevenson-Moessner, 65–86. Minneapolis: Fortress, 2000.

Ní Aoláin, Fionnuala, Dina Francesca Haynes, and Naomi Cahn. *On the Frontlines: Gender, War, and the Post-Conflict Process*. Oxford: Oxford University Press, 2011.

Nsonwu, Maura Busch. "God-Talk and Kin-Talk in the Survival Epistemology of Liberian Refugee Women." PhD diss., University of North Carolina at Greensboro, 2008.

Nussbaum, Martha. *Women and Human Development: The Capabilities Approach*. John Robert Seeley Lectures 3. New York: Cambridge University Press, 2000.

Oduyoye, Mercy Amba. *Beads and Strands: Reflections of an African Woman on Christianity in Africa*. Maryknoll, NY: Orbis, 2004.

———. *Daughters of Anowa: African Women and Patriarchy*. Maryknoll, NY: Orbis, 1995.

Orsi, Robert. *Between Heaven and Earth: The Religious Worlds People Make and the Scholars Who Study Them*. Princeton: Princeton University Press, 2005.

Olupona, Jacob, and Sulayman S. Nyang, eds. *Religious Plurality in Africa: Essays in Honor of John Mbiti*. Religion and Society 32. New York: Mouton de Gruyter, 1993.

Payne, Jason. Interview by author, Raleigh, North Carolina, March 2, 2012.

Pillay, Anu. "Truth Seeking and Gender: The Liberian Experience." *African Journal of Conflict Resolution* 9.7 (2009) 91–100.

Pillay, Anu, Marpue Speare, and Pamela Scully. "Women's Dialogues in Post-Conflict Liberia." *Journal of Peacebuilding and Development* 5.3 (2010) 89–93.

Poling, James. *The Abuse of Power: A Theological Problem*. Nashville: Abingdon, 1991.

Pray the Devil Back to Hell. DVD. Directed by Gini Reticker. Fork Films, 2008.

Rambo, Shelly. *Spirit and Trauma: A Theology of Remaining*. Louisville: Westminster John Knox, 2010.

Bibliography

Ramshaw, Elaine. "Making (Ritual) Sense of Our Own Lives." In *Injustice and the Care of Souls: Taking Oppression Seriously in Pastoral Care*, edited by Sheryl A. Kujawa-Holbrook and Karen B. Montagno, 291–304. Minneapolis: Fortress, 2009.

Republic of Liberia Truth and Reconciliation Commission. *Consolidated Final Report*. www.trcofliberia.org/resources/reports/final/volume-two_layout-1.pdf.

———. "Volume Three: Appendices Title 1: Women and the Conflict." https://www.trcofliberia.org/reports/final.

Ross, Fiona. *Bearing Witness: Women and the Truth and Reconciliation Commission in South Africa*. London: Pluto, 2002.

Samura, Sorious. "West African Journeys: Part Three." http://www.bbc.co.uk/worldservice/documentaries/2009/04/090430_west_african_journeys_three.shtml.

Scanlon, Helen. "Foreword." *African Journal of Conflict Resolution* 9.2 (2009) 5–8.

Scanlon, Helen, and Kelli Muddell, "Gender and Transitional Justice in Africa: Progress and Prospects." *African Journal of Conflict Resolution* 9.2 (2009) 9–28.

Scully, Pamela. "Expanding the Concept of Gender-based Violence in Peacebuilding and Development." *Journal of Peacebuilding and Development* 5.3 (2010) 21–33.

———. "Feminist Theory, African Gender History, and Transitional Justice." *African Journal of Conflict Resolution* 9.2 (2009) 29–43.

———. "Should We Give up on the State? Feminist Theory, African Gender History and Transitional Justice." *African Journal of Conflict Resolution* 9.2 (2009) 29–44.

———. "Vulnerable Women: A Critical Reflection on Human Rights Discourse and Sexual Violence." *Emory International Law Review* 23 (2009) 113–24.

Sharp, Melinda McGarrah. *Misunderstanding Stories: Toward a Postcolonial Pastoral Theology*. Eugene, OR: Pickwick, 2013.

Shaw, Rosalind. "Memory Frictions: Localizing the Truth and Reconciliation Commission in Sierra Leone." *International Journal of Transitional Justice* 1 (2007) 183–207.

Shoop, Marcia Mount. *Let the Bones Dance: Embodiment and the Body of Christ*. Louisville: Westminster John Knox, 2010.

Sideris, Tina. "Problems of Identity, Solidarity and Reconciliation." In *The Aftermath: Women in Post-Conflict Transformation*, edited by Sheila Meintjes, Anu Pillay, and Meredith Turshen, 46–62. New York: Zed, 2001.

Sirleaf, Ellen Johnson. *This Child Will Be Great: Memoir of a Remarkable Life by Africa's First Female President*. New York: HarperCollins, 2009.

Smith, Linda Tuhiwai. *Decolonizing Methodologies: Research and Indigenous Peoples*. New York: Zed, 1999.

Soskice, Janet Martin. *The Kindness of God: Metaphor, Gender, and Religious Language*. Oxford: Oxford University Press, 2007.

Steinberg, Jonny. *Little Liberia: An African Odyssey in New York City*. London: Cape, 2011.

Stepakoff, Shanee. "The Healing Power of Symbolization in the Aftermath of Massive War Atrocities: Examples from Liberian and Sierra Leonean Survivors." *Journal of Humanistic Psychology* 47 (2007) 400–412.

Townes, Emilie, ed. *A Troubling in My Soul: Womanist Perspectives on Evil and Suffering*. Bishop Henry McNeal Turner Studies in North American Black Religion 8. Maryknoll, NY: Orbis, 1997.

United Nations. "Landmark Resolution on Women, Peace and Security." http://www.un.org/womenwatch/osagi/wps/.

Whitehead, Alfred North. *Process and Reality*. New York: Free Press, 1978.

———. *Adventures of Ideas*. New York: Free Press, 1933.

Williams, Delores S. *Sisters in the Wilderness: The Challenges of Womanist God-Talk*. Maryknoll, NY: Orbis, 1993.

———. "A Womanist Perspective on Sin." In *A Troubling in My Soul: Womanist Perspectives on Evil and Suffering*, edited by Emilie Townes, 130–49. Maryknoll, NY: Orbis, 1993.

Wilson, Michael. *Health Is for People*. London: Darton, Longman & Todd, 1975.

World Health Organization. "Fact Sheet: Violence against Women." http://www.who.int/mediacentre/factsheets/fs239/en/index.html.

Young, Laura A., and Rosalyn Park. "Engaging Diasporas in Truth Commissions: Lessons Learned from the Liberia Truth and Reconciliation Commission Diaspora Project." *International Journal of Transitional Justice* 3 (2009) 341–61.

Index of Names

Amadiume, Ifi, 124
Arkoi, Rufus, 116
Asad, Talal, 48n21

Baker Fletcher, Karen, 145, 145n38
Bender, Courtney, 15, 125
Boone, Sylvia, 84
Bop, Codou, 27n40, 40n7
Brison, Susan, 12n31, 52n26n 59, 60, 60n33, 67, 85–86, 85n48, 155–56
Butler, Judith, 70, 71n15, 109–10

Cahn, Naomi, 89
Cole, Catherine, 46–47, 47n16, 81–82
Coleman, Monica, 7–8, 133, 134, 136, 144–49
Cooper, Etweda "Sugars," 24
Cooper, Helene, 18–19
Cooper-White, Pamela, 32
Copelon, Rhonda, 104
Cruz, Joelle, 82, 83

Das, Veena, 30, 48, 49n24, 64–65, 68–69, 79n36, 107, 110, 111, 151–52
Doe, Samuel, 18, 19–21, 44, 45, 123, 164, 165
Douglas, Kelly Jones, 145

Ellis, Stephen, 18, 21n21, 83–84

Farley, Wendy, 155
Fineman, Martha, 14n2XX
Flomo, Vaiba, 24

Flueckiger, Joyce Burkhalter, 8, 133, 135–36
Fuest, Veronika, 23n26m 113
Fulkerson, Mary McClintock, 15–16, 28, 126n27, 136n13

Gandolfo, Elizabeth, 71, 126, 127–29
Gbowee, Leymah, 5, 17–18, 24–25, 29, 59, 106, 107, 112, 121–22, 123, 127, 152, 154–55, 160
Geertz, Clifford, 137n15
Grigsby, Samuel 50–51, 65–66, 77, 92, 93, 94–95, 106, 128–29, 131–32, 138
Gyekye, Kwame, 30

Haynes, Francesca, 89
Herman, Judith, 46, 78, 78n33, 79n34, 108–9, 110
Hucks, Tracy, 7–8, 133–36

Johnson, Prince, 20, 39
Jones, Felicia (Pastor), 31, 36, 53–55, 72–73, 93–95, 164
Jones, Jackson (Pastor), 115n3
Jones, Janet, 93–94
Jones, Serene, 15–16, 59, 154

Karmara-Umunna, Agnes M. Fallah, 22n24, 27, 109, 119n11
Kenneth, Asatu Bah, 24
Kirk-Duggan, Cheryl A., 126n27
Kirmayer, Laurence J., 77n30

Index of Names

Lartey, Emmanuel, 31–32, 161n17
Lassiter, Katharine, 60–61, 68, 71n15
Lederach, John Paul, 153

MacIntyre, Alasdair, 135–36
MacKinnon, Catherine, 104
Magesa, Laurenti, 30, 74–75
Mahmood, Saba, 133–34, 136n12
Meah, Aletha, 19, 20, 21n20, 36, 37–38, 49, 50–58, 65–68, 72, 81, 93–97, 103–4, 108–11, 114, 115n4, 116–18, 120, 135–64
Meintjes, Sheila, 89, 126n30
Merry, Sally Engle, 3, 14, 105–6, 105n20, 159n13
Miller-McLemore, Bonnie, 126, 128
Moon, Hellena, 33
Moran, Mary, 18, 41n9, 84, 113, 113n2, 118n6, 122–23

Neuger, Christie, 32, 57n28, 58n29
Ní Aoláin, Fionnuala, 89
Nussbaum, Martha, 124

Oduyoye, Mercy Amba, 12n31, 32, 75–77
Olupona, Jacob, 30
Orsi, Robert, 76, 77, 156n10

Paynes, Laura, 5, 21–22, 37–40, 43, 44, 49, 50–58, 63–68, 70, 72, 79–83, 90–98, 108–11, 140n20, 147, 150, 152–54, 161–65
Pillay, Anu, 26–27, 47–48, 89, 90, 126n30
Poling, James, 3

Rambo, Shelly, 28, 46, 64n1, 156
Ramshaw, Elaine, 158
Reticker, Gini, 23

Scully, Pamela 14n2, 23n27, 89, 100n13
Sharp, Melinda McGarrah, 83, 84–85, 115n4
Sharpe, Jenny, 87n3
Shaw, Rosalind, 78, 78n31, 79, 79n35
Shoop, Marcia Mount, 62, 68–69, 76n28, 132, 132n1
Sideris, Tina, 111
Sirleaf, Ellen Johnson, 5, 5n13, 20, 25, 107, 114
Smith, Linda Tuhiwai, 8–9, 84
Steinberg, Jonny, 37n4, 116
Stepakoff, Shanee, 61

Taylor, Charles, 20–25, 112
Terrell, Joanne, 145
Turshen, Meredith, 89

Whitehead, Alfred North, 146
Williams, Delores, 142–45, 147
Wilson, Michael, 156

Index of Subjects

Accra Peace Conference (2003), 23, 25, 121
Addiction, 42
Advocacy, 22, 33, 102, 105n20
Agency, 60–61, 147
    Bodily practices as, 133
    Definitions of, 69
    Forgetting as, 78–79, 85
    Narrative, 78
    Ritual, 158
    Speech and, 79n36
    Theory of, 63
Alcohol, 27, 42, 43n10, 63
    As coping mechanism, 85
    Forgetting through, 78, 79n34
Alcoholism, 38, 42, 43, 78, 167
Alternative narrative, 47, 50, 60
Americo-Liberians, 18–19
And Still Peace Did Not Come, 27, 109, 119n11
Arrogance
    Organizational, 160
Attention, remembering as, 62

Baby dedications, 114–17, 120
Baby showers, 72, 97
"Breaking the Silence," 99, 102, 166
Brutality, 18, 21, 91
Burial. *See* Unburial
Burning villages, 2

Captivity, 22, 39, 66
CEDAW, 104, 105, 106
    Ratification of, 105n21

Check-points, 21n21
    Rates of deaths at, 21
Children, 41, 119, 120–21
    Blessing of, 114, 121, 140
    Caring for, 19, 41, 101, 102, 115, 117, 118, 118n6, 128, 129, 151, 166
    Dedication of, 114, 117
    Displaced, 20, 22, 23, 39, 41, 43, 99
    Educating, 69, 88, 90, 152
    FCC and, 139n19
    Harm to, 113, 120
    Homeless, 22, 38, 39–40, 99–100
    Importance of, 54
    Inability to produce, 115, 118n7
    Of Israel, 140–41
    Killing of, 25, 119n11, 120, 121
    Lost, 119
    Protecting, 122, 123, 153
    Raising, 48, 57–58, 62–63, 88, 92, 96, 115–16, 117
    Rape of, 25, 26. *See also* Rape
    Refugee, 2n4, 37, 167
    Relationality through, 121
    Risk of, 117–20
    As "second chance," 117, 120
    As soldiers, 21, 21n21, 24, 112, 116
    Surviving, 69
    Trauma and, 41–42, 43, 63, 91, 102, 113, 166
    TRC and, 47
    Violent, 21–24, 76
    War inexperience of, 34, 40
Christian Women's Peace Initiative, 29–30

Index of Subjects

Church
  As family, 38, 42, 49, 137
Coalitions, 24–25
Combatants,
  Children as, 21. *See also* Children as soldiers
  Women as, 21, 27
Communion, 131–32, 137
Community Dialogue Process, 107. *See also* Justice
"Congo" Liberians, 18, 44
Conscription, 21, 27
Contender, 65

DDR, 24
Diaspora
  Role of in national transitions, 26
  TRC and, 26
  Violence in, 37
  Witnesses and perpetrators in, 26
Dignity, 33
  TRC and, 47
  Women and, 23
Dissociation, 78, 78n33, 79nn34–35

ECOWAS, 20, 21
Ecumenical Women, 15, 15n5
Emory University, 2
  Reproductive Health and Religion Project, 2
  State at Regional Risk initiative, 1, 1n1
Empathy, 59, 60n33
  Narrative and, 52
  Others and, 59, 60, 67, 69
  For traumatized self, 59
Empowerment, 35, 37, 52–63, 135, 157
  Books, 61
  Communal, 63
  Definition, 53, 63
  Girls and, 126–27
  Groups, 5, 41, 49–58, 56n27, 61, 65, 69, 77, 80–81, 132, 144, 147, 151, 154, 157, 158, 163, 167
  Theological language of, 63
  As transformation, 60
  Youth, 72, 90, 165

Family separation, 20. *See also* Children, displaced; Trauma
FCC, 93
  As family, 96–97
  Locations of, 94–95, 139n19
  Making a way, 141, 144
  Origins of, 94
  Prayer practices of, 76
  Vision for, 94–95, 139–40
  Youth rebuilding at, 80
Feminist theory, 6, 9, 15–16, 28–32, 59, 89, 104, 11, 123–24, 128, 133, 155
  Challenging public/private divide, 124
  Religion in, 124
Fictive genealogies, 118, 118n6
Forced displacement, 21n22
Forgiveness, 56, 73, 93–94
Friendship Community Church, 5, 36
  Demographics of, 36
  History of, 36
  Leadership of, 36
  Shared suffering in, 48

Gang(s)
  Post-conflict, 37
  Violence, 37, 97, 144
  Youth involvement in, 79–80, 96, 116
Gender equality, 14, 15, 28, 124
Global Network of Women Peacebuilders, 4n12
God
  -bearer, 127
  Blessings of, 74, 117, 142
  Caring of, 2, 7, 31, 101–2
  Deliverance by, 21, 66, 167
  Faith in, 52, 55, 57, 72
  Forgiveness of, 93–94
  Hating, 101–2
  Healing of, 2, 73
  Image of, 67, 70
  Involvement of, 75, 75n24, 76, 150
  Language for, 21n20
  Love of, 97, 114
  Partnership with, 42
  Power of, 79

Index of Subjects

Presence of, 2, 43, 57, 60, 62, 63, 66, 67, 129, 130–31, 145–46, 150–51, 155, 156
Redemptive gloss and, 28
Remembers, 130–31
Survival and, 9, 33, 35, 56, 57, 66, 143–44
Witness of, 2
Women and, 114
"God was there," 2, 3, 10, 30, 35, 63 *See also* "Making a Way"
Gratitude, 43, 66, 73n19, 139, 156
Grief, 150, 166
  Holding, 76n28
  As privatizing, 70
  Public, 71n15
  Relationality and, 70

Hagar, 142–44. *See also* "Making a way"
Healing 157, 162. *See also* Practices, Transformation, Trauma
  And alternative narratives, 67
  Bodily, 7, 10 [ch3]
  Community, 52, 63, 70
  Daily life and, 68–69
  Definitions of, 31, 38
  Everyday, 7, 10, 12, 35, 63, 69, 108–9, 151
  Faith and, 43, 45, 56–57, 157
  Feminist practical theology and, 15–16
  Framework for understanding, 28
  Gardening for, 64
  By helping, 108
  Language about, 4, 6, 16–17, 33
  In life and death, 151
  Lived, 33
  Men and, 52
  Narratives and, 17, 50
  Nature of, 2
  Non-narrative practices of, 69
  In North Carolina, 7
  As partnership with God, 42
  Peace and, 7, 9
  Practices. *See* Practices
  Prayer practices, 10, 31, 72–73, 74–77
  Process of, 31, 68–70, 157

Reconciliation and, 6
Reframing victimization for, 60
Relational, 5, 35, 45, 60, 108, 154–55
Religion and, 30, 48
As repair, 68
Ritual and, 61–62, 68
Subject formation and, 61
Talking and, 44, 46, 50, 51, 52n26, 55, 57, 59, 64, 77, 80, 81, 103, 154, 159. *See also* Storytelling, Witnessing
Theodicy and, 156
Theology and, 10, 31
Transformation and, 46
Trauma and, 5
Of trauma healing groups, 37, 37n5, 49–58
Trauma, with art therapy, 10, 51, 54–55
Healthcare
  Education through, 92, 161, 165
  Empowerment through, 53
  Refugee resettlement and, 37
  Truth commissions and, 49
  For survivors of sexual violence, 87
Hope, 102, 137, 140
  Agency and, 85
  Choosing, 108
  Faith and, 157
  For FCC, 147 *See also* FCC, "Making a Way"
  Hardship to, 11, 120, 121, 129, 151, 161
  Imagination and, 74, 76, 85
  Loss of through war, 25
  Memory and, 86
  Narratives of, 77, 80, 132, 143, 148–49, 151, 154, 155, 161
  Objects of, 73–74, 85
  Parenting with, 136. *See also* Baby dedication, Children
  Practices of, 36, 122, 129, 132. *See also* Practices
  Prayers of, 33, 76. *See also* "Making a Way"
  As relational, 110, 114, 121, 129, 154

Index of Subjects

Hope *(cont.)*
    Religion and, 17, 49
    Sermon of, 139–40
    Stories of, 61, 67–68
    Trauma to, 57
Human rights, 13, 110 *See also* CEDAW, CSW, TCR, UNSCR, WIPNET
    Documents, 106, 124 *See also* CEDAW, SCR 1325
    Gender-based violence and, 14
    Instruments and frameworks, 104, 107, 111, 133. *See also* SCR 1325, TCR.
    Literature, 17
    Local frameworks for, 105
    Neglect of, 10
    Organizations *See* LWI, UN, UNCSW, UNHCR, UNFEM, WIPNET
    Place in book's framework, 9
    Practical theologians and, 159, 161
    Practices, 108, 110
    Process, 105–6
    Religion and, 3, 4, 13–15, 16, 31, 88, 108, 125, 159
    Violations, 25n35, 47. *See also* TRC
    Vulnerability and, 14n2
    Women and, 104–8, 124, 125
    Women's leadership in, 33, 107–8

ICAN, 4
IDP, 23
Immigrants,
    Life of, 10, 91–103
Imprisoned, 1, 19, 22, 56, 99–100
INPFL, 21
Interdependence, 70
    Loss and, 70
Internet, 41n9, 121
Interview participants, 164–67
Interview protocol, 168
IRHAP, 30, 160
    Participatory methodology of, 160

Justice, 9, 81–82 *See also* Community Dialogue Process, TRC
    Faith and, 134
    Feminist scholarship and, 6–7
    Gender, 4, 14

    God and, 146
    Identity and, 71
    Interiority and, 155
    Localized, 147, 160
    Pastoral theology and, 32
    Postcolonial, 83
    Practices of, 32, 105
    Religion and, 7
    Right relationship and, 75, 126–27
    Social, 15
    Tragedy and, 76n28
    Transitional, 38, 46, 89, 107
    Unexpected arenas of, 48. *See also* Das
    Visions of, 2–3, 76
    Women and, 107, 111, 123

Killing, 18–19, 20, 21n22, 56–57, 96, 120

Legal system, 46, 159
    v. religion, 3, 30, 87–88, 124
Liberia
    American's knowledge of, 44, 63
    Life in, 1, 43–45, 115
    Reason for focus on, 4
    Ties to U.S. 17–18
    U.S. Slavery and, 17
Liberian Civil War, 17, 20
    Context of, 10
    Deaths in, 20, 26. *See also* Killing, Rape
    Displacement during, 2
    History of, 17–18, 20–27, 40, 56, 66.
    Religion and, 6
    Stabilization after, 5
Liberian
    Community in New York, 37n4
    Community in North Carolina, 36
LFS, 36, 37
LURD, 23, 24, 112
LWI, 25
    Letter-writing campaign, 25

"Making a way," 7, 11, 20, 33, 35, 62, 94, 96, 108, 113, 133, 136–37, 140, 141–49, 151
    Transformation as, 141, 149

Index of Subjects

Worship as, 148
Martyrdom, 46. *See also* Witnessing
Maternality
   Healing and, 126
   Protection of, 122
   Protest power and, 122
   Vulnerability and, 128
Memorialization, 7, 59, 86, 87, 127, 158
Memory, 55–58, 127 *See also* Migration
   Books, 61
   Boxes, 56, 58, 69, 158
   Collective war, 35
   Community and, 34, 86
   Controlling, 52
   Directed forgetting and, 78n31, 85
   Displacement, 79n35
   Empowerment and, 24, 63, 71
   Identity and, 34, 40, 68
   Narrative, 67–68
   Peace and, 65–67
   Public acts of, 77
   Remembering and, 62
   Repairing, 85
   Resistance, 71
   Shaping, 86
   Shared, 63
   Trauma and, 12, 12n31, 38, 45, 49, 67, 78
   Truth of, 12, 12n31, 77
Migration, 10, 34–63, 118. *See also* Diaspora; Resettlement
   Definition of, 35
   Experiences of, 10, 144
   Memory and, 34–63
   Stories of, 36–45
Motherhood, 114–15
   Hardships of, 113, 120–21, 143. *See also* "Making a Way"
   Healing and, 128
   Relationality and, 121
   Tragedies of, 118–20
   Violence and, 128
   Vulnerability and, 126–28
Mothering. *See also* Children
   Essentializing, 126n30
   Faith practice of, 128–29
   Hardships of. *See* Motherhood
   Importance of, 113

   Pains of, 118n7
   Power of, 122
   Practices of, 11, 62, 112–30
   As religious practice, 128
   Scholarship on, 128
   Status of, 24
   Transformation and, 126–30
   Vulnerability of, 126–29
Mothers
   Collective identity politics of, 112–13
   Power of, 112–13
MSF (Médicins Sans Frontières), 99
Murder *See* Killing
Mutual support, 44, 97
Narrative, 85. *See also* Healing, talking; Practices, storytelling; TRC, testimony; Witnessing

NPFL, 20, 21

Othering, 84

Parenting
   Practices, 114–16, 115n4, 125, 126, 128–29, 136, 154. *See also* Mothering
Participatory research, 8–9, 83–84, 160
Pastoral theology, 31–32, 33, 83
   Four paradigms of, 161
Peace, 16, 17, 28, 45, 51, 65, 66, 88, 106–8, 155. *See also* Practices
   Definitions of, 9, 65–67
   FCC goal of, 93
   Jesus and, 67
   Learned, 9
   Lived, 9, 155
   Memory and, 65–67, 127
   Mothers and, 113, 120–23
   Prayer for, 29, 67, 74
   As process, 25, 153
   Self and, 155
   Unity and, 94
Peacebuilding, 153–54
Peacebuilding literature, 89
Peacebuilding practices, 45, 120–23
   Women's, 4, 31, 124

Index of Subjects

Pentecostal Prayer, 73
   Practicality of, 75
   Reinvention through, 75
Phone tree, 41n9
Politics
   As talk only, 81, 90, 92
   Over women/religion, 88, 90
Post-war needs, 103, 152
   Of children, 90–91
   Financial, 92, 97–98, 97n12, 100–101, 153
   Healthcare, 92
   Social services as, 152
   Of women, 90 *See also* Trauma
   Of young people, 90, 92
Practice(s)
   Of care, 7, 48, 51, 69, 71, 77, 88, 97, 114, 115. *See also* Memory box; Mothering
   Christian, 11, 131–49
   Community, 45, 63, 97
   Contemplative, 86
   Empowering, 59. *See also* Empowerment, Transformation
   Everyday, 35, 64, 125, 129
   Faith, 129, 130–49
   Gardening, 64
   Of healing, 10, 16, 35, 44
   Hymn singing, 29, 72–73, 137, 138, 140, 141
   Indigenous understanding of, 8
   Of justice, 32
   Of mothering, 11, 129
   Of peace, 10, 32, 33, 48, 62
   Of prayer and meditation, 24
   Of resistance, 61, 71, 126–29
   Storylistening, 33, 60n33
   Storytelling, 32, 51, 57, 59, 61, 63, 65–68
   Of surviving violence, 16, 39, 57
   Of transformation, 60, 63, 151–53
Pray the Devil Back to Hell, 4, 23, 24
Prayer, 7, 9, 10, 24, 29, 33, 58, 63
   Chaotic, 76
   Forgetting through, 77, 79
   Of forgiveness, 93–94
   Grief and, 127, 130
   Healing and, 131–32, 154, 158

   As participatory, 51, 73, 76
   For peace, 29
   Pentecostal, 73–74, 75
   Phone, 72
   As redress, 24, 125
   Re-membering, 86, 149
   As transformation, 77
   Warriors, 71–77, 166
   Women's prayer meeting, 5, 65, 71–77, 94
Process theology, 144, 145n38, 146
Purge. *See* Killing

Rape, 1, 18, 21n22, 23, 25, 26, 99, 101
   Children of, 27
   Of children, 25, 26, 99–100
   Death after, 26
   Feminist political theory and, 124
   God and, 2, 30
   Hagar and, 143
   Human rights and, 104
   Memories of, 77n30, 85
   Taboo of, 102, 166. *See also* "Breaking the Silence"
Reconciliation, 87–89, 103. *See also* TRC
   Community, 88, 103
   Healing and, 6, 9, 30, 103, 111
   Justice and, 48
   Memoir of. *See And Still Peace Did Not Come*
   Peace and, 87
Recovery programs, 64
"redemptive gloss," 28
Refugee camp, 23, 36, 41, 61, 80, 101, 119, 165, 167
Refugees, 2, 36, 103. *See also* Immigrant
   Assistance for, 95
   "Double flight," 101
   Empowerment and, 37, 61
   Ex-soldier, 116
   FCC and 95–96
   Statistics about, 2n4
Regional stability, 1, 5
   As transformation, 5
Religion, 2, 3, 29, 31, 48, 124, 125. *See also* "Making a Way"
   African, 6, 24, 30, 70, 74, 134–35, 141, 145n38

Index of Subjects

Anthropologists of, 8, 135
Anti-feminist, 14, 124
Culture and, 14
As danger, 16
Definition of, 30
Everyday, 15, 16, 33, 74, 125, 157
Healing and, 30, 33
Health and, 6, 160
Human rights and, 3, 4, 15, 33, 48, 88, 133. *See also* Human rights
Ignoring, 88
As instrument of change, 2, 3, 16
Language of, 13
As life, 30–31
Parenting and, 125
Peace and, 3, 45, 113
Place of, 48n21
Practices of, 15, 30, 74, 125n27, 132, 134, 135, 136. *See also* Practices
As repair, 48
Self in, 70
Transformation and, 11–12
Violence and, 3, 9, 10, 16, 17, 29, 31, 33
Women and, 3, 8, 9, 29, 125, 129, 132
Re-membering, 62, 68, 86
Body and, 68–69
Community, 86
Repairing, 68
Community, 38, 86, 88, 90, 92, 110, 129, 151, 155, 157
Everyday life, 36, 49, 62, 157
Memory, 77
Through mothering, 113
Practices of, 85
Self, 68, 88, 110, 151–53, 157
Wounds, 35, 155
Research methods, 8–9, 133, 160, 163–64
Resettlement, 35, 97
Difficulties of, 36–37
Empowerment and, 37
Reasons for, 36
Resilience, 17, 34, 57, 68, 71, 154
Definition of, 85–86
Rights. *See also* Human rights

Feminist theory and, 31
Religion and, 31
Womanist theory and, 31
Ritual, 35
Agency, 158
Authority, 25
Forgetting through, 78, 79
Healing through, 68, 158
As memorializing, 7, 35, 52, 59
For peace, 25, 125, 155
Symbolization and, 61
Thick description of, 137n15
Secrecy, 82–83, 84–85
As alternative democracy, 123
Dual-sex societies and, 84
Liberians and, 84
Political corruption and, 83
Sande and, 84
Sorcery and, 84
Tribalism and, 84
Trauma and, 82
Selves-in-relation, 61, 68, 70–71, 156
Shame
Women and, 23, 81
Shelter, 97–98
For children, 39–40
Domestic violence, 2, 3, 19, 23, 97–100
In Liberia, 98–100, 166
Prayer for, 75
Underground, 100
Singing, 72–73, 141. *See also* Practices, hymn singing
Solidarity
Healing and, 16
Human, 109–10
Practices of, 127–28
Vulnerability and, 127
Of women in war, 89n8
Space
Conversational, 33, 82
Healing, 32, 89–90
Institutional, 14
Peacebuilding, 153
Practices and, 32, 77
Processing, 50
Of religion, 48n21

Index of Subjects

Space *(cont.)*
   Religious, 76–77
   Research, 160
   Safe, 97, 100. *See also* Shelter
   Trauma and, 78n30
   Truth commissions and, 49
   Worship, 93, 95, 137–38, 139n19, 141, 164
Storytelling. *See* Practices, storytelling
Storyweaving, 67–68, 81, 155
Stripping (women) 121–22
Subject formation, 60–61
Survival strategies, 89, 89n8, 142. *See also* Hagar
Survivor mission, 108–10, 111
Symbolization, 61

Talk
   As healing, 44, 68, 147, 154, 159. *See also* Practices, storytelling; Storyweaving
Theology, 31
   Of complexity, 28–29, 70, 161
   As experience, 31
   Practical, 31–32, 33, 161
Thick description, 72, 137, 137n15
Traditional African Religions, 6, 74, 134
   Life after death in, 74
   Petition and, 74–75
   Prayer in, 74
   Tragedy, 76, 76n28
   Attention to, 156–57
   Social action and, 109
   Transformation of, 129, 155–57
Transformation, 1, 5, 11, 60, 150. *See also* "Making a way"
   Bodily, 71, 133–35
   Communal, 5
   Context of, 6
   Definition of, 35, 132–33, 135, 148, 151–57
   Feminist, 17, 58–59
   Healing as, 4, 6, 7, 9, 33, 46, 48, 62, 63, 65 130, 136 *See also* Empowerment; Practices
   Health and, 17
   Individual, 5
   International, 35. *See also* TRC

   Justice and, 6–7, 32, 89
   Language of, 33, 61, 129
   Migration as, 35
   National, 5
   Pain and, 75
   Political, 28
   Practices of, 64–86, 131–49
   Prayer and, 71–77
   As process, 141, 153–54, 157
   As reconciliation, 6
   As relational, 69, 151, 154–56
   Religion and, 5, 6, 12, 62
   Self-, 63
   Stability as
   Talking about, 50, 59, 65
   Theorizing about, 35, 61
   As thriving, 6
   As tragedy. *See* Tragedy
Trauma, 25. *See also* Violence
   Agency and, 85
   Absurdity of, 85
   Amplification of, 82
   Children and, 41
   Contraction of, 82
   Coping with, 3, 61, 85, 108–9
   Dissociation, 43n10
   Effects of, 44, 78n33, 100
   Empathy and, 59
   Engagement and, 109–10
   Forgetting, 77–79, 78n31, 80, 82, 85, 86
   God's presence in, 2, 35, 60, 157
   Healing group, 31, 34–40, 37n5, 44, 49–58, 82
   Healing program, 10, 34, 37, 61, 79, 91
   Immigrants and, 10
   Memory and, 12, 12n31, 46, 49, 67–68, 76–77, 78, 82, 85, 127
   Moving on from, 25, 28, 34, 77–78, 81, 86
   Narratives, 60, 77n30, 80, 81
   Nightmares, 41–42, 102
   Participating in, 160
   Peace despite, 9
   Recovery from, 85–86
   Saints and, 156n10
   Secondary, 24, 50

Index of Subjects

Secrecy and, 82–83
Sleeplessness, 41–42
Transformation and, 70
Trekking, 2
Violence and, 23, 33
TRC, 1n3, 2n4, 21n22, 23, 25–26, 25n35, 46–47, 70, 87
    Data from, 2n4
    Definition of, 46
    Establishment of, in Liberia, 25–26
    Importance to diaspora, 26
    Limitations of, 48, 49, 87
    Mandate of, 25n35, 47
    Memorialization practices and, 7
    Shared narratives and, 46, 47n16
    Testimony and, 46–47, 49n24
    Traumatic memory and, 78
    Women and, 47, 58, 107

ULIMO, 21
Unburial/reburial, 87n3
UNCSW, 3, 13, 64, 106, 111
UNFPA, 14
UNHCR, 101
UNIFEM, 5, 13, 87
Unity
    FCC goal of, 94, 103
UNSCR 1325, 4, 4n10, 104–5, 107

Victim
    Narratives, 12n31, 56. *See also* TRC
    Perpetrator and, 28, 49n24, 50, 56, 154
    Stereotypes, 12n31, 23n27, 68
    Support, 99. *See also* Shelter
    Violations, 25n35. *See also* Killing, Rape, TRC
    Kinds of, 1n3, 21n22, 26–27, 104
    Rates of, 21n21
Violence. *See also* Burning; Memory; Prison; Rape; Shelter; Trauma; TRC
    Absurdity and, 85
    Captivity, 22
    Community weakening by, 70
    Conflict-related, 3
    Domestic 2, 3, 58, nn30, 97–98, 104, 124
    And everyday, 68–71

    Faith communities and, 158. *See also* FCC
    Forced displacement as, 21n22
    Gang 1, 37, 79, 96, 97, 116, 144
    Gender-based, 1, 2, 3, 14, 19, 22–23, 52, 64, 97, 98, 99, 101–2, 105, 107, 124
    Gender equality and, 13
    Gender relations after, 89n8
    Healing and, 38, 46
    Impact of, 38, 48, 68
    Invisibility of, 65
    Loss of livelihood and, 47–48
    Monitoring, 104
    Peace and, 66, 104
    Persistence of, 68
    Post-war, 37
    Rates of, against women, 14
    Religion and, 10, 11–12, 13–14, 29, 33, 57, 88, 132, 136, 159
    Relationship and, 64–65, 156
    Ritual and, 158
    Self-sufficiency of, 27
    Sexual, rates of, 26. *See also* Rape
    Solutions to, 14, 38
    Stories, 47, 90–103
    Surviving, 3, 16, 30, 86, 127, 136, 157. *See also* Healing, Practices, Reconciliation
    Telling of, 31, 50–51, 59, 61–62, 64, 80, 84. *See also* Practices, storytelling; Testimony
    Theological language about, 63
    By women, 28
    To women, 5, 11, 14, 16, 23, 26, 28, 32, 33, 40n7
Victimized subject, 68
"Vulnerable subject," 14
Vulnerability, 68, 70, 71, 86, 103, 126, 127. *See also* Motherhood; Shelter; Solidarity
    Definition of, 14n2
    Empowerment through, 127–29

War
    Aftermath of, 28
    Experience of, 96. *See also* Captivity; Rape; Trauma; Witnessing, to violence

Index of Subjects

War *(cont.)*
    Opportunities for transformation of, 28
WIPNET, 23–25, 29, 106, 112, 124–27
Witnessing, 46, 59, 52n26, 76n28. *See also* Practices, Storytelling; TRC
    Faith community as, 49
    God and, 2, 63
    Life after trauma, 62, 64
    Martyrdom and, 46
    Protection and, 100
    As protest, 123
    Survival and, 46
    To violence, 59, 64–65, 66, 76, 103
Womanist theology, 7, 8, 11, 31, 133, 144–45
    Process thought and, 146
    Salvation in, 145
    Spirituals and, 126n27
    As verb, 146–47
Women
    As accomplices to violence, 27, 28
    As activists, 27, 28, 123
    As alcoholics, 27, 42–43
    Authority of, 25
    Biological function of, 114–15
    As combatants, 27
    Democracy and, 123
    Essentializing, 126n30
    Healing task of, 25, 30, 32
    Invisibility of, 88–89
    Peacebuilding and, 88–89, 107. *See also* Practices
    Religious identities of, 8
    Religious lives of, 7, 88. *See also* Practices; Worship
    Religious practices of, 29, 31, 32
    Resistance by, 123
    Ritual authority of, 25n31
    As sex workers, 27
    Stripping, 121–22
WONGOSOL, 87, 91
"World War I," 22n24
"World War II," 22n24, 23
Worship, 11, 15, 31, 36, 73, 77, 93, 95, 115, 132, 137–42, 147–48, 167. *See also* Practices

www.ingramcontent.com/pod-product-compliance
Lightning Source LLC
Chambersburg PA
CBHW051743230426
43670CB00012B/2133